THE WHOLE TRUTH, AND I

❖

A IS FOR ADMISSION addresses virtually every issue you have, including:

• **What is the AI?** The Academic Index is the "trade secret" of certain Ivy League admissions committees: It's a precise mathematical formula that's used routinely to rank most applicants.

• **Do minority students really have a better-than-average chance of getting into an Ivy League college?** A IS FOR ADMISSION explains how minority applicants are actually gauged.

• **Are certain applications tagged for special consideration by the admissions staff?** Absolutely. Find out whether your profile fits into one of these privileged categories.

• **How are essays and interviews appraised?** Here are the criteria for powerful, winning essays and instructive advice for interviews.

A IS FOR ADMISSION also tells you if going to an elite private school—or a public high school—will help you, whether where you live makes a difference, which high schools have the highest acceptance rates, your odds for acceptance if you're deferred or wait-listed by a top school, and much more.

"Just about anything you would need to know to be accepted into an Ivy League school can be found in this very detailed, very specific volume. . . .Hernández knows what she's talking about."
—*Library Journal*

more . . .

A
IS FOR
ADMISSION

THE INSIDER'S GUIDE TO GETTING INTO THE IVY LEAGUE AND OTHER TOP COLLEGES

MICHELE A. HERNÁNDEZ

GRAND CENTRAL
PUBLISHING

NEW YORK   BOSTON

Grand Central Publishing
Hachette Book Group
237 Park Avenue
New York, NY 10017

Visit our Web site at www.HachetteBookGroup.com.

Printed in the United States of America
Originally published in hardcover by Hachette Book Group.
First Trade Edition: September 1999
10 9

Grand Central Publishing is a division of Hachette Book Group, Inc.
The Grand Central Publishing name and logo is a trademark of Hachette Book Group, Inc.

The Library of Congress has cataloged the hardcover edition as follows:

Hernández, Michele A.
    A is for admission : the insider's guide to getting into the Ivy
League and other top colleges / Michele A. Hernández.
        p. cm.
    Includes index.
    ISBN 0-446-52319-4
    1. Universities and colleges—United States—Admission.
    2. Universities and colleges—United States—Entrance requirements.
    I. Title.
LB2351.2.H45   1997
378.1'61—dc21   97-26446
                                                                        CIP

ISBN 978-0-446-67406-5 (pbk.)

Book design by Giorgetta Bell McRee

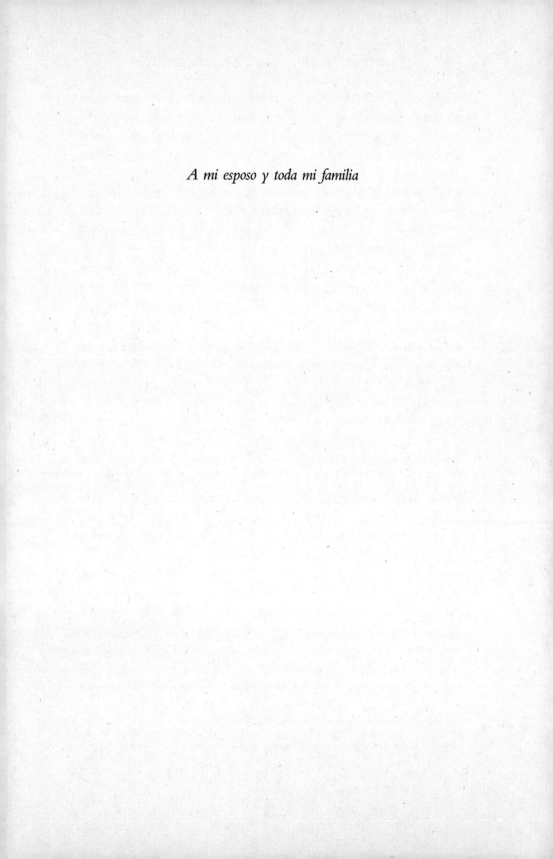

A mi esposo y toda mi familia

Acknowledgments

A book of this scope is by nature a collective effort. I would first like to thank my parents, whose generous support put me through Dartmouth College in the first place, and my sister Jennifer, the artist in the family. Thanks to my colleagues at Dartmouth and to all my friends from Dartmouth who encouraged me early on in the project. I would be remiss not to mention my colleagues from other colleges, with whom I shared the experience of working in admissions. My former colleague from the Putney School, Harry Bauld, inspired me through his own terrific writing and successful book on college essays. I owe thanks to author and editor Sol Stein, who read an early chapter of the book, and to J.C., for his invaluable help and advice. Thanks to Stephanie Bartling, who gave me feedback on an early draft, and to my friend Gordon Silverstein, who shared his journalistic expertise. Thanks also to Michael Blackman, who also shared with me his perspective and insight on college admissions.

I am greatly indebted to my former high school English teacher Bud Pollak, who not only taught me how to write in the first place, but also read through an early manuscript and made many helpful changes. My appreciation to longtime friend Phyllis Wharton in her role as reader extraordinaire; she told me point-blank which sections put her to sleep and made many suggestions, all of which were for the better. I can't thank enough my old friend from the Latin Institute at City University in New York, Will Clurman, an amazing Latinist and study partner, without whom this book would have never found its publisher. This brings me to the person to whom I probably owe the greatest debt of gratitude, my agent, Robin Straus, who believed in the project from day one and has been the greatest source of inspiration. Thanks to Rick Wolff for his faith in the book, to Carol Ross, Esq., for her expert legal advice on the manuscript, and to copy editors Lucy Maher and Carol Edwards for their careful attention to detail.

Many people helped me to update and improve the paperback edition. Thanks to Dr. James Murphy who took the time to make many helpful corrections, as well as to recommend the book to scores of friends. Thanks also to the entire faculty and administration at North Broward Preparatory Schools, particularly my close friend and colleague Bruce Bayliss, who shared his extensive knowledge of education in general, and the IB program in particular. Finally, thanks to my husband, who in many ways made this book possible and supported me all the way through its writing and my first pregnancy, both at the same time. As for the book, any remaining factual errors are entirely my own.

Contents

CONTENTS

Author's Note

The content of this book is based entirely upon my years as an admissions officer at Dartmouth College. In that capacity, I have read thousands of applications, and have had a front-row seat in seeing how the Ivy League admissions process works.

All of the student essays, applicant profiles, and case studies cited within are based on composites of the scores of applications that have come across my admissions desk. None are quoted directly in this book.

Introduction

Ah, the Ivy League. Its name evokes a kind of mythical vision of endless success, money, and happiness; fame and fortune; success or failure. I'll never get a good job if I don't go to an Ivy League school. . . . How many times have you heard the same refrain? Our son is very smart—he's applying to *Ivy League* schools. What well-heeled parents wouldn't kill for that Ivy League sticker for their rear windshield? After all, the Ivy League is *the* ultimate status symbol, the privileged club, the in conversation at cocktail parties. And then there are those families for which the very name Ivy League conjures up images of a privileged world or an exclusionary society that will, on the basis of some extra-academic criteria, issue an automatic rejection to their children. The unfortunate result of this bit of outdated image making is that many bright students from modest backgrounds will eliminate themselves prematurely from a selection process in which they definitely have a chance.

On first view, perhaps the fear expressed by these families is understandable, since the Ivy League can be—and I must stress the superficial nature of this assessment—the hallmark of snootiness for the high-toned set. In an often-quoted cover story in *New York* magazine, one mother summed it up as follows: "There's almost a fetishistic sense of power, being able to associate your child with one of these schools . . . especially at one of these East Side dinner parties . . . the women don't work, so all they talk about is school. It's like belonging to the same country club or something."* Somehow, if your child goes to an Ivy League school, or so goes the theory, others will naturally assume you must be smart, too, for how else could your kids have done it themselves without a little help from the gene pool? Clearly, there is an aura imparted to those who venture forth into Ivy League territory.

*Ralph Gardner, Jr., "Poor Little Smart Kids," *New York,* March 18, 1996, p. 37.

Most people assume that the Ivy League originated as an intellectual alliance of the top universities in the United States. However, this view is far from the truth. While there are various opinions as to exactly when the term *Ivy League* was first used, most sources agree that the term was penned by a sports writer for the *New York Herald Tribune* in the mid 1930s. By 1945 this Ivy League football conference included what we now know as the eight Ivy League institutions: Brown, Columbia, Cornell, Dartmouth, Harvard, Princeton, the University of Pennsylvania, and Yale. By standardizing eligibility requirements, academic standards, and financial-aid practices for athletes, the athletics directors of the Ivy League could maintain minimum standards for their athletes while preventing ringers from coming in and dominating on the gridiron, especially if they were unable to perform at a high level in their classes. By forbidding athletic scholarships, the athletic directors forbid coaches from "buying" their athletes. Instead, they had to attract student athletes who were interested in getting a solid education in addition to playing football.

The true Ivy League was founded in February of 1954, when the athletic directors broadened their rules to include all sports, not just football. Today, the term refers to the above-named eight institutions, which are still bound together by athletic accords regulating the acceptance of athletes for their NCAA Division I teams (with the exception of football, which is NCAA Division I-AA).

Throughout the years, more colleges were added to the list of exclusive colleges. The women's colleges, once affiliated with the original Ivies, are known today as Barnard, Bryn Mawr, Mt. Holyoke, Radcliffe, Smith, Wellesley, and Vassar. They are also called the "Seven Sisters." Amherst, Swarthmore, Williams, and Wesleyan make up the so-called little Ivies, although not everyone agrees on the inclusion of all four colleges.

For the purposes of this book, which focuses on how to get

accepted at a top-rated, or "highly selective," college, I am going to use the term *Ivy League* both as a specific term that refers to certain admissions practices found only in the Ivy League and also as a general term that refers to the most highly selective institutions in the country. I am defining highly selective as colleges that accept 30 percent or less from the applicant pool. As you might imagine, there is quite a variety, even among the eight Ivy League schools, in terms of the selectivity factor. By selectivity, I mean the total number of students that are accepted divided by the total number of students that applied. If ten students applied to a college and five were accepted, the selectivity factor would be 50 percent—one out of every two students.

I suspect that some parents reading this will think back to the days when they applied to colleges. Most people applied to only a handful of colleges and were often admitted to their first choice without much competition. Even law school and medical school applications were much less competitive. The rules that applied in those days are no longer valid. There is an enormous difference between how the admissions process used to be prior to 1970 and how it is now. How and why did this process change?

Prior to 1933, Dartmouth actually had a list of private high schools from which it accepted applicants. These were known as "feeder" high schools because the college counselors would call up the admissions officers and tell them which students they should accept, thereby feeding their students into the specific college via a direct pipeline. If the counselors abused the trust put in them by admissions officers, they were sometimes removed from the feeder list. In the 1920s, these high schools included some of the prestigious New England preparatory schools, such as Phillips Academy at Andover, Massachusetts, and Phillips Exeter Academy at Exeter, New Hampshire, as well as such New York City high schools as Horace Mann. Dartmouth decided in 1921 to institute a "selective process of admissions" because of the increased number of applicants.

Dartmouth is, in fact, considered the first college to have instituted such a selective policy, which was soon copied by other colleges.

Still, the selectivity factor was not comparable to today's levels. It took World War II and the glut of soldiers returning from battle to move the colleges in the direction of truly selective admissions. The proverbial "old boy network" was the modus operandi for decades, right up until World War II. The turning point in admissions procedures is generally considered to be 1945, in that the procedures instituted in the post–WW II years were very similar to those used today. As far as standardized testing is concerned, Dartmouth started requiring the SAT tests for admissions purposes in 1951, and later, in 1958, three achievement tests, or SAT IIs, as they are now called. During the 1950s, the influence of prominent alumni in admissions decisions decreased dramatically, while the Ivies also began to use waiting lists to accommodate the increasing number of applicants.

The process slowly evolved through minority recruitment in the 1960s in the wake of the civil rights movement, and steadily increasing competition, but not until the last five years has the selectivity increased to such a dramatic level. In order to set the stage for the following chapters, let me provide a list of the most highly selective colleges in the United States, along with their acceptance rates. First, there are the Ivies, in order of selectivity:*

Harvard:	13%
Princeton:	13%
Columbia:	17%
Yale:	18%
Brown:	18%
Dartmouth:	22%
(University of Pennsylvania:	31%)
(Cornell:	34%)

*I have taken these acceptance rates from *Peterson's Competitive Colleges: 1998–1999.* Keep in mind that these 1998 numbers actually refer to the class from the year before.

The other U.S. colleges and universities that fit into my artificially created highly selective category are:

USMA (West Point):	14%
Stanford:	15%
U.S. Air Force Academy:	15%
U.S. Naval Academy:	17%
Amherst:	20%
Georgetown:	21%
Williams:	21%
Cal Tech:	23%
Swarthmore:	24%
MIT:	25%
Rice:	27%
Northwestern:	27%
Duke:	30%

I think it comes as a surprise to find that there are only twenty or so colleges (depending upon which year you use, the number will vary slightly) among the thousands of colleges and universities in the United States that are extremely difficult to get into, if we use my arbitrary cut off of 30 percent as the dividing line. All the Seven Sister schools are slightly less selective, ranging from 39 percent to a not-very-selective 65 percent, although one must remember that all-women's colleges are somewhat self-selective in the first place. It is no secret that certain Ivies are easier to get into than other Ivies, not so much because of the overall strength of the college, but more because of size, number of spaces in the freshman class, and number of applicants. The numbers vary slightly from year to year.

Every year, more than 110,000 students apply to Ivy League colleges, but fewer than 26,000 are accepted. How can you make sure you'll get one of those precious offers of admission to Harvard, Yale, Dartmouth, Princeton, or the rest of the Ivy League? This book is the only one available that reveals the actual Ivy League admissions process from a true insider's perspective.

In my case, I worked for four years in the Dartmouth College admissions office. Therefore, I feel uniquely qualified to write this book. The reader will have the benefit of all my insider's knowledge of the elite Ivy League process. I'll take you inside the daily routine of a typical Ivy League admissions committee as it sorts through thousands of competitive applications.

Reading this book will reveal to you the intricacies of that process and will greatly improve your chances of being accepted at an Ivy League or other highly selective college. Once you understand how each part of the application is read and interpreted by an admissions committee, you will learn how to best present yourself and make yourself stand out among the thousands of highly qualified applicants. You will also learn the secret formula used by all the Ivy League schools to compare students from different high schools and different regions. Learning how to use this formula will give you a much better idea of your chances of getting into an Ivy League school in the first place and how to improve those odds.

Even if you are only a middle schooler (or a parent or teacher of one), this book will be an invaluable guide to planning your courses and standardized testing schedule with an eye toward that elusive ticket to the Ivy League. I devote most of the book to a step-by-step look at the application process, going through the application section by section, explaining how each section is read, indicating what the admissions committee is looking for, and telling you exactly who "they" are. "They" know everything there is to know about you; this book helps you learn more about them and how to turn that knowledge to your advantage. Finally, I show how certain "tip" factors are used in the admissions process and how these colleges really treat legacies, recruited athletes, minority applicants, prospective donors, and other VIPs. You will find out how you can use these special categories to your advantage.

Not everyone has access to a knowledgeable college counselor, but anyone can become an expert on Ivy League admissions by fully understanding how different factors are considered. Even the best college counselors often can offer only general advice and do not have the resources to help every student. The vast majority of these counselors have never worked in an Ivy League admissions office and therefore have a limited grasp of what really goes on in the Ivy League admissions process.

The big question remains: Can *you* get *your* child into an Ivy League school? I'm sure many of you are parents who picked up this book to see what the trick is, the quick fix. It is to you and your children, in particular, that I am addressing this book. The bottom line: *You* cannot get your child into an Ivy League school. Your son or daughter is the only person who can get into an Ivy League school. With perhaps some rare exceptions, neither position, nor wealth, nor an elite prep school, nor connections can single-handedly guarantee admission to an Ivy League school. In fact, some of these factors could work against the applicant in the Ivy admissions process. There is never anyone who is guaranteed admission. There are cases of valedictorians with double 800 SATs who are not admitted into their top-choice colleges, just as there are lower-ranked students with mid-500 scores who are admitted.

My goal in this book is to explain enough about the admissions process so that any counselor, parent, or student can see whether it makes sense to apply to an Ivy League school. This book is not aimed at guaranteeing admission to an Ivy League school. However, it will teach you how to maximize your chances and show you how to present yourself in the best possible light. The rest lies in the hands of those who read your application. In chapter 1, I will examine exactly who those people are and what it means for you.

1
The Target Audience

———◆———

The most natural thing to assume is that you are writing your application so that brilliant Ivy League–educated people can read it and laud your humor, charm, and intellectual prowess. But have you ever stopped to think why these brilliant educators would be working in an admissions office, rather than in an upper-level teaching or administrative capacity?

THE TYPICAL ADMISSIONS OFFICER

In most highly selective admissions offices, two very different kinds of admissions officers can be found. Though I admit to stereotyping, most admissions people would probably agree with the basic truths surrounding these two groups.

The first group would include highly talented recent college graduates from either that particular college or another highly selective college. These individuals tend to be very bright, people-oriented, interested in education as a broad field, and anxious to gain some valuable job experience before moving on to a teaching position or perhaps a graduate program. Although they are not very experienced in admissions, they know the caliber of students who are accepted into highly selective colleges because of their firsthand experience with their supertalented classmates. They are, for the most part, extremely qualified to judge candidates in terms of their intellectual potential. Finally, they tend to have a risk-taking capacity that allows them to break the rules here and there when they really believe in a candidate. As a group, they are in touch with current students on a day-to-day basis, since they run most of the student programs, such as hosting and tour guiding.

The second group is composed of the "lifers," people from all walks of life who for some reason got into admissions and have been doing it for so long that they tend to be a little out of touch with the current quality of students. For the most part, they have much less interaction with actual college students and can be slightly out of touch with present-day realities. They may consist of graduate students; former teachers; spouses of professors and college staff; and career administrators. The majority of this group did not graduate from any highly selective college, let alone an Ivy League one.

Since they, for the most part, did not attend highly selective colleges themselves, they sometimes have a harder time recognizing truly great applicants. In some extreme cases, they have to learn a formula for quality applicants and then apply this formula to the applicant pool. In effect, these officers have learned to recognize truly intelligent applicants through repeated viewing. Of course, there are exceptions in this category. I feel fortunate to have worked with some of the brightest people in admissions, not only those at Dartmouth, but also admissions officers from other top colleges whom I traveled with during recruiting seasons. However, these high-quality officers are the exception, not the rule.

As you can imagine, there is little motivation for a talented young graduate to spend more than a year or two in an admissions office before moving on to other academic endeavors, such as law school, medical school, or a Ph.D. program. Thus, there is always a huge turnover in the first group, while the older guard, the career admissions officers, remains the staple of most Ivy League offices. With the exception of Harvard and sometimes Princeton, usually under 50 percent of those working on Ivy League admissions staffs (and here you can include Williams, Swarthmore, and Amherst, to name just a few) attended an Ivy League college. Even if you consider the current deans of admissions at the Ivies, very few attended an Ivy League institution themselves.

I hope by now the point is clear: For the most part, Ivy League hotshots are *not* the ones reading your application. You will note the conspicuous absence of Rhodes scholars or well-known educators on admissions staffs. Many of the people who will be judging you went to less prestigious colleges and sometimes begrudge those who have had more opportunity than they have had. As my former colleague from the Putney School in Putney, Vermont, and former Brown admissions officer Harry Bauld writes in his hilarious book on college essays, "This is your audience. Study them well. Not exactly the Nobel Prize panel."

What I am trying to say without shocking you too much is that the very best of applicants will often be brighter than many of those who will be evaluating them.

THE IMPLICATIONS

The main fact you should keep in mind is that sometimes admissions officers will miss subtle points because they are not always extremely perceptive readers, or because they are reading too fast, or because they are trying to highlight one main point from a letter, or because they are just plain exhausted from reading applications for seven to eight hours a day for months at a time. Unfortunately, many admissions officers are not expert readers (many more have degrees in education than in an academic discipline), and most of them are not scholars or intellectuals. Add to this problem the above factors and you can understand why oftentimes subtle points are overlooked even though they can be crucial to understanding a student's academic potential.

Let me give an example that took place at Dartmouth during a reading retreat, when the whole admissions office gets together, discusses strategies and priorities for the upcoming year, and then reads through actual case studies from the current year's class. All thirteen of us prepared the five case studies the night before so we could read our write-ups aloud and then see how people voted. The biggest disagreement concerned an extremely subtle case of a girl who came from a very humble background. She knew early on that she wanted to be a veterinarian, and she had started working ten hours a week and all summer for two years in a vet's office to obtain firsthand experience. Veterinary medicine was her passion, and you could see throughout all her class work and activities that she was preparing for a career in the field. All her recommendations stressed that she was very quiet but that when she did contribute to class, she almost always offered a tremendous and insightful thought that really turned the classroom into a live arena for debate. One even referred to her as something like a "creative whirlwind of ideas." Though all her teachers said she was modest and quiet, no one said that she was a low-impact person who just blended in with the scenery. On the contrary, they all pointed to the fact that she just didn't blather on and on about what she knew, as some students did, but, rather, that her idea was to follow the discussion intently and then to interject her point as things became more interesting.

What became immediately evident in our follow-up discussion was that nearly all the old-guard people in the office immediately latched onto her teachers' remarks about the quiet aspect of her character, stressing that she would be a low-impact person at Dartmouth and would never add to class discussion because she'd be afraid to speak up. In other words, they totally ignored the body of the recommendations, which stressed that she always had meaningful contributions and that she just waited until the right moment to share her thoughts. Based on this information, only two out of thirteen people voted to accept her.

As you can see from this example, it takes a much more comprehensive reading to get beyond the formula (which in this case was the word *quiet*) and to delve into the meaning of what the recommendations were saying, which was that *at first glance* you might think she was quiet, but, in fact, she was one of the most valuable presences in class discussions.

WHAT CAN YOU DO?

The most obvious point is that teachers, guidance counselors, and students should avoid being too subtle. Remember, most recommendations are read quickly and the reader is skimming for main points. Rather than writing a long, detailed letter that chronicles the entire intellectual development of the student ("When Jim was in ninth grade, his writing was not very good; then in tenth, I noticed some improvement. . . ."), just get to the point. How is the student *now*? Hit your main point hard: "In my class of twenty-five honors-level students, Jim is by far the finest writer and thinker." If you want to convey the idea that even though Jim is quiet, he is not a wallflower, be direct: "Although Jim is a quiet person, his insights are so powerful that when he does contribute to class, he changes the way others think about an issue." If the recommender I described above had been more direct, there would not have been such a high potential for misunderstanding.

The same rule applies to the student. Don't try to hide your accomplishments behind a wall of modesty. If you are captain of your team, come out and say so. If you are president of an organization that is citywide, explain briefly that your role goes beyond that of the average club president. If your science experiment won a major competition, write about it and explain how high the level of competition was. I will offer more specific information in later chapters, but keeping your audience in mind will always help your chances of admission.

THE MONEY QUESTION

Despite the fact that most people are convinced that wealth, fame, and position in society will be looked upon as positive factors in the Ivy League admissions process, this is simply not the case anymore. The tendency at all the Ivies is to reward students from very humble backgrounds who have gone above and beyond their means in order to succeed academically. Since for the last several years the Ivies have been trying to shed their image as snobbish enclaves for wealthy and privileged students, they scrutinize applicants who have never had to work for anything.

In the majority of cases, coming across as a preppy, well-off kid will work against you in two ways. First, you will alienate many admissions officers who might hold your upbringing against you, especially if they come from a more modest background, and second, you are putting yourself right into the Ivy mold that these colleges are trying to break away from.

During my years in admissions, I was sometimes surprised by the bias Ivy officers held against privileged students, especially those who went to fancy private high schools. I disagree that there is something inherently undesirable about having smart students from wealthy families on Ivy campuses. In my opinion, having a wide mix of socioeconomic backgrounds on every campus is an important part of diversity. Just as poor students didn't choose to grow up poor, few rich students choose to grow up wealthy. I disagree strongly that being privileged should automatically count as a strike against the student. However, the reality is that it often does, so it is necessary to take this into account when writing college applications.

How does all this relate to *your* presentation of your application? The first thing to avoid is the tendency to brag about your privileged upbringing. You'll notice that most colleges have you start by filling in your parents' college backgrounds and professions. I know that when I filled in these boxes, I was convinced that the admissions committee would be impressed by my parents' backgrounds and jobs. I thought I would get "extra points" because I came from a family that valued education. In fact, I thought the committee would see that I had a good chance of succeeding since I came from a successful family. I could not have been more wrong.

The main reason colleges ask this question is to see if you qualify as a "legacy" at their college, meaning that either your mother or father graduated from their school (see chapter 12 for more details). Another reason is to see if you have come from a much less sophisticated background and therefore would have lower standardized test scores and perhaps a less polished application. What these questions are *not* there for is to impress the reader, some of whom have been known to harbor grudges against kids who "have it easy." It's a matter of preconceived notions and expectations, as well as personal biases.

If an officer is reading the application of a student from Groton whose father went to Harvard Medical School and is the chief neurosurgeon at a major hospital and whose mom has a Ph.D. in clinical psychology and is in private practice, he starts out by expecting a lot of the student. Clearly, the student comes from a family where there has always been enough money to put a child in the finest nursery schools, kindergarten, after-school activities, and so on. Undoubtedly, they have been able to afford private tutors for both standardized tests and high school subjects. If the officer then sees that this applicant has mid-600 SAT scores, a *B* high school average, and has been involved in extracurricular activities such as lacrosse, sailing, and horseback riding, he is bound not to be very impressed. The officer's thoughts would run as follows: He has had every possible advantage and still only managed mediocre [by Ivy League standards, that is] grades and scores and has never really gone beyond the classroom to seek additional academic challenges.

Now let's look at a student with similar achievements from a totally different background. The first thing the officer sees about Susan is that neither parent went to college; her father is an auto mechanic and her mom is a postal clerk. She goes to a poor inner-city high school where only 15 percent of the population goes on to four-year colleges. Before the officer even starts reading her application, he mentally adjusts his expectations and attitude. No need to feel threatened or jealous of the advantages she might have had. Despite her background, and the fact that she could not afford SAT prep courses, she was always a reader from early childhood. She scores 660 on the verbal, 650 on math, and ends up ranked tenth in her class of 110 students (let's say she earned mostly *A*'s, with a few *B*'s), taking the hardest course load available to her. She is captain of two athletic teams, has done significant community-service work, and teachers say she adds that extra spark to class discussions. Susan would get the vote of any highly selective admissions committee because she rose to the top with limited resources and managed to stand out. The readers can feel good, thinking that they are helping out someone less fortunate by giving her that ticket to an Ivy League school so she can succeed in life.

Some of you may take my advice too much to heart and be tempted to lie or invent. I am not suggesting that path. I am a firm believer that the cream always rises to the top and the best kids shine, no matter where they are from. What I *am* saying is that you don't need to be overly specific. You have to state where your parents were educated, but when it comes time to put down their jobs, you might want to be somewhat vague. For example, if your father is the president and CEO of a big-name investment bank, the committee is going to be expecting quite an amazing applicant, one who has gone beyond his comfy lifestyle to make himself known. You might just write down "banker" for occupation. It's not a lie, but at the same time, it doesn't create such a high expectation in terms of wealth and privilege. Rather than saying "chief neurosurgeon," why not just M.D.? Rather than "chief partner in a major law firm," just put "lawyer." I'm not suggesting you deceive the readers; rather, I'm proposing that you be modest and exercise a level of humility in both your personal part of the application and the description of your parents' jobs.

Unless someone in your family is planning on using his position (let's take the CEO of a major investment firm) to erect a large building on the campus, the admissions office does not need to know exactly what your parent does. That way, an officer will be unable to judge you unjustly because of your background. You are merely protecting yourself from this unfair treatment. Better to let the committee wonder about your background and thus consider you entirely on your intellectual merit.

There are a few exceptions to this rule. The highly selective colleges are always glad to have some very high-profile students or celebrity kids at their institutions, because they get free publicity. When the son of a Disney CEO attended Dartmouth, the college received tons of good, free publicity. When Amy Carter went to Brown, people suddenly knew all about the school and its curriculum. However, a very small percentage of students will fit into this category, so if your parents are merely wealthy or partners in law firms or business firms, the highly selective colleges will not be impressed. However, if your father is a famous actor or the President of the United States, the admissions office might be more favorably impressed. In any case, all VIP cases (see chapter 14) first go through the alumni/development office, not through the admissions office. At some point, the two offices communicate. The bottom line is that in 98 percent of all cases, there is no reason to overstate your parents' position in society on your application.

In some cases, it will be obvious that you come from a privileged family just by your choice of high school and your address. If you go to a fancy private high school in New York City and live at a chic, recognizable address, you might as well write whatever you want, because your background will be quite evident anyway. In later chapters, I will go into more detail about how to present yourself without being overly coached or polished, but for now, I want to set out a constructive timetable for the years leading up to college, especially for the benefit of families who do not have access to an informed college counselor.

2
The Timetable Through High School:
Is Kindergarten Too Early?

———•———

Many parents are convinced that if their children do not get into a first-tier nursery school or kindergarten, they won't get into college. This is not an exaggeration. One has only to look at the influential cover story in the March 1996 issue of *New York* magazine on this very topic. The article begins, "At New York's elite private schools, the obsessive scramble to get into an Ivy League college is getting increasingly desperate, sending hysterical ripples down into nursery schools." The lead is picked up a page later when the author writes, "For many, the mad scramble to get into the Ivy League starts in infancy, with an utterly mad scramble to get into the right nursery school. 'I have had conversations with New Yorkers who have kids who are 18 months old asking what preschool should they send their child to to get on a good track for Amherst,' said Jane Reynolds, Amherst's dean of admissions who, sitting on her campus in western Massachusetts, doesn't know the difference between Episcopal, for example, and All Souls, two of the city's hottest preschools."*

I believe, and I speak from my experience of reading the ap-

*Ralph Gardner, Jr., "Poor Little Smart Kids," *New York,* March 18, 1996, p. 33.

11

plications of both U.S. and foreign students, that inherently smart children who are stimulated by learning can learn just as much from reading at home as they can in the fanciest schools. It is no surprise that the students who get 800 on the verbal SAT scores are always the ones who were read to a lot and then developed a real love of reading as they grew up. Even if they were not challenged in school, these children could read in their spare time and thus learn many of the skills necessary to succeed in college.

I believe that if you can read and write well, the rest will follow. Those who are gifted in math but who are weak readers and writers will ultimately stand a lesser chance of acceptance at top colleges (unless they apply to very technologically oriented colleges such as Cal Tech and MIT), since it is far more typical to see a strong math/science student than to see a standout humanities student. My advice to parents is not to fixate on which prekindergarten or kindergarten school offers the best programs.

The truth is, it's not the level of competitiveness in these early years that makes children smarter later on, but, rather, the intellectual stimulation and reinforcement they get at home from their parents and siblings. A love of learning and reading is almost always instilled in students in the home, not in the school. There are plenty of brilliant students who were sent to very ordinary, not particularly distinguished schools all their lives and still manage to shine, just as there are many average students who have attended the finest schools from prekindergarten to high school.

Therefore, in terms of stimulating your children's minds, instilling a love of reading, and developing lifelong interests, kindergarten age is not too early to begin but it *is* too early to obsess over finding the top-notch kindergarten program in your area.

MIDDLE SCHOOL/JUNIOR HIGH

As parents, if you know your children are able to handle the challenge and the teachers agree, select all available honors-track courses when they are offered. That way, by the time your children enter high school, they will be taking the most advanced courses. Especially in high schools that weight grades (that is, assign added point value to advanced-level classes), students will not be competitive unless they are taking a challenging course load. In this respect, students are judged relative to the norm in their high school. If at high school X, most of the top students take five Advanced Placement or International Baccalaureate classes,* students will not be seen as competitive if they take only three such classes, even if they have higher grades than the person taking a more demanding schedule of classes. There are some high schools that count all their course work as honors and therefore limit the number of APs or IBs a student can take. So, at that particular high school, three APs or IBs might be the limit. It is the college counselor's job to fill in the appropriate box under "Strength of course load" ("Less demanding than average"; "Average college-bound program"; "More demanding than average"; "Most demanding available") correctly.

Sometimes the admissions officers know a high school so well that they can add to the college counselor's assessment through careful examination of a high school record. Many highly competitive colleges keep files or notebooks on high schools. Georgetown, for example, has its officers write an extensive report on every high school they visit, complete with notes about grading systems, representative course loads, where students typically attend college, and any other

---

*Advanced Placement courses (usually referred to as APs) are one category of advanced course work available at many high schools. You can receive college credit for such courses by taking the nationally administered AP tests, which are graded on a scale of 1–5, with 5 being the highest. Some schools offer the International Baccalaureate degree, or IB, which is counted the same as AP for admissions purposes and has a corresponding worldwide test scored on a scale of 1–7, with 7 being the highest.

material that would help them to evaluate students from that high school. They even keep track of which students have been accepted over the past few years and what their class rank and/or GPA was. In cases like these, an informed officer might know that the joint English/art double-period class at a certain high school is actually much harder than AP English, or that AP physics has a much harder teacher than AP biology. Remember that admissions officers are each assigned regions—a collection of states or areas around the country—and are expected to read about and visit these areas. For example, my region for three or four years included all the schools in Westchester and Rockland counties in New York, as well as schools in Ohio, Florida, Indiana, and some other areas, so I had a chance to get to know the schools in those areas well. Many of the old guard who have been in admissions for a while will not only be familiar with the subtleties of specific course loads but will also know who the strongest teachers are and what their recommendations are like.

HIGH SCHOOL

I will talk more specifically in chapter 9 about how to present yourself and your strengths, but for now, I will discuss some basics so you know exactly when you need to do what. One of the most important things you need to do in the eighth or ninth grade is to take a challenging course load while at the same time pursuing your academic interests. When you get to high school, you don't want to get off to a slow start academically. If you are taking all honors classes and start out in ninth grade not working up to potential, you will not be noticed by teachers and you might be dropped into a less competitive track. While admissions officers definitely look for grade trends (that is, if you had a weak ninth-grade year but achieved all *A*'s after that), you don't want to dig yourself a hole you can't climb out of. To top it off, if you start by getting *C*'s in honors classes, teachers won't be that impressed by you, and if you have the same teachers or their colleagues in later years, your reputation might precede you.

There is no doubt that teachers talk among themselves, especially about extreme cases—that is, their worst and best students. You want to be in the latter category so that teachers in the upper grades will look forward to having you in their classes. Though grading aims to be objective, if teachers have heard from their colleagues how brilliant you are, they are going to be predisposed to recognize your talents early on. In a sense, your academic strength and the impression you make on teachers during your early years of high school can have a huge impact on how you do academically in your later years and on the respect accorded to you by faculty.

WHAT IF YOU ARE THE SHY, QUIET TYPE?

If you know you are extremely shy and are hesitant to speak up in class, you need to confront this problem early on. It wouldn't be a bad idea to take a speech class or elect an activity like Model United Nations or debate so you can learn how to present oral arguments in front of a crowd. I have read hundreds of essays about how students overcame their natural shyness through debating or other kinds of leadership positions, and I am convinced that this kind of activity helps. The problem is that if you are a straight *A* student, teachers will not praise you as much if you are very quiet, because you might not add much to class discussions. In fact, one of the boxes on the teacher recommendation form is "Effective participation in class," and if your teacher checks off "Rarely participates," you run the risk of having admissions officers say, "Well, if he rarely participates in his high school classes, what will he add to his college classes?"

Try to make an effort early on to speak out in class. As obvious as this sounds, it always helps to be prepared for class.

Often, especially in larger classes, teachers will ask basic questions from the homework assignment, and they are not looking for a complex answer, just a factual response. If you make it obvious by constantly answering these questions that you have done the reading assignments and that you are interested in the class, teachers will take note.

You'll notice that many naturally brilliant students are chronically unprepared for class because they tend to rely on what they already know instead of trying to keep up with assigned work. This means that even if you are in a class with older and more advanced students, you can still stand out and get the teacher's attention by displaying a love of the subject and a high level of preparation. Go out of your way, especially if you are in a large class, to volunteer at least one or two well-thought-out comments in class. If you are particularly interested in something, request additional reading. Down the road, teachers will comment, "She used to come to my office to discuss literature. I got her started on Jane Austen, and then she proceeded to tackle Victorian literature, always returning to tell me what she thought."

WHAT ABOUT GRADE GRUBBING AND WORKING FOR THE GRADE?

In short, try to avoid grade grubbing. If you are unhappy with a grade, my advice is to work harder on the next paper and talk to the teacher, but make it clear that the grade is not what matters, just the process of learning the material. Don't have your parents go marching in to complain that you will never get into a good college with B grades; don't tell teachers that you have never gotten a B before, so they must be wrong. Be humble, participate in class, and impress your teacher with your sense of maturity and character. The last thing you want to come across as is a spoiled whiner who can't accept low grades.

Remember that teachers will also be filling in boxes on your character and commenting on it in their recommendations. All of their academic praise can be undermined by one reference to "working for the grade." The best thing teachers could say about you is, "Unlike all the hypercompetitive students I had in my calculus class, Phil really steered clear of all that and let his interest in math carry him through the class." That is the kind of comment that is noticed by an admissions staff. Needless to say, it also makes you stand out much more from those of your peers who seem much *less* interested (by comparison) in learning the material. The worst thing that teachers could say on your college application is that you are constantly pestering them for a higher grade. From an admissions standpoint, grade grubbing is the antithesis of what the highly selective colleges are seeking. The grade grubber is *not* interested in learning for learning's sake, but, rather, in learning as a utilitarian process for getting ahead.

Keep in mind that the operative questions admissions officers always ask are these: "What will they add to our college? What kind of impact will they have?" The number-one student with average test scores who achieves through slavishly hard work but doesn't contribute much to classroom discussions and is barely noticed by teachers except for good testing ability is *less* attractive because his major contribution will be studying really hard and trying to get good grades in college. In contrast, the more interesting, dynamic applicants will be the ones who are achieving and contributing in the classroom, pushing their professors, and raising the level of discussion.

I'd urge students to take a strong look at themselves and their motivations for achieving. Are your parents forcing you to do hours of homework when you'd be happier shooting hoops in the driveway? Do you dread the thought of plowing through novels for your English class? Why do you want to get *A*'s? Are you truly interested in your classes, or do you view them just as stepping-stones to *success*? I put the word *success* in italics because I'd like to highlight an obvious fact: You don't even have to go to college, much less an Ivy League school, to be successful. Plenty of self-made millionaires (if money happens to be how you define success) made their money through hard work and insightful marketing. If your goal is to make money but you don't enjoy studying or reading, don't waste your time by trying to get into an Ivy League or highly selective college. I say this because the beauty of an Ivy League/highly selective education lies in the intellectual atmosphere and the collegial bonds formed among students interested in similar ideas and fields. It does not lie in the prestige of having a diploma from Princeton or Dartmouth on your wall. You would be much better served at a more trade-oriented school where you could major in something practical rather than theoretical. Similarly, if you are achieving only to please your parents so they can brag about you to their friends, you need to think seriously about wasting their money (more than $100,000) at an Ivy League school, when it is clear that you would struggle or, at the very least, not appreciate the opportunities.

TIME TIPS FOR TAKING TESTS IN HIGH SCHOOL

Let's assume that you are taking competitive classes at your high school. As early as ninth grade, you need to be thinking about taking SAT II subject tests. Everyone makes a big deal of the SAT I, but don't forget that the Ivies place equal weight on the SAT II subject tests (which until recently were known as achievement tests). You will see in later chapters just how important both of these tests are.

The big difference between the SAT I and the SAT IIs is that you really can study for the latter. Unlike the SAT I, the subject tests (SAT IIs) last only an hour and cover a very narrow range of material, which can be prepped for. Even if your high school class in a specific subject wasn't very strong academically, you can buy a prep book for any subject test and teach yourself areas not covered in class. These tests are offered in many more areas than you would imagine: Chinese, Japanese, French, Spanish, Italian, two levels of math, writing, literature, biology, chemistry, physics, American history, and so on. Most of the Ivy League schools require three of these subject tests.

The good news is that there are at least twenty different tests (with new ones being added every year). Select only the ones you are good at. If you are terrible in math, don't take the math subject tests. If you love American history, review the material covered on the exam and take it. Do check the requirements for each college you are applying to, because some vary slightly in terms of testing requirements. The most important advice I can give you is to take the SAT II subject tests at the end of the year, immediately after completing the corresponding class. If you take biology in ninth grade, don't wait until the following fall to sign up for the test; take it in June, right after you finish the class. The other crucial thing is to start early—that is, in the ninth grade. Ideally, you will want to take four to six tests so that when colleges select your three strongest, they will be excellent.

As a reference for parents, students, and counselors, I have provided a timetable for all four high school years that is geared towards gaining admission to a highly selective college.

ACADEMIC PLANNING

FRESHMAN YEAR

- Try to ensure that you are in all or nearly all of the advanced-level classes that are available.

- Make your voice heard in class so teachers can get to know you better.
- Sort through all the extracurricular activities available in your high school, with an eye toward participating for four years in those that truly interest you. Colleges like to see long-term commitment. It is fine to start something and then drop out, but try to have at least two or three in-depth involvements that will be three- or four-year commitments.
- Set up a schedule for yourself so you don't fall behind. The study habits you develop as a freshman will be the basis for your success later on.
- Many ninth graders are young and somewhat immature. Avoid the temptation to leave academics behind to join the slacker group. Remember, a really weak ninth-grade year will lower your overall rank by senior year.
- During your spring break, buy one or two SAT II preparation books with actual tests so you can begin to review and study for the appropriate tests.
- Try to find a one-month or perhaps two-week college program at one of the top summer schools so you can pursue a subject you might not have had time to find out about in high school. Don't commit to the whole summer, because you want to have fun, too, while getting your feet wet academically.
- Over the summer, *read, read, and read* in your spare time: novels, newspapers, scientific journals, et cetera. By reading many different literary styles and genres, you will be doing the best kind of preparation for the SAT verbal section. This is much cheaper than taking a Stanley Kaplan course, and it is equally effective in many cases. The more you read, the more your vocabulary and reading comprehension will increase and the more you will be able to raise your score on the SAT verbal section.
- Start a list of your extracurricular involvements that you can add to each year.

Sophomore Year

- Keep reading novels, magazines, quality newspapers, or any other challenging texts in your spare time.
- The more familiarity you have with the SAT I, the better you will do when you take the test. Rather than waiting until junior year, take the PSAT this year as a practice. Colleges never see PSAT scores, just SAT scores.
- Are you enjoying your sports or other extracurricular activities? Do you have any new interests you want to pursue? Now is the time to change around a little but still have a solid three-year commitment by senior year.
- Keep up with your homework. If you are doing less well than you expected in a particular class, talk to the teacher and ask what you could do to improve. Stress that it is not the grade that is worrying you, but, rather, your own disappointment with how you are doing.
- By spring break, evaluate your strong subjects and begin to study for one or two SAT II tests.
- In June, take two or possibly three different SAT II tests.
- During the summer, continue reading all different kinds of materials. This is when you will have the free time to brush up on your reading and boost your vocabulary and reading comprehension before the barrage of junior-year testing.
- This is a good summer to get a job. Colleges love to see a sense of responsibility, as well as the fact that students have not had everything handed to them. Though everyone will want to be a lifeguard or a camp counselor, try to pick a job that's less cushy, such as working in a retail store or on a construction crew. If you have a particular talent, try to line something up commensurate with your academic skills, such as working in a computer store or for a local paper. If you are an athlete, work on your training here, too.

- To avoid the junior panic, try to fit in three to five college visits over the summer—in June or July, not August, when every other student in the country will be mobbing campuses. Sit in on the information sessions, take a tour, and talk to students. The more you get done this summer, the less panicked you will be the following summer.

JUNIOR YEAR

- This is the big year for testing. Luckily, if you have been following this schedule so far, you have not saved all your testing for this year and you will have several scores to choose from.
- Take the PSATs when they are offered at your high school. Remember, your status as a National Merit semifinalist or National Merit finalist will be determined by your PSAT scores, not your SAT scores.
- This should be your hardest academic year, since you will ideally be taking many honors, AP, or IB classes. Colleges look upon your junior year as a crucial one. This is the year when you really want to focus and go for the very best grades possible. Let your academic interests direct you. If you get involved researching a paper, feel free to go beyond the basic course requirements in pursuing your topic. This is the year you want to impress your teachers and excel in all your classes. Pursue your interests outside of class, as well.
- Take the SAT I for the first time. You will have other chances to improve these scores. Sleep well the night before and eat a healthy breakfast the morning of the test.
- After getting through the SAT I, take one or two more SAT II tests in the spring. Start preparing for them the month before by taking practice tests and filling in gaps in your knowledge.

- Save college visits and interviews for summer so that you don't have to miss classes.
- If you have found a good academic program already or have a good idea for a new one, this is the perfect summer to participate. Be adventurous.
- If you really can't afford one of these programs or are unable to get scholarship assistance, continue to work over the summer, since work is considered an important factor in your admission.
- Sometime during the summer—and I would *strongly* suggest June or July, not August, when the entire country will join you—visit colleges that you are interested in. Attend the group information sessions, go on the tour, and talk to students at each college. This way, if you do decide to apply early decision, you will have had time to visit all the colleges you are interested in.
- Everytime you visit a college, fill out a visitation sheet at the admissions office so you will be on the mailing list for an application.
- If you are really interested in a college, schedule an on-campus interview a few weeks ahead of time. Schools are much less busy in June and July, so that is an ideal time. If you wait until the fall of your senior year, you will have to miss classes, which is not advisable, since your fall grades are crucial this year.
- At the end of the summer, narrow down your college list and be sure to request applications from all the colleges you are considering.
- Before school starts, try to do as much research as you can on the colleges that interest you. Read about them in college guidebooks (go to your public library and spend some time reading through these books), surf the Internet, and talk to college-age friends who might be around during the summer.
- Think about applying early decision if you have had time to make a final decision about your first-choice college.

- Evaluate your testing record. If you already have high scores on the SAT I, don't bother taking it again. If you think you can improve, take the test one more time in the early fall.
- Evaluate your SAT IIs, as well. If you don't have three scores you are happy with, retake one or two of the tests in October or November.
- Send your scores to the colleges you are applying to.
- Start working on your college essays so you don't have to dash them off in a hurry later on. You will have to write several essays and drafts in order to produce a strong essay.

Senior Year

- Keep up your grades! Colleges look at your senior grades, even for spring term. This is no time to slack off after so much hard work.
- If you are applying under either an early-decision or early-action plan, work on your application so you can postmark it by the deadline, usually November first or fifteenth.
- If you are not applying early decision, you have up until the February test dates to take and improve upon your SAT Is and SAT IIs.
- Get your applications done by January 1st.
- Take a deep breath—you have made it this far!

Whew! Even if you are able to do half the things on this list, you will be ahead of most college applicants, who typically save everything to the last minute. With careful planning, you can have a much calmer high school experience and avoid the panic of taking tests late in the year in a desperate attempt to get a few high scores. If you have had a chance to visit colleges and have a clear first choice, early decision or early action might be a good option for you. We will turn to these options in the following chapter.

WHAT ABOUT SAT PREP COURSES?

Before closing this discussion on high school planning, I will address the question of prep classes such as Princeton Review, Kaplan, or other private classes geared toward preparation for standardized testing. As much as I would like to offer an authoritative statement—for example, "I believe you should never take a prep course," or "To be competitive, you must take a prep course"—this kind of oversimplification is impossible. The real issue is familiarity with the test. The more familiar you are with the format of the SAT I, the types of questions asked, the amount of time you should devote to each question, the better you will do. This is why students who take the test more than once almost always raise their scores each time, even if only by a little bit.

If you are disciplined enough to take practice tests (which you can request directly from the Educational Testing Service in Princeton, New Jersey), you will become intimately familiar with the test and will probably not need a prep course. If, however, you are the kind of student who would never be motivated enough to practice on your own, a prep course would give you the discipline to study the test and to take practice tests.

When I was a high school student, I thought to myself, Why should my parents have to pay hundreds of dollars for a prep course when I could devote a few weekends to taking practice tests, reading a few guidebooks with helpful test hints, and becoming intimately familiar with the test? By the time I took the SATs, I knew exactly how long I should spend on each question, which sections I could move through quickly and which ones I should take more time on, and how many I could leave blank and still score over 650 or 700. It took some time and some independent study, but in the end, I know I would have been bored to death in a prep course, when all the information I needed was in printed form in any good bookstore. On the other hand, I had some friends who could not find the time or the motivation to read about helpful hints for the tests, and who were incapable of spending a few hours in their house taking practice tests. For them, I think prep classes were helpful in disciplining them to learn as much as possible about the test.

You will notice that I haven't focused very much on the issue of learning the actual material on the test. This oversight is intentional, because it is my personal belief that the main purpose of prep courses is to familiarize students with the test and to teach test-taking techniques that can go a long way in raising a score. What they are *not* tremendously helpful for is teaching the material for the SAT I, because it is fundamentally an aptitude test, not a knowledge-based test. This difference is most obvious on the verbal section.

Whether you prepare on your own or take a prep class to help you with the verbal section, you will not become a more insightful reader, only a more insightful test-taker—this distinction is crucial. The verbal section is designed to see how strong a reader you are, how you think and reason, and how you process information in prose form. As any SAT instructor can tell you, learning test-taking techniques and familiarizing yourself with the test can raise your score up to a certain point, especially if you are starting from a low level. It is not uncommon, either through private study or an organized prep course, to raise a verbal score from 450 to 600 or from 570 to 680. What is almost impossible is to jump into the 720 to 800 range, even if you are starting in the high 600s. With a few exceptions, the students who score over 740 or so are simply voracious readers, students who have been reading seriously since they were very young and have continued to do so all their lives.

Every time I have seen a student with an 800 verbal score,

there has been confirmation throughout the application that the student is a reader—teachers mention it, the student often talks about loving literature from a young age and reading a lot throughout middle school and high school, and guidance counselors allude to it. No amount of test-taking preparation can earn you an 800 verbal score, because that requires a lifetime devoted to reading. That is why in my timetable I mention that students should increase their reading load two years prior to taking the SAT I, since that will go much further in helping to raise a verbal score than taking a prep course.

The SAT I math section is a little different. Although it is designed to test aptitude, it is possible to prepare for the math section to a greater extent than the verbal section. Again, you won't get an 800, but even a weak math student can learn enough tips, patterns, and finite material (after all, the math SAT I is not based on an infinite curriculum; it covers the same topics over and over, using slightly different examples and problems each time) to score over 600. Depending on the student and his mathematical background and motivation for private study, he can determine the necessity of taking a prep course or studying on his own. Many students have such a natural math ability that a course would be superfluous; all they need to do is familiarize themselves with the format of the test so they don't have to waste valuable time reading the somewhat complicated directions.

In short, prep courses can be helpful for many students, although they are certainly not necessary. What students need to do is know the test format, directions, and strategies extremely well so that they can go in and do their highest-level work. The best strategy for determining the necessity of taking a class is to take an actual SAT I test at home, score it, and examine your score. If you are scoring between 300 and 600, either a prep course or private study will probably raise your score, sometimes significantly. If you are already scoring over 650, you probably just need to brush up on a few areas, practice more, and become intimately familiar with the test.

3

Early-Decision and Early-Action Policies

———•———

If you are looking for a way to increase your chances of getting into an Ivy, one possibility is to apply early decision, or early action, if a college has an early-action plan. *Early decision* means that you apply around November first to one college and hear around December fifteenth whether or not you have been accepted. If you are accepted, you are committed to attending that college. Early decision is known as a "binding" plan, because if you are accepted, you are bound to attend.

Early action is similar in terms of time frame, but you are not committed to attending; hence, this is considered a "nonbinding" plan. Of the eight Ivies, only Harvard and Brown have early-action policies—the other six have early decision so I will focus mostly on the implications of early decision in this chapter. The acceptance rate is invariably higher for early-decision candidates at most of the Ivies, but you have to be sure that the college is *truly* your first choice. What would be the point of applying early decision to Princeton, getting accepted, and then deciding that you want to attend Harvard? If your heart is set on attending an Ivy, make sure to visit all the colleges and to set up interviews with time to spare. I would suggest the spring and summer after your junior year, so by the time September rolls around, you have a clear first choice. If you can honestly say to yourself that you prefer one college over all others, applying early decision is a fantastic idea. If, on the other hand, you are torn between several colleges, it is *not* a good idea to apply early decision, because the disadvantages outweigh the advantages.

At Dartmouth, the odds of getting accepted early decision are roughly 30 to 32 percent, whereas for regular decision, the odds drop to below 20 percent. Dartmouth usually gets around 1,300 to 1,400 early-decision applicants and accepts around 350 to 380. For almost all of the Ivies, the admission rate is about one in three for early decision or early action and the freshman class is typically made up of 30 percent early-decision applicants and 70 percent regular-decision applicants.* Until recently, about half of the Ivy League schools had early-action programs and the other half had early-decision programs. In 1995, Princeton and Yale switched from early-action programs to early-decision ones. Their statistics were significantly different from the other Ivies for the class of 2000 in that they accepted almost half of their entire freshman class under the early-decision policy; the other half were regular-decision applicants. I suspect they will cut back a little bit on this high percentage, but only time will tell.

Currently, the only Ivies that remain early-action schools are Harvard and Brown. Even though Harvard has an early-action, and therefore nonbinding, policy, the yield on its early-action students who are accepted is 88 percent. That is to say that roughly 88 percent of those students who are accepted

---

*For the class of 2000, these are the early-decision numbers as reported by the Ivy (and MIT) directors during the annual Ivy League meeting in the spring of 1996: Princeton accepted 38 percent of early-decision applicants and filled 48 percent of the freshman class. Yale admitted 38 percent of the early-decision applicants—18 percent of the class. Cornell admitted 38 percent of early-decision applicants and filled roughly 25 percent of the freshman class. Dartmouth admitted 31 percent of early-decision applicants and filled 35 percent of the class. MIT accepted 37 percent of those who applied early action (75 percent of those students decided to attend MIT) and filled 36 percent of the freshman class. Brown admitted 23 percent early action, 32 percent of the freshman class. The University of Pennsylvania accepted 35 percent of the early-decision applicants and filled about one-third of the class. Columbia admitted 33 percent of the early-decision applicants and filled about one-third of the class. Harvard accepted 25 percent of the early-action applicants (88 percent of those students decided to attend Harvard) and filled up 48 percent of the class. Amherst filled up 37 percent of the class, Swarthmore, 26 percent, Williams, 34 percent. See *New York Times,* November 27, 1996.

early action to Harvard say yes to the offer, while around 12 percent choose to attend other colleges.

How does the early-decision pool of applicants differ from the regular-decision pool? In almost every case, the early-decision pool is much more homogeneous. Dartmouth, for example, receives many more applications from candidates in the middle of the academic range than it does in the very high end or the very low end. Why is this? Firstly, I surmise that the most spectacular applicants know they will get into almost any college they apply to, so those very highly qualified applicants don't feel the need to apply early and almost all prefer to apply to multiple Ivies, see where they get accepted, and then choose from among those colleges. Of course, I am generalizing somewhat, because not all highly qualified applicants fall into this category. Secondly, most minority applicants tend not to apply early decision, usually for financial reasons. Finally, many students for whom financial aid is a major concern opt not to apply early so they can compare scholarship offers from a variety of colleges. Therefore, many of the applicants for early decision tend to be affluent white students.

Since the early-decision pool is noticeably more homogeneous, and since all the colleges aim for overall diversity (see chapter 16), it does not behoove a college to accept more than 30 percent or so of its applicants early, because then only "special category" cases will be accepted regular decision.

So what is the benefit of early decision from the college's standpoint? To some extent, the college can set a standard for the incoming class, not to mention the fact that every person it accepts has a definite place in the class—the yield on early-decision applicants is 100 percent. Thus, the colleges can control exactly what the class will look like—students cannot turn down the offer of admission. It is good for a college to get a solid body of students who are excited to attend. All the early applicants to Dartmouth want to go to Dartmouth over all other colleges and must attend if accepted. They are usually very excited about the college once they are accepted and tend to be some of the most loyal alumni. Many legacies (that is, those whose mother or father attended Dartmouth) apply early, so for fund-raising reasons, it is good to have a slightly higher percentage of legacies in the early-decision pool. Finally, probably the most important benefit of early decision has to do with athletics. Coaches have lists of those candidates they wish to have admitted and they want to get as many as possible of those accepted early so they don't have to worry about yield later on. With some early-decision admits, they are guaranteed a certain number of students for their teams without having to fight with other colleges over them.

Keep in mind that you should always check directly with colleges about their early-decision or early-action plan. Though at almost all the Ivies you have a statistical advantage by applying under one of these early plans, that is not the case at all of the colleges, most noticeably Cornell, which does not grant favor to those applying early decision. Their acceptance rate is usually almost identical for both early-decision and regular applicants (38 percent versus 34 percent) and they do not give much weight to the fact that Cornell is a first choice for those students applying early.

POSSIBLE OUTCOMES FOR EARLY APPLICATIONS

At some of the Ivies, applicants are either accepted or deferred, while at others they can also be rejected. At Dartmouth, about a third of the early-decision applicants are rejected outright, about a third are deferred until regular decision, and about a third are accepted. If a student is rejected, that should be interpreted as a realistic indication from the college that he was not a competitive applicant and would not have been admitted on a regular-decision basis, either. If a student is deferred, his file will be read again under regular decision, but typically only about 5 to 10 percent of those who are deferred will ultimately be accepted, because the competition only gets fiercer for regular decision. Sometimes a student is deferred because the college feels that it needs more information: additional scores, senior grades, or additional recommendations. Sometimes a student is deferred because he simply doesn't stand out that much, yet is too strong to be rejected outright without upsetting the high school or community. A valedictorian with low test scores will usually be deferred, not rejected, unless test results are extremely low. Students who are accepted are guaranteed a place in the class, providing that their grades do not drop dramatically and they don't get into any kind of serious disciplinary trouble.

Schools always reserve the right to revoke an acceptance, so once you are accepted, it is wise to continue to have a strong senior year and to avoid trouble of any kind. At Dartmouth, usually two or three students a year have their acceptances revoked for academic reasons, while the same number have theirs revoked for disciplinary reasons.

WHAT CAN YOU DO IF YOU ARE DEFERRED?

The problem with being deferred is that you will not know if you were a polite defer (that is, a valedictorian with low test scores who will probably not be admitted anyway but was deferred to show that he was strong enough not to be rejected outright) or a realistic defer (that is, someone who looked pretty strong, but the college wanted to wait for more scores and/or midyear grades to see how the person performed while carrying a challenging senior course load). Most colleges will talk to applicants, so I definitely recommend that the student call the admissions office himself, ask to speak to the regional officer in charge of his high school, and try to get a sense of what his weaknesses are and if there is any advice the officer would suggest. It shows a greater maturity on the applicant's part to call himself, rather than delegating this task to a parent, so leave your parents out of the loop. Since sometimes admissions officers will be more candid with guidance counselors, a student might encourage his guidance counselor to call, as well, to fish for information.

Remember that officers cannot disclose specific information in your file, so you must read behind the lines. If an admissions officer starts reciting statistics about average testing, he probably is trying to say that your testing is on the low side, putting you into the category of high rank, low standardized testing. If she says that nothing is wrong but you are right in the middle of the applicant pool, you will probably not be admitted unless scores and/or grades go up dramatically. Most likely, the officer is trying to tell you that your grades and scores are good but that you do not come across as an intellectual standout. If she says that you are close but the college wants to see what the rest of your senior year looks like, you probably have a better chance and your task will be to have a stellar remainder of your senior year.

After speaking to an admissions officer, reaffirm your interest by writing a brief letter to the college saying that you are still considering that school as your top choice (you can do this at the end of February or early March, since no one will even pick up the deferred files until mid-March, when all the early-decision or early-action candidates are reviewed, usually all at once in a two- or three-day review session). Then update your file by having the guidance counselor send updated grades and any new awards or accomplishments (or you can include those in your letter). What you should avoid is sending reams of new material, because the officers do not have time to read copious amounts of new information.

At most, I would suggest sending one extra letter of recommendation from a senior-year teacher, a brief update on new information (major awards like a Westinghouse, midyear grades, athletic honors), and a paragraph or two saying that you were disappointed but that this college is still your first choice. Do not call and harass the officers for months, do not have the partner at your parents' law firm pester the admissions office, and do not send information every few weeks.

In mid-March, at most of the highly selective colleges, the regional officers receive a big pile of all the deferred applications from their region, which normally includes several different states. Typically, I had between twenty-five and thirty-five deferred students in my region. For a day or two, I would sort through these applications by first rereading both my original comments and the other readers' comments, then sorting through the new information in each folder (this information would be right in the front of the file). In 95 percent of the cases, the student would actually look less competitive when compared to the regular-decision applicants, whose files we had spent the last three months reading. In 5 to 10 percent of the cases, there might have been a major change, such as new testing, which brought the academic ranking up (see chapter 4); a new athletic ranking, which suddenly placed the student as a top recruit in a sport; an impressive senior record; or a major national award like a Westinghouse finalist, of which there are only a few in the entire country. I would then take what I considered the most compelling cases (five or so), make a brief list with a short explanation for the director, and submit this list and the selected files for his review. He would then go through all the regional officers' recommendations and select those whom he found to be the strongest applicants in the entire applicant pool.

In summary, the odds are against your getting in once you have been deferred, but as long as you have a realistic picture of your chances, you should still feel free to take the positive steps outlined above in order to do everything in your power to increase those chances. Sometimes an officer will remember you or have been impressed after making a personal contact with you, so calling and following up in writing will serve to keep your name in the forefront of his mind. (Annoying the officer by calling constantly will only make him less likely to select you above all others.) Ultimately, if you were not a stand-out intellectually to begin with, no awards, grades, or recommendations will change the impression generated from your entire high school record, but if you were close, there is a much higher chance for admission if you follow these steps.

Now that you are familiar with some of the admissions plans in the Ivies, let us turn to the admissions decisions themselves. I will take you inside the decision-making process so you will have a more informed idea about how decisions are made.

WILL I GET LESS FINANCIAL AID IF I APPLY EARLY DECISION OR EARLY ACTION?

Because of misconceptions and rumors about how financial aid is awarded at the Ivy League schools, many students hesitate to apply early decision because they mistakenly think they will get less money. Of course, there are various scenarios, so let me explain a little bit about how Ivy League financial aid works, particularly in respect to early decision or early action. First of all, the Ivies are forbidden by the athletic rules that tie them together to award athletic scholarships. Because admission to the colleges is so competitive, very rarely are merit scholarships available. At Dartmouth, absolutely no merit scholarships are awarded.

Due to a lawsuit a few years back, all the Ivies must use a slightly different method for calculating financial-aid packages and are not allowed to communicate with one another or with the admissions officers about financial-aid packages. Even so, these packages are usually within a few thousand dollars of one another. Because I am not a specialist in financial aid, I will not elaborate on exactly how financial-aid packages are calculated, especially since it is done slightly differently at each college. To generalize, most, but not all, highly selective colleges try to ascertain how much money a student needs in order to be able to attend, then try to design a financial-aid package that will cover full tuition and room and board. The reason behind the similarity between Ivy League financial-aid packages is that the methodology these colleges use is almost identical. In fact, because of their athletic ties, the Ivies must be able to justify their formulas in case a coach challenges their methodology.

Since all of the Ivies are 100 percent "need-blind" (that is, they do not take into account the applicant's ability to pay) with regard to applicants for admission, they are bound to look at all students the same way, regardless of when these students apply for admission. In other words, there will be no difference between the amount of money awarded to an early-decision applicant and to a regular-decision applicant.

Why, then, do some Ivies on the average generate slightly more favorable financial-aid packages than others? The general rule in the Ivies is that all colleges must use the appropriate formulas and be able to justify and defend their awards, but if a college has extra money, it is allowed to add money, *as long as it is done equitably among all financial-aid recipients*. Thus, if Princeton, because of its large endowment, decided that it was going to add an extra two thousand dollars to a scholarship, it would have to do so in every single case for all students who qualified for scholarship aid. Even so, they would still have to treat early-decision applicants and regular-decision applicants the same way. What the colleges are expressly forbidden to do is to throw in an extra two thousand dollars in order to get a highly coveted athlete to enroll at their college.

WHAT'S THE BOTTOM LINE?

If you are applying only to Ivy League schools, you will get exactly the same package early decision or early action as you would in regular decision. In addition, you would probably get the same amount of financial aid at all the Ivies, give or take a few thousand out of the thirty-thousand-dollar-plus tuition, so you might as well apply early if you have a clear first-choice college. Even if you did get slightly more money from another highly selective college, it would most likely be a small and insignificant amount over a four-year period.

But what if you are also planning to apply to other colleges that *are* allowed to offer either athletic scholarships or merit-based scholarships? Then you might want to wait until regular decision so you can compare your full-tuition scholarship at Notre Dame or your full merit-based scholarship to the University of Connecticut to the much smaller financial-aid package you would get at an Ivy League school. However, keep in mind that the Ivies *cannot* (that is, are not allowed) to match any merit-based or athletic-based packages, so you will *not* get any more money if you appeal your award to one of the Ivies.

The only time an Ivy League school will honor an appeal is if the other awarding college has similar methodology—in those cases, they will usually try to match the scholarship offer. Some colleges for which the Ivies will match offers would be Swarthmore, Williams, Amherst, Bowdoin, Bates, Middlebury, and so on—provided that those awards were not merit- or athletic-based.*

In conclusion, in the majority of cases, you will not be hurt at all in terms of financial aid by applying early decision. The Ivies do not run out of money, nor do they change their methodologies midstream. Only in the last case I mentioned would it behoove you to wait until regular decision for financial-aid reasons. In short, applying early decision has many advantages, but it is only for those who are certain in

*This is not a hard-and-fast rule. The schools can always decide not to honor an appeal. It is not an automatic process. In general, the applicant would have to provide new information in order for an appeal to be granted in the first place. It's worth a try, but there is no guarantee.

November of their top-choice college. In the best of cases, you will know before Christmas whether or not you have been accepted, and in the worst of cases, you will be denied and will have to apply to a broader range of colleges for regular decision.

4

The New SAT I
and Recentering

In the first part of this chapter, I will describe in detail how the SAT I has changed and what the effects of "recentering" are in both layman's and more technical terms. In the second part of the chapter, I will explain what effects these changes have had on highly selective admissions. Anyone over the age of eighteen should read this section carefully, because the SAT I that you took has undergone dramatic changes. Therefore, it is impossible to compare old scores with new scores.

When the SAT was first developed, the median score was set at 500 for both the math and the verbal. Keep in mind that the median represents the midpoint score, so if half the class scored over 50 on a test and half scored under 50, the median score would be 50. Thus, in 1950, if you got a 560 on the verbal and a 480 on the math, you were above the national median in verbal and below it in math. In other words, it was fair to say you were stronger in the verbal area. However, in the last forty years or so, the number and composition of people taking the SAT has increased dramatically and the median has changed, so that now both verbal and math have different median scores, neither of which is a 500. In 1995, the median verbal score was 428, while the median math score was 482. Thus, in 1995, if a student scored 540V and 540M, he was *not* equal in these two areas—in fact, that student was stronger in verbal, since the verbal median was actually lower than the math median.

Why did the median score change from the original 500V, 500M scale? The simple answer is that the population of test takers changed dramatically in both number and composition. In 1941, ten thousand students from private secondary high schools took the SAT, averaging 500V, 500M. The incredible thing is that from 1942 until 1995, all SAT takers were compared with this class of 1941, even though by 1995 more than 2 million people took the SAT, a third of whom were minority students. Needless to say, these 2 million students made up a much more diverse group of test takers than the 1941 group.

Another side effect of not adjusting the test scale was that there was not an even bell-curve distribution over the score range 200 to 800. The curve peaked and then glided down toward 800, but not all scores were represented. If you had a perfect score on the verbal section, you would get an 800, but then one or two wrong answers and you'd be down to 760, then 720, and so on—with no one getting 790, 780, or 770. It was nearly impossible to get over a 700, since you had to make very few mistakes, and each mistake would take you down by a much larger margin in this high range than it would if you were going from a 500 to a 490. In other words, a raw-score (your raw score is equivalent to the total number of the questions you answered correctly minus one-quarter of all the questions you answered incorrectly) difference of one point might cause a thirty-point drop on the high end of the scale, whereas in a lower range, it might not cause any difference in the final reported score. Thus, on the old scale, only .1 percent of all test takers scored between 750 and 800 on the verbal section. In order to get a perfect 800, you had to answer every question correctly. Only .9 percent scored between 700 and 750 on the old verbal, so in total, a paltry 1 percent of all test takers scored over 700 on the verbal, whereas a whopping 75 percent of test takers scored below 500. In the math section, only 4.2 percent of the population scored over 700.

Although from experience I knew when I took the SAT that the high scores on the verbal section were stretched out and the low scores were scrunched together, I didn't really understand why until recently—that is, until I read the special report prepared by the College Board (distributed in May 1995) for the Ivy League deans of admissions to explain how score recentering would affect the Ivy League applicant pools. After I read the official explanation, I immediately understood why no one ever has the slightest idea what the College Board is talking about. Let me summarize the main points of their explanation regarding why the old SAT was scored unfairly.

When the statisticians at the Educational Testing Service equated raw scores with scaled scores, they always found a few (about 1 percent of the test-taking population) that fell below the 200 score minimum. Because no score can be reported lower than 200, all of these low scores were reported as 200. Likewise, in the upper range, it was almost impossible to get a perfect raw score, so the statisticians were forced to extrapolate raw scores in the upper end to reach a scaled score of 800. Since these scores were basically stretched out over the high range, there were gaps, so that a raw score of 78 might correspond with an 800, but then the next-highest score (77 raw) would be 760, then 740, and so on. Thus, a difference of two points on the raw scale resulted in a difference of sixty points on the actual scale.

Believe it or not, this "two raw points equals sixty scaled points" formula was not true all along the scale, only at the high end. In the lower ranges, since the scores were not so compressed, a two-point raw-score difference would only equal a real score difference of maybe ten, twenty, or thirty points. The problem was the lack of a consistent relationship between raw score and scaled score, a fact that caused many scoring inequities on the old SAT. The extrapolated scores in the upper range were apparently not based on actual data, so high scores were not consistent with scores in other parts of the test range.

In simpler terms, it was impossible to equate each raw score with a scaled score between 200 and 800 because some students would have scored *under* 200 (not allowed), while no one would have scored over 700. To remedy this situation, ETS had to extrapolate at the extreme ends of the scale based on their own judgment, one that seems not to have been based on hard data. I do not mean to criticize their procedures, but there seems to be a disturbing lack of mathematical method in their assignment of scores in both the very high and the very low ranges. It almost sounds as if they had to fudge the data to some extent.

From all this, what we really need to understand is that on the old scale, most people scored in the middle range, and many of those scores were bunched together, so that the difference between a 530 verbal and a 500 verbal might have been only one or two questions on the entire three-hour test. In addition, very few scored over 700 in either verbal or math. Finally, a 600 verbal score was not directly comparable to a 600 math score, since the median for both tests was different.

In any case, because of all the inequities in scoring, the College Board decided in 1995 to set the median once again at a true 500 for both verbal and math. This decision also had the benefit of restoring the true bell curve, which peaked at 500 and gently sloped down in both directions toward 800 and 200. Remember, the old curve was no longer a perfect bell curve, so there is no way to establish a one-to-one correspondence between old scores and new scores. In other words, you can't just add a certain number to the old scores in order to calculate the new scores. Instead of just adding fifty points to old scores to get new scores, you have to use the College Board's conversion tables equating all old scores with new scores.

In general, since both the verbal and the math median were below 500, scores on the recentered test look higher, although the percentile remains the same. At Dartmouth, for example, the class of 1999 had an average of about a 640 verbal and a 710 math (unrecentered scores), while the class of 2000 had a

705 verbal average and a 710 math. The verbal is really almost the same (there was a real rise of maybe five points), even though it *seems* much higher, since recentered verbal scores jump as much as sixty points, while the recentered math scores are very similar, with a slight real rise. As you can see, the math hardly changed at all in the upper range, while the verbal changed somewhat dramatically because of recentering.

Rather than listing the complete official ETS conversion table for original SAT Is to recentered SAT Is (which is available from the College Board and from most high school guidance counselors), I have excerpted scores in various ranges for the sake of example. To assure yourself that there is no constant number you can use to change old scores to new, look at some of the following conversions from old scores to new scores:

Original Verbal	Recentered Verbal	Original Math	Recentered Math
800	800	800	800
790	800	790	800
780	800	780	800
770	800	770	790
730	800	730	730
720	790	720	720
670	730	670	660
660	720	660	650
650	710	650	650
600	670	600	600
590	660	590	600
580	650	580	590
400	480	400	440
300	380	300	340
200	230	200	200

Notice that on the verbal scores, the conversion just in the examples I cite above can vary from zero points to eighty points, depending upon where you are on the scale. The math conversion can vary from zero to as much as forty points, again depending upon where you are on the scale.

If you want to see more sobering statistics about the new SATs, you need only to look at Harvard's numbers on the recentered SAT I for the class of 2000. Of the over 18,000 applications they received in 1995, 9,400 students received higher than a combined SAT of 1,400; 1,600 received perfect verbal scores of 800; and 1,900 had perfect math scores of 800. Before recentering, only about twenty to thirty students *worldwide* scored a perfect 1,600 combined, whereas with the new test, Harvard alone turned down 165 (out of about 365) applicants with perfect 1,600 combined SAT I scores. Nationwide, about 545 students scored 1,600 in 1996.

Many people have not gotten used to the new scores, especially if they had older children who took the old test. In 1995, the governor of New Hampshire, Stephen Merrill, falsely compared the new state average (935) with the old state average (924) and concluded that New Hampshire students had shown a marked jump in intelligence since the previous year, when in fact the scores were nearly identical, if not lower once adjusted for recentering. He went so far as to say, "The SAT results are a tribute to the excellence of the teachers of New Hampshire and our outstanding educational system,"* although he forgot to mention that more than 25 percent (compared to under 15 percent for most states) of the students in New Hampshire attend private schools (St. Paul's and Exeter, to name the two most prestigious), in which most of the students are from out of state to begin with, and that New Hampshire has one of the lowest minority populations of any state in the country. If the governor could make such a math-

*See Lois K. Shea and Ralph Jimenez, "Study Finds Lifestyle Has Big Influence on SAT Score," *Boston Globe New Hampshire Weekly,* September 3, 1995.

ematically egregious error, imagine what the average parent could invent. "Your younger sister must be smarter, since her scores were higher"—even if their scores were identical. If you are trying to compare various siblings, use the conversion tables at least to equalize scores within your family. For example, if your first child had a verbal score of 670 and a math score of 710 and your second child (taking the recentered test) scored a 720 verbal and a 700 math, they had the very same math score, while the first child had a higher verbal score, even though it looks lower. Notice how at first glance the latter scores appear higher, but this is not the case.

There has been tremendous confusion over the new scores, which was exacerbated by the fact that the College Board, the year before recentering, also changed the duration of the test (an extra half hour was added), the name of the test (instead of Scholastic *Aptitude* Test, it is now called Scholastic *Assessment* Test), and certain sections of the test (they eliminated the antonym/vocabulary part, made the vocabulary more context-based, and added more reading passages) from what they had been for the last forty years or so. No wonder there has been so much confusion.

IMPLICATIONS FOR SELECTIVE ADMISSIONS

The most obvious result of recentering is the fact that what used to be considered an unusually high score on the SAT I is now just an average score. To be exact, for years a combined score of 1,400 was considered the dividing line between normal scores and extremely high scores for highly selective colleges. This is no longer the case. The average combined score for the admitted class of 2000 at Dartmouth was over 1,410. In fact, for the class of 2000, the *average scores of all 11,400 applicants* who applied to Dartmouth (this includes all the weakest applicants in the pool) was 662V, 677M, almost 1,340 combined. For the class of 2001, the average was even higher: 664V, 683M.

While it used to be extremely rare to see students with verbal scores over 700 (remember, only 1 percent of all students taking the unrecentered test scored over a 700, and those students could not have missed more than three or four questions on the whole test to achieve that score), now it is much more common. In fact, *half* of the members of the class of 2000 scored over 710 on the verbal section, about the same as the number who scored over 710 on the math section.

Here is an SAT I breakdown of the acceptance rates at Dartmouth for the class of 2000:

	Verbal SAT	Math SAT
399 or less	0%	0%
400–449	1.6%	2.4%
450–499	4.1%	6.3%
500–549	5.4%	5.4%
550–599	7.5%	7.1%
600–649	10.1%	9.5%
650–699	14.8%	15.1%
700–749	28.2%	24.4%
750–800	52.2%	44.0%

All these statistics taken together mean that parents, students, and counselors need to readjust their standard for excellence dramatically in terms of scores. When a college counselor or a parent calls an admissions officer to ask whether or not a student has a chance of being admitted, he usually starts out by announcing that the student has very high SAT I scores. The problem is, when the officer asks what he means by "very high," he usually says, "Over fourteen hundred," which, as we have just seen, is not only not "very high"; it is actually below the class average.

If I had to come up with an artificial number of what constituted truly impressive combined scores on the recentered SAT I, I would say over 1,490 or 1,500. Those are still considered very high scores, ones that are not easy to attain, no matter how bright a student is.

I hesitate to give this example, because, as always, it is not the combined score that matters as much as the breakdown. It is still, as it has always been, more impressive to see high verbal scores than high math scores, since most students at the highly selective colleges will be doing much more writing and reading than math. Verbal ability is still a good indicator of how strong a reader the student is. The ability to read well will ultimately have a bigger impact on most college students than the ability to do SAT I math very well, especially since the level of SAT math is not particularly high. There are many students who do terribly on the SAT I math and yet who manage to get the highest score of 5 on the AP calculus exam. If any math is useful at the college level, it is calculus, not the basic math covered on the SAT I. Therefore, SAT I scores of 750V, 630M would be much more impressive for most highly selective colleges than a 640V, 780M, even though the latter score has a higher combined total by forty points.

The final point I want to make about interpreting SAT I recentered scores is that because most admissions officers are not gifted in math, there is still the tendency to use the 700 cutoff as the magic number between good and excellent scores, even though, as we have seen, the average score is over 1,420 combined. What I mean by this is that all admissions officers should be intimately familiar with the information in this chapter (although I'm sure if you handed out a pop quiz that asked officers what percentage of SAT I takers scored over 700 on both the old and the new SAT, hardly anyone would know the true numbers), but few have intellectualized and internalized the new system to the point that they can be completely consistent. Remember, probably 99 percent of all current admissions officers took the old SAT I, the nonrecentered test. In their own personal histories, 1,400 has always been a high score. It is extremely difficult to consider applicants under a totally different system from the one you had in high school. In the past, a 670V was a good score, not a great score. Now that same 670V is a 730V, which somehow seems higher, even though it is actually not.

Oddly enough, and I saw this during my last two years in admissions, officers still respond to any scores over 700 by saying that they are strong, whereas if the scores are in the mid to high 600s, they tend to refer to them as average. This is simply not accurate. In Ivy applicant pools, a 700V, 700M is now an average, even below-average, score, although some officers will not be able to draw the correct conclusion when analyzing student scores.

Despite this inability on the officers' part to be 100 percent accurate in interpreting your scores 100 percent of the time, they will undoubtedly improve as the years go on and they see years' worth of recentered scores. In the meantime, all applicants should be aware of the reality of SAT I, which is that if you want to stand out in the Ivy applicant pool, you should aim for a combined score of about 1,490 or higher,* or at least a verbal score over 730 or so, which would allow you to have a modest 650 math score and still look strong in the applicant pool.

One final point regarding SAT Is: How many times should a student take them? As I mentioned earlier, scores will generally go up a few points each time the student takes the test, as the student's familiarity with the test increases. The problem is, once a student has taken the test two or three times, scores usually plateau, so there is no need to keep on taking

---

*Remember that there is no perfect score that will guarantee admission, and, as we shall see, the SAT I is evaluated with regard to socioeconomic background, so that while a 610V, 630M might be low for a well-educated, well-off applicant, it might be very high for an economically disadvantaged applicant.

them. All the highly selective colleges and Ivies will take into account only the single-highest verbal score and the single-highest math score, whether the student takes the test once or ten times. Keep in mind, though, that the colleges get the scores reported on an official printout from ETS that will list all the scores, including the dates of all the tests (SAT I scores cannot be supressed—meaning that scores are only reported to the student, but are withheld from colleges—although SAT II scores can if the student requests it). Though they will *officially* look only at your highest (and use those in the formula discussed in chapter 6), they will see the other scores, too. It does not necessarily make a strong impression on officers if they see that a student has taken the SAT I six or seven times, because they might think to themselves, Doesn't this student have anything better to do with his time? After all, testing isn't everything—maybe the student should have spent the extra time doing better in high school.

There is a certain resentment or even suspicion regarding students who take the test many times. There is really no need to take the test more than two or three times at most, in my judgment. It makes the student look score-obsessed, and it also shows the range of improvement—so I might note that the student originally had a 500V and got it up to a 620, a good jump (although I would probably assume it was after taking a prep course), but still not impressive in the overall pool of applicants, despite all the effort. My suggestion is to take practice tests in your own house as often as you want, but take the actual SAT I only once or twice, three times at the most, if for some reason you anticipate a major rise.

Now that we have made a thorough study of the SAT I, let us turn to the equally important SAT II subject tests.

5

The Importance of the
SAT II Subject Tests

The official advice that admissions officers give when asked about the importance of testing is usually a variation on the following: "For admissions purposes, the most important academic component of your application is your four-year high school transcript, since that represents four years of effort. SAT Is and IIs are not as important because they represent only an afternoon's worth of work and don't tell us as much about how you think."

I have heard this advice since 1985, when I applied to college, but after having worked in admissions for four years, I have come to doubt its veracity. I am not accusing admissions officers of outright lying. In fact, I think most (including myself) really believe deep down that your high school transcript should be more important than your testing record. However, there are several reasons why I believe test scores (particularly SAT IIs) take precedence over high school transcripts.

The first reason has to do with how high schools represent your place in the class. Since many high schools do not like to rank their students because they think it fosters too much unhealthy competition, the tendency is to try to provide colleges with less information rather than more. For example, if colleges know that you are ranked number three out of three hundred students in your high school and that rank represents some kind of weighting for advanced courses, they are positive that you are indeed at the very top of your class. But what if your high school reports only your GPA as 93, with no further information on where that GPA would put you, even approximately, in your class? (Luckily, some high schools, even though they do not officially rank, will at least provide some kind of grade-distribution information that allows officers to approximate fairly accurately how that student measures up to his classmates.) I hate to say this, but when high schools try to withhold information in this way, colleges tend to assume that the high school is hiding something (perhaps at this high school, the grading is very inflated and that student would be only in the top 20 percent of the class, low by Ivy standards) and sometimes regard the applicant with a suspicious eye. After all, if that student's GPA truly put him close to the very top of his class, why didn't the counselor volunteer that information on the high school's part of the application?

What can highly selective colleges do if they have absolutely no way to judge whether this hypothetical 93 GPA is truly excellent or just average for this high school? As you might guess, they are almost forced to ignore the entire high school transcript and rely instead on test scores. Since the high school transcript in this example has no meaning (in that the student cannot be placed in the overall context of the class), it becomes almost a nonfactor in the admissions process—four years of work wiped out in a single blow. Test scores now take a primary role.

Lack of information provided by the high school is only one reason why testing is important. What about very small high schools that have only from ten to thirty members of the senior class? How can admissions officers give the same weight to a student who is number one out of a class of four hundred as they do to another student who is number one out of a class of fifteen? Although it is certainly in no way the student's fault for being in a small high school, clearly he has not had to face the same kind of intense competition as the student in a larger class. In this case, scores can be used to compare both of these students, even though they are in very different high school situations.

Finally, what about the consistency of teacher recommendations? Since officers cannot possibly know every teacher personally, they have no way of standardizing what teachers say. Obviously, not all teachers are equal in ability, nor are they comparable in their own ability to judge a student's intellectual strength. How can officers weigh one teacher's recommendation against another's? The obvious answer again is by using SAT II subject tests in conjunction with what teachers write about a student.

Admissions officers use the SAT II tests to sort out a standard that can be applied across the entire country. Let's say they are reading an application from Montana of a student who is ranked number one out of three hundred in the senior class. Let's also assume that the admissions officer is not at all familiar with this particular high school. Teachers all say positive things about how strong the student is. The Spanish teacher says that this is the most talented language student he has ever had, while the biology teacher says that science is this student's real strength. So far so good. Turning to the SAT II subject tests,* the student has scored the following: 570 biology, 490 Spanish, 600 writing. Suddenly, the admissions officers are forced to reevaluate the teachers' comments: If Ricky is the strongest Spanish student the teacher has ever had and yet he scores only a 480, well below the national average, either the teacher has really never had a good student or the class itself is so weak that it could not possibly begin to cover the basic material on this test. The same applies to the biology score: Ricky just cannot be that good a science student if he scores only a 570. These tests cover finite amounts of material and are relatively straightforward to prepare for.

*SAT II subject tests, like the SAT Is, have also been recentered and are scored on an 800 scale, with 500 being the median score.

Now when admissions officers compare this student to another valedictorian at a different high school who gets all *A*'s and scores three subject tests in the 700s, they are forced to draw different conclusions. If one of this student's teachers say she is the finest Spanish student and the student actually scores 750, the comments are taken a little more seriously. In fact, because this student has compared favorably to the top students in the country who took this test, more credence is given to the level of the high school and to the competence of the teachers.

A straight-*A* student with very weak subject tests in many cases represents an extremely diligent student or a very poor test taker. This type of student tends to have good study habits and has learned how to do the necessary work in order to obtain an *A*. However, I would go so far as to say that many of these students are working up to 100 percent of their capacity and just do not compare to the brightest students in the country, who are their competition for a place at an Ivy League school. Diligent and hardworking yes; brilliant and/or insightful, no. On the other side of the coin, a *C* student with very high testing usually represents a very smart but lazy student who obviously has the ability to do well but does not work up to capacity.

In short, it is fair to say that these subject tests are the true equalizers in the admissions process. The real function of these subject tests is either to back up all the evidence present in the file or to contradict this evidence. They are still examined relative to your socioeconomic background (more on that in subsequent chapters), but admissions officers can get a sense of how strong the high school is, how qualified the teachers are, and how well the student has covered the material. Doing very well on the SAT II subject tests will help show your academic strength when considered against the national pool of applicants. Doing poorly will show that you are not up to the competition of applicants from around the country who have higher scores.

The Ivies will look at your three top tests, although some might require one specific test, such as the writing or the math level 1, so do not limit yourself just to math and science. Follow your natural strengths. Since math is not always required, don't suffer through math level 1 and 2 if you hate math and are not very adept at it. I say this because part of these subject tests is being able to do a good amount of work in a short time frame. Call the College Board in Princeton, New Jersey, and get the full list of available tests—all this is public information published in various College Board brochures. The earlier you know what is offered, the better off you will be selecting appropriate tests.

SOME IMPORTANT OBSERVATIONS

1. I have mentioned the case of the poor tester, that student who is extremely bright but falls apart under strict time constraints. (I am not including learning-disabled students in this category because they can request untimed SAT testing so that time does not affect their scores.) What can you do if you are a poor test taker? The best advice I can give you is to study the material so well that you can work faster than your normal speed. The "poor tester" excuse is sadly one that is not looked upon very sympathetically by Ivy League admissions officers. After all, they reason, if a student does not work well under pressure and tight time constraints, how will they handle the rigors of Ivy League classes? The majority of classes at the Ivies have exams, many of which are timed, and final exams tend to be two- to three-hour tests, much like the SATs.

Poor testers should keep in mind that the main difference between SAT Is and IIs is that the latter are *much* easier to prepare for, not to mention that there is a direct correlation between level of preparation and score. As you will discover, it is much harder to prepare for the SAT I, since it is designed to test aptitude. For example, the verbal part of the SAT I—no matter how many Stanley Kaplan tricks you learn—will still be difficult if you have never really been a reader. Remember, the SAT I is still fundamentally meant to test *aptitude,* while the subject tests are meant to test *knowledge* of a specific subject. Therefore, you must go out of your way to prepare for the SAT II subject tests.

2. Another surprising observation, especially for teachers, is that test scores tend to get more weight than do recommendations, even though officers would seldom admit that this is, in fact, the case. As in the examples I cited previously, if a teacher recommendation seems to be out of sync with a subject test, usually the subject test is taken as gospel. My personal opinion is that in some cases, the subject tests are good indicators. For example, in biology, a 450 score really does indicate that the student did not learn the biology curriculum very well. Of course, it could also mean the student had the flu the night before he took the test, or that while he learned a tremendous amount of biology, he didn't learn the exact material required for the College Board's test. It could simply mean that the student was a deep thinker and spent too much time puzzling over the implications of the questions, rather than just tearing through the exam without giving it much thought.

The most striking example of a test that has little bearing on a student's true talent is the writing test. Although admissions officers will value your score of 750 on the writing test, I maintain that the test has little to do with a student's real writing ability. Even the essay part of the test is so formulaic that it encourages very linear, structured writing, not the kind of creative writing that could distinguish a brilliant writer from a standard one. To look at it another way, Ernest Hemingway probably would have scored an 800 on the writing test because of his organized, spare, and direct prose. On the other hand, one of the greatest English-language writers of all time, James Joyce, probably would have scored only a 500 at best because of his unorthodox style and unconventional use of vocabulary. I doubt that William Faulkner, with his complex sentence structure, would have done well, either.

3. The last important observation is that despite what Ivy League admissions officers will admit if you ask them, most value high scores and decent grades much more than decent scores and high grades. There is something undeniably impressive about a student who scores over 750 on the verbal and math portion of the SAT I and who scores in the high 700s on three SAT II subject tests. Perhaps part of the reason is because very few people working in Ivy League admissions offices scored this well on these tests, so they unconsciously rank the student above their own intellectual level and therefore consider him very smart.

It used to surprise me that even the director of admissions at Dartmouth would make excuses for students with extremely high scores. I am not talking here about *C* students, but about students who did modestly well in high school (top 15 percent rank or *B*-category grades) and had astoundingly high test scores. Often during committee deliberations, I would hear the director say, "With those scores, I bet Caroline was just bored with her classes and her teachers, since she is obviously smarter than some of them. I bet she would take off if challenged by other brilliant people in an Ivy League classroom." You would never hear the same argument for someone with a number-one rank and all low 500 scores. The comments would run more like this: "Despite the impressive rank, we can only assume that this high school is very weak or that Tom is a real grind, who would continue to do here what he did in high school—plug away at his work and get good grades without adding any intellectual insights to the classroom."

As harsh as it sounds, most Ivy League admissions officers equate high scores with brilliance and would rather take a chance that an underachieving but brilliant student will blossom in college, rather than take a chance that a very diligent student would add significantly to the classroom.

The truth is that the Ivies admit very few students with even high-500 test scores, perfectly respectable as those might be. The highly selective colleges compete with one another for high test averages, which are reported each year in numerous college guides. No admissions director wants the testing average to go down, since, superficially, the conclusion is that the students at that particular school are getting weaker. All admissions directors know that students compare the different colleges by looking at testing averages. To attract the best students, it helps tremendously to have impressive standardized-testing averages.

In short, for all the reasons I have set forth in the last two chapters, I cannot overstate the importance of standardized testing, despite what admission officers might tell you. In the following chapters, you will see even more graphic evidence of why scores are so important in the admissions process at Ivy League schools.

6

The Academic Index (AI)

In this chapter, I will reveal one of the central mysteries of the Ivy League admissions process, the academic index, or AI.* No matter how many books you have read on admissions, you will not see a reference to this index, because it has always been a kind of trade secret. I am now using the term *Ivy League* intentionally—although you can apply this formula to all highly selective colleges, the formula itself is used solely at the eight Ivy League schools. The AI is a formula that combines the averages of student test scores (both SAT Is and SAT IIs) and high school rank in class (represented by an Ivy League invention, the converted rank score, or CRS). The AI is represented on a scale of 1 to 240, with 240 being the highest. In order to have a sense of the AI scale, please bear in mind as you read this chapter that the average applicant to Dartmouth typically has an AI of around 200, while the average AI of the matriculating class is about 211.

Most of the highly selective colleges use two ratings for each student, an academic ranking and an extracurricular/personal rating. Each officer assigns a ranking to every student and that ranking is represented as a fraction, academic over extracurricular/personal. For example, if a school had a 1 to 9

*Curiously, AI does *not* stand for athletic index. Insiders use the term AI, so I will refer to it this way throughout this book. It was originally intended to prevent any of the schools in this athletic league from accepting students who were tremendous athletes but were below a certain academic standard.

scale, with 9 representing the highest rating, a student could receive any combination from a 1/1 to a 9/9. Using this 1 to 9 scale, a 5 would be the average applicant in the Ivy pool.

Let's take a look at how this ranking system is used. For example, a student may be ranked as a 9/6. This would mean that the student is in the highest-possible academic category (probably at the very top of his class, with very high test scores and lots of academic power) and has an above-average to excellent involvement and leadership in extracurricular activities. In contrast, a student with a rating of 3/4 would be a below-average candidate academically for the Ivy League. The numbers show decent extracurricular involvement, but probably the student occupied few leadership positions. The 9/6 would be a certain admit, while the 3/4 would probably fall short of admission.

Selective colleges give much more weight to the academic ranking than to the extracurricular/personal rating—typically, between 70 to 85 percent of the final decision will be based entirely on the academic ranking. This academic ranking is directly proportional to high school achievement and standardized testing scores. High school achievement in the Ivies can be measured by the CRS, which is integral to calculating the AI. The CRS tries to establish a uniform method for comparing high school rank or standing for all students applying to college. In most of the Ivies, the AI is directly proportional to the student's academic rating, even if the school does not base its ranking strictly on the AI calculation.

Before we delve into the intricacies of the AI and CRS calculations, it will be helpful to define a few key terms and concepts. The most important is the concept of *weighting,* which can be applied either to rank or GPA. Basically, if a high school weights grades, it adds a certain point value to advanced courses such as honors or AP classes. There are many different ways to weight grades, but one typical one is to add .5 points to the final grade achieved in an AP class, so if the student earned a 4.0, he would receive a grade of 4.5 for that class.

If grades are reported on a 1 to 100 scale, sometimes two to three points are added for advanced courses, so a 94 would be weighted to a 97. Since every school has a different system, it is impossible to give a range of GPAs—unweighted grades tend to be reported on a straight 4.0 or 100-point scale, while weighted grades can be reported on a scale that goes up to 4.5 or higher or over 100 in a 100-point system.

For high schools that weight the final *rank,* usually the grades on the transcript are reported exactly as they are (in an unweighted form), but honors or AP classes are taken into account when class rank is computed. In these high schools, if two students had a 4.0 but one student took more APs than another, that student would be ranked correspondingly higher in the final class standing.

For Ivy League purposes, the most helpful way of reporting grades is really a weighted rank, which tells the colleges how hard your courses are *and* how you have done in relation to the rest of your class—both at the same time. The next best thing would be unweighted class rank, since colleges can see how your grades compare to your classmates' and they can use the school profile or the guidance counselor's explanation to figure out how hard your course load has been. GPAs by themselves are not very helpful if the college cannot calculate roughly where that GPA would put you in relation to your classmates. With these basics in mind, let's turn to the subject at hand, the AI.

Knowing your academic index, along with having a complete understanding of how applicants are evaluated, will give you a good idea of what your chances are for gaining admission to an Ivy League or highly selective college. One crucial fact before we begin: You must learn how the AI is used before you can fully understand how it can help you estimate your chances of being admitted to an Ivy League school. With this understanding in mind, I have organized this chapter into five parts: calculating the AI; inequities and other problems with the AI; how to override the AI to make it more equitable; academic ranking systems; and what you might be able to do about improving your chances for admission.

CALCULATING THE AI

As I've already mentioned, the AI is the sum of three factors: (1) the average of your highest SAT I math and verbal scores, each rounded to two places (800 and 800 would be 80 + 80 = 160, not 1,600); (2) the average of your three highest SAT II subject tests (also rounded to two places, so that 750 = 75, 640 = 64, 500 = 50, etc.); and (3) your converted rank score (CRS). In 1996, the formula was changed slightly, but since the change was not very dramatic and only intended for recruited athletes, I will not elaborate here. These factors are set forth in the AI Blue Book, which is used by all Ivy League admissions officers, or at least by the systems technicians, who are the ones who actually do the math and then input the results into the computer for the officers to see. Here is my rendition of the formula used for calculating the AI:

$$AI = \frac{[SAT\ (V) + SAT\ (M)]}{2} + \frac{[SAT\ II + SAT\ II + SAT\ II]}{3} + CRS$$

Again, note that the average test scores are rounded to two places so that an 800 becomes 80, and so on. In addition, the highest scores are used, so if a student took the SAT I three times, only the single-highest verbal score and the single-highest math score would be used for the calculation.* Since

*In some areas of the country, such as many midwestern states, a test called the ACT is taken instead of the SAT I. The Ivy League does have a provision for this substitution: First the single ACT score is converted to an approximate SAT I score and that number is doubled to stand in for both the math and the verbal sections for use in the formula. In other words, instead of using the average of the SAT Is, the ACT conversion is used twice. If a student takes both the SAT I and the ACT, for AI purposes the college will use whichever score is higher, but remember that in any case the officer will see both the SAT I and the ACT score, so tak-

the highest-possible CRS is 80, the highest-possible AI is 240. Thus, if a student scored double 800 on the SAT I, 800 on all three SAT II subject tests, and was valedictorian in a class of 350 students, that person would have a perfect AI of 240.* Of course, this is extremely rare, but it gives you an idea of the very top end of the academic scale.

Let's look at another basic example. Suppose a student has a CRS of 67 (next, we will look at how the CRS is calculated), SAT I scores of 700V, 800M, and SAT IIs of 600, 650, and 700. The average of the SAT I scores is 750, but we have to round it to two places—hence, 75. The average of the SAT IIs is 650; rounded to two places, it is 65. And the CRS is 67. Therefore, in this case, the AI is 75 + 65 + 67 = 207.

The first two components of the AI—the average of the highest verbal and highest math SAT I and the average of the highest three SAT II scores—are very easy to calculate. Let's focus on the third component, the converted rank score, or CRS, since this is much harder to calculate. As the name suggests, the purpose of the CRS is to transform class ranks generated in a variety of different ways, from a variety of different high schools, into one uniform scale. This common scale facilitates comparisons between students graduating from different high schools. Eighty represents the highest-possible CRS score.

Earlier in this chapter, I explained weighted grades and weighted ranks. There is an established order of preference for determining CRS in the Ivy League. This means that the systems technicians in every Ivy League office calculate the CRS by first looking for exactly how each school reports rank. They are bound by Ivy League regulations to use the following order of preference:

---

ing both tests merely to try to beat the formula is a wasted effort. A perfect ACT score of 36 converts to 800V, 800M; 35 = 780/780; a 34 = 760/760; a 33 = 740/740; a 32 = 710/710; a 31 = 690/690; a 30 = 670/670; 29 = 650/650; down to the minimum of 15 = 370/370.

*80 (the average of the verbal and math scores for the SAT I) + 80 (the average of the three SAT II subject tests) + 80 (the converted rank score for being number one in a big class) = 240.

1. Exact rank (weighted if available; if not, unweighted)
2. Decile, quintile, quartile rank
3. Weighted grade point average (as provided by the high school)
4. Unweighted grade point average (as provided by the high school)
5. Unweighted grade point average (as calculated by the systems technicians in each Ivy League office)

This means that if a high school reports both an exact rank and a weighted grade point average, the Ivies would be bound to use only the rank, since that factor has a higher preference. If a high school reports both weighted and unweighted rank, the Ivies are bound to use the weighted rank. Here is how your CRS is computed for each of these different scenarios.

CASE 1: RANK

The first component the systems technician looks for is your class rank. Your class rank is either weighted or unweighted, if your high school ranks at all. A weighted class rank adjusts your class rank for the degree of difficulty of your course load. For example, suppose you took very demanding AP courses during your junior year and your high school employed a weighted ranking procedure. If, after adjusting your grades in these courses, you ranked sixth in a class of 120 seniors, your weighted rank will be reported as 6/120. If your high school does not adjust your grades for their degree of difficulty, it is using an unweighted ranking procedure. As I have explained, the Ivy admissions officers are obliged to use the weighted class rank, if this is reported.

To find your CRS, first ask your guidance counselor where you are ranked as of your senior fall, when you will be applying to colleges (or as of junior spring, in order to get a rough idea); then look in the appendix at Table A for the number of people in your senior class. Again, let's suppose that you are ranked sixth in a class of 120 and that your high school reports only the unweighted rank.*

There are two ways to figure out your CRS from an exact rank. The quickest and easiest for an individual (as opposed to a computer) is to use Table A. Find the section of the table that reflects the size of your class, go down the left-hand column to find your rank, and then look at the right-hand column to find your CRS. If you look under the heading "Class Size 100–149" and then look for number 6 in the left-hand column, you will see that the CRS in the right-hand column is 67. The way the computer calculates your CRS yields the same result. It is worth running through one example so you can assure yourself that both methods yield the same result.

The computer uses the following simple formula:

$$Z = \frac{(2 \text{ x absolute rank}) - 1}{2\text{x class size}}$$

After the computer calculates this decimal (Z), it then locates the resulting number in Table B in the appendix to ascertain the CRS. In the case above, we would use 6/120 as the rank and apply it to the formula as follows:

$$CRS = \frac{(2 \text{ x } 6) - 1}{2 \text{ x } 120} = \frac{11}{240} = .0458 = 67$$

Note that once you compute the decimal value, when you look at column "Z" in the table, you always pick the next-highest decimal, which corresponds to the lower CRS. In the case above, the student would get 67 out of a possible 80 CRS points no matter which method was used to compute the CRS.

---

*Note, the Ivies use the best rank available. Since, in this case, the weighted rank is not reported, the unweighted rank is used in the computation of the CRS. The formula itself makes no allowance for weighted or unweighted ranks.

Case 2: Percentile Rankings

What if your high school does not provide a weighted or an unweighted rank? In that case, things get more complicated, and the next option is used. Let's take a new example and say your high school reports a decile ranking, such as "within the top 10 percent," or a quartile ranking, such as "within the top 25 percent."*

How do the Ivies determine class rank when only percentage information is provided? The short answer is that the AI Blue Book tries to define as precisely as possible what the phrase "top 10 percent" means and then multiplies the appropriate percentage by the size of the class to obtain a "best guess" of what the true class rank might be. In other words, since colleges cannot tell if you are at the very top of the top 10 percent of students (let's say number one out of a class of one hundred students) or at the very bottom of the top 10 percent (number ten out of one hundred students), they try to be fair by putting you in the middle of the distribution, which in this case would be number five out of one hundred students, even though that is clearly an approximation of "top 10 percent" and not an exact rank.

The language of the AI Blue Book is about as clear as the tax code, but here is the technical description of what the Ivy officers must do in order to arrive at your CRS. First, the reported top decile, quintile, or quartile is translated into a percentile. Next, the midpoint of that percentile must be found. The resulting percentile is then subtracted from 100 and the result is divided by 100 to yield a percentage. In formula form: $100 - x\% \div 100 = \%$. The resulting percentage is multiplied by the number of students in the graduating class to obtain an

---

*There are ten deciles, four quartiles, and five quintiles. To be ranked in the top decile means that the student is superior to at least 90 percent of his classmates. A student in the top quintile is superior to at least 80 percent of his classmates and a student in the top quartile is superior to at least 75 percent of his classmates.

imputed class rank. The imputed class rank is used in conjunction with Table A to obtain the CRS.

Describing the process might make it sound more complicated than it actually is. Let's look at the following example in order to clarify the sequence. A person who graduates within the top 10 percent of the class could have graduated in the top 1 percent (so he would be better than 99 percent of the students) or ahead of all but 10 percent of his classmates (in which case he would have been better than 90 percent of the students). A statement that the student graduated "within the top 10 percent" is not specific enough to locate precisely where within the distribution of class performance a student lies. Unless the exact position in the distribution is indicated, the members of the Ivies have agreed that the *midpoint* of the relevant distribution is used—in the example above, the midpoint would be number five out of one hundred students, since that represents the midpoint between number ten and number one of one hundred students. Consulting Table A, you can see that the resulting CRS would be 68.

So for purposes of the formula, a student who graduated in the first quartile, or top 25 percent of the class, did better than 87.5 percent of his classmates, 87.5 percent being the midpoint between 100 percent and 75 percent. Let's say that the student's graduating class had 445 students. The student's imputed class rank is 56/445. This is found by subtracting 87.5 from 100, dividing the result by 100—yielding .125—and multiplying .125 by 445 (56). By consulting Table A, you find that 56/445 equals a CRS of 61. Demonstrate to yourself that someone in the second decile in a class of 153 would be determined to have a rank of 23/153, or a CRS of 62.*

*The second decile means that the student is between the top 90 percent and the top 80 percent of the class, so we take the midpoint, which is 85. Thus: 100 minus 85 equals 15, and 15 divided by 100 yields .15. Then we multiply .15 times the size of the class, 153, which yields 23. Thus, the imputed rank is 23/153, which, if you look at table A, is equivalent to a CRS of 62.

CASE 3: NO RANKING AND NO PERCENTILE INFORMATION PROVIDED

When your high school does not provide rank or percentile information the Ivy League AI Blue Book suggests that officers do everything possible to force a rank using the high school profile.* If it is impossible to tell from the high school profile and the high school will not help, the general conversion table must be used (see Table C in the appendix).

It is quite possible that you attend a high school where rank and percentile information is not provided. Surprisingly, the computation of your CRS in this last case is quite simple. Table C converts your GPA or letter grade directly into a converted rank score.

On a final note, the AI Blue Book has a separate section of tables from several high schools with unconventional grading systems, sometimes on a 1 to 12 scale, or a 1 to 6 scale—there is quite a range. These high schools either have their own special CRS tables that systems technicians in each Ivy office must refer to when calculating CRS or they use methods that are not specific enough for determining rank, so the Ivies simply recompute a GPA or perhaps have directions to use either the weighted or unweighted GPA—it is different for every school. Some of the high schools in this special category are: Brearley School (New York, NY), Brooks School (North Andover, MA), Burke Mountain Academy (East Burke, VT), Choate Rosemary Hall (Wallingford, CT), Collegiate School (New York, NY), Darien HS (Darien, CT), Fairfax County Public Schools (Virginia), Friends Academy (Locust Valley, NY), Gilman School (Baltimore, MD), Greenwich High Schools (Greenwich, CT), Groton School (Groton, MA),

---

*Just about every private and public high school in the country has a school profile. It usually contains a description of what kind of socioeconomic area the school is in, where the students get accepted to college, average test scores, and so on. If you are ever considering moving to a new area and you want to investigate schools, call up the guidance office and request the profile that is sent to colleges.

Gunnery (Washington, CT), Head Royce School (Oakland, CA), Hillsborough HS (Tampa, FL), Holmdel HS (Holmdel, NJ), Hopkins Grammar Day Prospect Hill School (New Haven, CT), Horace Mann School (New York, NY), Hotchkiss School (Lakeville, CT), Kent School (Kent, CT), Lakeside School (Seattle, WA), Lexington HS (Lexington, MA), Longmeadow HS (Longmeadow, MA), Milton Academy (Milton, MA), Montgomery County Public Schools (Maryland), Newton North HS (Newton, MA), Phillips Academy (Andover, MA), Phillips Exeter Academy (Exeter, NH), Pingry School (Hillside, NJ), Princeton Day School (Princeton, NJ), Princeton HS (Princeton, NJ), Ransom Everglades School (Miami, FL), Regis High School (New York, NY), St. Alban's School (Washington, DC), St. Ann's Episcopal (New York, NY), St. Mark's School (Dallas, TX), St. Paul's School (Concord, NH), St. Stephen's Episcopal (Austin, TX), Stratton Mountain Academy (Stratton Mountain, VT), Tabor Academy (Marion, MA), Taft School (Watertown, CT), Townsend Harris (Flushing, NY), Trinity School (New York, NY), United Nations International School (New York, NY), Western Reserve Academy (Hudson, Ohio), Wheeler School (Providence, RI), and the Wooster School (Danbury, CT).

If you attend one of these high schools, you can still use the methods I have outlined in this chapter, because they will yield very similar results, but if you really want an exact number, see if your college counselor knows what the special table is for your high school or what method the Ivies use. If your counselor does not know, just revert to the standard method for calculating CRS.

INEQUITIES

The factors in the AI formula are weighted equally. Thus, the first thing that should strike you is that *two-thirds* of this formula is derived from test scores, while only one-third is derived from a student's high school GPA or rank. This is in direct contrast to what all the Ivies say in their literature—that is, that the most weight is given to academic performance in high school, followed by test scores. As I have stressed in the preceding two chapters, test scores are very important. Now you can begin to see exactly why this is so.

Moreover, the CRS is not comparable in all cases (and therefore, neither is the AI, since the CRS is one of its three components). This is because it is calculated in different ways, depending upon the information provided by the high schools. As you have just seen, it can be calculated using methods ranging from exact rank (sometimes weighted, sometimes unweighted), to GPA (sometimes weighted, sometimes unweighted), to approximations derived from deciles, quartiles, or quintiles, to recomputed GPAs.

What are the inequities involved in calculating the CRS using exact rank? To answer this question, let's take a closer look at Table A and compare several number-one-ranked students. Consider the case of two valedictorians, one from a small graduating class and the other from a large one. One striking fact that you will notice is that if you come from a small high school, your CRS will automatically be on the low side. Thus, the number-one student in a class of twenty-four seniors can obtain a maximum CRS of only 70 out of a possible 80. If the second student was ranked at the top of a class of three hundred or more students, he would earn the highest-possible CRS: 80.

You might think that you'd get additional credit if you graduated from a very large high school, but this is not the case; no additional credit is given if you graduate from a high school with more than three hundred students. You will earn the same CRS if you are number one in a class of three hundred students or number one in a class of two thousand, even though in the latter case the accomplishment is more impressive. Through no fault of your own, you will be handicapped in terms of the AI if you attend a small high school and your high school reports a rank rather than a GPA. In general, students in large high schools, whether public or private, fare better than those in small high schools if their school reports an exact class rank.

What are the inequities involved in calculating the CRS using decile, quartile, and quintile approximations? The first problem is that officers are using *approximations*. Because the midpoint only approximates the student's actual location in the distribution, high schools using percentile, quartile, or other relative ranking measures will inadvertently hurt their very best students, because the true rank of these students will generally be understated by the approximation. In other words, in the example we have used before of the number-one student in a class of one hundred students, numbers one through four will be hurt by the approximation, since it assumes that their rank is number five, the midpoint of the first decile. On the other hand, high schools that use these relative ranking measures will enhance the prospects of relatively weaker students, because the true rank of these students will be overstated by the approximation. In this same example, numbers six through ten would be helped, since their rank is "raised" to number five.

My own high school, with its typical senior class size of around 120 to 135 students, has inadvertently handicapped its top students since the school board abolished rank a few years ago. Now the school uses a decile system, so usually the highest CRS possible is around 67 of the full 76. Thus, the very top students from this school are starting out with a nine-point handicap, which, as you will soon see, can be the difference between a top academic ranking and a mediocre academic ranking. How is this decile rank computed?

As we see from Table A, the number-one student in a class of between 100 and 149 students would have a CRS of 76. But if only "first decile" is reported, even this top student can get only a maximum CRS of 67, since the midpoint of the first decile is used yielding an imputed rank of 6/120, or a CRS of

67. (Once again, the midpoint of the first decile is 95, subtracted from 100 is 5, and divided by 100 is .05. Multiplying .05 by the class size of 120 yields 6, so the imputed rank is 6/120 and Table A shows that the corresponding CRS is 67.)

Finally, what are the inequities in calculating the CRS using straight GPA? To answer this question, we need to examine Table C closely. A student with a 95 GPA* would get a whopping CRS of 77 out of a possible 80. But what if that student had only been ranked in the second decile if the high school had reported a decile rank? If the high school did not report that decile, the student would be awarded a CRS of 77, even though in this case the CRS would be tremendously inflated. In other words, it makes a big difference in this case if your high school reports GPA rather than just a decile. The student in this example would receive a boosted CRS just because the high school reported a GPA instead of a decile ranking. Conversely, the student would receive a much lower CRS if the high school used decile ranking rather than GPA, even if he had a rather high GPA.

To make matters worse, the most striking thing about Table C is that it makes absolutely no allowance for weighted or unweighted GPAs. In other words, what if your high school only has a 4.0 scale and you have a perfect 4.0? Unfortunately, you could only get a CRS of 77 out of a possible 80, since the only way to get a 4.3 GPA and a CRS of 80 is to have a weighted average that would bring your CRS up to its full value.

In an even more pointed example, what if a student from one high school has a *weighted* 93 average, while a student from another high school has an *unweighted* 93 average? (Assuming that they are taking the exact same number of AP classes.) Common sense tells us that the student with the unweighted GPA really has a higher GPA (and deserves a higher CRS), since no credit has been given for honors or AP classes; but,

*All these averages are presumed to be out of a total of 100 points. On a 4.0 scale, a 4.0 is an *A* average, 3.0 a *B* average, 2.0 a *C* average, and so on.

according to the CRS formula, both students would get exactly the same CRS, 73 out of a possible 80. Finally, what if the rating scale goes up to a number higher than a 4.3 GPA? Let's say a student had a 4.4 weighted GPA, but that only represented a student in the second decile, because the highest weighted GPA at this high school was a 5.2. According to the table, any student with a GPA of 4.3 or above would get a CRS of 80, even if his average was nowhere near the top GPA at the high school.

HOW TO OVERRIDE THE CRS IN UNFAIR CASES

In practice, admissions officers do not blindly accept the CRS, since in many cases one ends up comparing apples to oranges. In many of the examples I gave in the previous section, an officer can override the CRS. Officers scrutinize the CRS, particularly in cases other than exact rank. If the CRS seems truly unfair, officers have the authority to raise or lower the CRS, and therefore the AI, accordingly.

How do admissions officers obtain their information so they can make fair adjustments? Even in the absence of rank and percentile information, many high schools provide detailed profiles of their classes to assist the admissions office. The profile might provide a histogram or bar graph so that it is possible to figure out where the student fits in the class.

Let's say the college counselor provided only a GPA—88 (B+)—since the high school had a no-rank policy. If the high school did not provide any kind of decile distribution, the admissions office has no way of knowing whether 88 represents a good GPA at that high school or a weak GPA. Officers would probably assume that it was not a very high GPA if the college counselor did not provide more information. The situation would be entirely different if the college counselor provided a grade distribution that looked like this: $A = 88$–92 (4 percent of class), $B = 83$–87 (12 percent of class), and so on. Suddenly, the officer could tell fairly accurately where the student falls in the class, even though the high school does not rank—in this case, an 88 average is rather high (judging from this profile, grading is tough at this high school) and would put the student in the *top 4 percent* of the class. In a case like this, the officer would give the student additional CRS points and raise the AI accordingly because just the 88 GPA does not give accurate-enough information—by itself, it would drop the student's CRS to a 67.

How does a shared rank affect the overriding of the CRS? If an officer noted after reading the profile that forty students in the high school shared a number-one rank,* he would probably knock the CRS/AI down manually because there is no way to pinpoint if those students really were number one or number forty. Conversely, if a student had a "first decile"–based CRS that only converted to 67 but the college counselor said something like "We don't formally rank our seniors, but if we did, Maria would be number one because she has the highest GPA in the class," the officer would boost the CRS several points (depending on class size), which would boost the AI.

In short, officers are always on the lookout for unfair use of the CRS. However, the less information the high school provides, the less the officer can exert influence to change the CRS. If there is no evidence one way or the other—just a GPA reported totally out of context—there is nothing the officer can do. In order to change the CRS manually, the officer must provide a quick written explanation so all who read the file can understand the rationale behind the decision.

---

*An annoying trend among big public schools is to call everyone with a 4.0 GPA "valedictorian," even if that means that twenty-two people will share the rank. In states like Texas, it is not uncommon to find as many as forty students sharing a number-one rank. If it were up to admissions people, they would end this policy immediately because it does not allow them to differentiate between the true number one and the solid students. In almost every case, this shared rank hurts the students rather than helps them, since officers have to rely more on standardized testing because the transcript tells almost nothing about how the student compares to others in the class.

There are some general rules I would like to provide for the benefit of college counselors regarding how best to report a student's class performance to highly selective colleges.

1. In high schools that have very small senior classes (under forty-five to fifty), the high school is better off reporting a weighted (or unweighted) GPA instead of a rank. As you can see from the CRS conversion tables, even if a student is number one but comes from a small high school that has only twenty seniors, that student's CRS will be quite low. The CRS is always abnormally low when using rank in a small class, even if the student is right near or at the top of the class.

2. In high schools that have large senior classes (over one hundred or so), it is much better to report an exact rank than to provide a decile, quartile, or quintile. If for some reason the high school board forbids reporting rank, the high school counselor can easily get around this prohibition by providing a grade breakdown: 94–99 (3 percent of class), 90–93 (4 percent of class), 85–89 (7 percent of class), and so on. In this case, a student with a 93 GPA would be roughly in the top 3 to 5 percent of the class. Notice that this approximation is much more accurate than just saying "top decile," which only states that the student is between the top 1 and 10 percent of the class.

3. For small high schools that report only a GPA, it is crucial to provide some kind of written explanation as to where in the class that GPA puts the student. What happens if admissions officers have no information at all, just a reported GPA of 92? As I explained in a previous chapter, if officers have no way of figuring out where a student stands in the class, they almost have to ignore the student's entire high school record. Thus, they have to rely more on the student's own writing, standardized testing, and teacher recommendations. Testing will get a disproportionate amount of weight, which almost always hurts the student.

4. Finally, high schools should be consistent for all students, even if a few different guidance counselors write the school recommendations (as is the case with large senior classes

where the class is split up among two to ten different counselors). Most officers keep notebooks, so if they know that a big public high school always uses rank, but for some reason the school reported three students in deciles but fifteen others with rank, they would have to call the high school to ask for the exact ranks of those three students. Schools should pick a system and then apply that system to all students, regardless of where they fall in the class.

ACADEMIC RANKING SYSTEMS

All the highly selective colleges use a ranking system of some kind for the academic criteria of every applicant, and usually the same ranking system for the extracurricular/personal criteria. As I have said, the final ranking is usually expressed as a fraction, with the academic ranking over the extracurricular/personal ranking. In this chapter, I am referring only to the academic ranking, but later we will consider the extracurricular/personal rating, as well.

In order to get an idea of how the ranking systems work, let's look at some representative examples from highly selective colleges. Harvard uses 1–6 for both rankings, with 1 being the highest; Brown uses 1–6 with 6 being the highest; Columbia uses 1–5; Cornell does not use a numerical ranking system—instead, they invite faculty to evaluate parts of the file; Amherst uses a 1–5 system, with 1 being the highest; both Dartmouth and the University of Pennsylvania use a 1–9 system, with 9 being the highest; Georgetown uses a 1–5 system, with 5 being the highest; Princeton uses a 1–5 system, with 1 being the highest (they also recompute a GPA for every applicant on a 4.0 scale that leaves out ninth grade); Yale uses a 1–4 scale, with 1 as the highest; and MIT rates 1–5 on both an academic and personal scale, using a system of cells such that one cell is 5/5, one is 5/4, one is 5/3, et cetera, for every possible combination. Stanford gives all its admissions officers a four-to-five-hundred-page manual when they start work; it explains the many different areas in which they rate students. They seem to avoid numerical ratings for the most part and to rely on prose descriptions in many different categories.

I'll use Dartmouth's ranking system of 1–9 (9 being the highest) as a representative example that can be effectively applied to all the highly selective colleges, even though the scales are not identical. Before looking at the numerical determination, study the prose descriptions of the different academic ratings at Dartmouth. They will also give the reader an idea of the competitive nature of the applicant pool.

A 9 ranking. Academic 9s are the crème de la crème of the entire applicant pool. Typically, they represent the top 1 percent of the total number of applicants and their most salient quality is an intense love of learning. Love of learning and the pursuit of intellectual endeavors in school is characteristically coupled with academic initiative outside the classroom. Often, these students take college courses or follow up on their interests by means of special projects, research, and independent study involving extensive reading and writing. Students in this category explore a wide range of subjects, from astronomy and classical archaeology to zoology, impelled by their own curiosity. It is not unusual for academic 9s to be valedictorian or salutatorian of their high school and taking challenging honors/AP classes. The intensity of these intellectual pursuits suggests that academic 9s have the potential to become leaders in the academic/intellectual field of their choice in the world beyond college.

A 7 ranking. Academic 7s are among the strongest in the applicant pool as well, but they tend to show a little less evidence of the academic intensity and love of learning than do academic 9s. Even so, these students still show an impressive inner drive to achieve and, indeed, are perceived as high achievers by peers and educators. In contrast to the 9s, these students' inner drive seems to stem more from a sense of competition than from a love of learning for learning's sake. For example, an academic 7 might underachieve in certain subjects on the grounds that proper motivation was not provided by the instructor or class environment. Though many students in this category perform extremely well in high school (roughly top two to five percent in their high school), lower performance could result from a sense of boredom experienced in a class perceived to be below their level. However, like academic 9s, these students pursue subjects beyond their high school classes, take college classes, follow up their academic interests through projects and research, and can be top students in certain subjects. In short, academic 7s are likely to make a big contribution intellectually to their college class.

A 5 ranking. Students in this category are considered to be average in the Ivy League pool of applicants. They are still impressive performers who might look very strong on paper: captain of a sport, high school rank within the top 10 percent, fairly high test scores, advanced classes, and so on. What might be missing in the case of these students is initiative, particularly in following up outside of class on exploration of subjects that interest them. They tend to lack the creative, intellectual spark. Academic 5s can be perceived as very diligent and dutiful students who possess a tremendous work ethic but lack the intellectual edge that can be seen in the case of 9s and 7s. The actual motivation for a student in the academic 5 category may not be clear—rather than love of learning, or the fascination with a particular subject, is it the thrill of besting their classmates that inspires them? One gets a sense that most of what they have done—the record of their achievements—has been geared toward getting into the "right" college. Still, these students are clearly capable of doing the required college work and do contribute to the life of a top college, as well.

A 3 ranking. Academic 3s represent the solid student who does fairly well in school (typically top 25 percent) in a variety of honors classes, AP classes, and some regular courses. However, the student does not stand out in any particular subject or area. In the case of 3s, there is little evidence of seeking out challenges or pursuing knowledge beyond the bounds of the classroom. At the end of a high school career, the student's true interests remain undefined and perhaps even unexplored. It is unclear what students in this category would add to the life of the college.

A 1 ranking. Academic 1s are, simply put, not competitive candidates for admission to an Ivy League institution. Typically, these students are taking light course loads compared to their classmates; they fall below the top 40 percent of their high school class, show little real interest in academic study, and do not display the kind of potential to contribute to the class that is typical of the higher stanine students. The academic 1's performance indicates little academic potential, which might be evidence of the fact that his real talents lie in another area.

To compare these descriptions to those of another Ivy League school, let's look at Princeton's 1–5 scale. Fred Hargadon, the director, has described their highest rating, a 1, as someone who has five or six test scores over 700, probably a 4.0 GPA, and at least twenty solid academic classes. An academic 2 rating represents a profile lower than a 1, and so on down to the lowest, 5. He estimates that 55 percent of all applicants to Princeton fall into the category of academic 2s and 3s, whereas only about 10 percent are academic 1s.* Notice that even without basing their ranking scale on the AI, test scores and high school grades are still the primary determining factors in the academic ranking. To be an academic 1, the student needs many test scores over 700.

FINE, BUT WHAT USE IS THE AI?

Remember, only the Ivies calculate AIs, since the formula was invented to compare athletes in the same league so an academic standard could be upheld. Theoretically, the AI is only for

*See Bill Paul, "Getting In: An Inside Look at Admissions and Its Dean, Fred Hargadon," *Princeton Alumni Magazine,* November 22, 1995.

athletes, but thanks to computers, it is relatively easy to compute an AI for every single student who applies to any Ivy League school. After all, the AI is supposed to be a formulaic method for comparing students from different high schools around the country against one uniform scale. So why not use it for non–recruited athletes, as well?

Let me be clear about the fact that not all the Ivies base their academic rankings directly on the AI as Dartmouth does. (Some do: the University of Pennsylvania uses the same 1–9 scale as Dartmouth does, also using the AI as the determining factor.) In fact, some of the Ivies do not even bother to compute an AI for every student. Why, then, is Dartmouth's AI-based ranking system useful to students, parents, and counselors as an approximation of the chance for admission at *any* highly selective college?

I would argue that if you were to look at those students to whom the Ivies assigned high academic rankings (using the descriptions that I have provided), there would be an extremely high correlation between high AI students and highly ranked students on each Ivy scale. This is because all the Ivies have nearly identical standards for evaluating their applicants, and these standards put a premium on test scores and class rank, as can be seen in the Princeton example. Even if the actual AI ranking system was not used, the Ivies cannot and will not change their basic system of evaluation because it is based on academic performance and, by definition, must be determined using this criteria.

This correlation is borne out by the many students who are accepted both to Dartmouth and to the other Ivies to which they applied. In the majority of cases, a student who is accepted by Dartmouth will be accepted by Yale, Princeton, Brown, Columbia, and so on. Conversely, it is rare to find a student who is rejected by Dartmouth but accepted by Yale, Harvard, or Princeton. Since the University of Pennsylvania and Cornell are slightly less selective, you might find students rejected by Dartmouth but accepted by Cornell and Penn, but you will rarely find the reverse. In fact, even though the other highly selective colleges, such as Amherst, Williams, and Swarthmore, do not even have an AI, you would find the same very high correlation. Thus, most students who are accepted by Dartmouth will also be admitted to most of the other highly selective colleges.

Even in non–Ivy League colleges, which do not use the AI, other numeric systems are employed. For example, Georgetown uses a similar ranking to the AI, but its ranking system gives more weight to class rank than to testing, unlike the AI. Its system is arguably fairer (and closer to the highly selective colleges' public declarations that high school performance is more important than testing) than the AI because Georgetown does not face the inconsistency problems involved in the different ways the CRS can be calculated. It uses only the numerical scale if the student has an exact rank. If the high school reports GPA or anything other than rank, the formula is simply not generated and not used.

In light of the extremely high correlation with regard to admission to many top colleges, we turn to Dartmouth's 1–9 academic ranking scale, which is based on the AI. The first reader to look at the folder would see the AI printed on the front and would then have to assign an academic ranking manually. For the class of 2000, these rankings were as follows: 1: 179 and below; 2: 180–188; 3: 189–199; 4: 200–209; 5: 210–215; 6: 216–220; 7: 221–224; 8: 225–228; 9: 229 and above. Because of a small change in AI calculation (too small to warrant a full explanation), the scale is slightly different for the class of 2001 and beyond: 1: 180 and below; 2: 181–192; 3: 193–202; 4: 203–210; 5: 211–215; 6: 216–220; 7: 221–224; 8: 225–229; 9: 230 and above.

I have provided a list of acceptance rates by academic stanine (Dartmouth refers to these rankings as "stanines") for the class of 2000, for which Dartmouth received almost 11,400 applications: Academic 9s were admitted at a 94 percent acceptance rate; academic 8s were accepted at 92 percent; 7s at 76 percent; 6s at 52 percent; 5s at 25 percent; 4s at 11 percent; 3s at 7 percent; 2s at 5 percent; and 1s at less than 1 percent.* Note the high correspondence between high AIs and high acceptance rates.

Even more interesting is the distribution among prospective applicants. Of the almost 11,400 applicants who applied for the class of 2000, only 2.2 percent were academic 9s; 2.7 percent were academic 8s; 4.6 percent were academic 7s; 7.5 percent were academic 6s; 11.8 percent were academic 5s; 22.5 percent were academic 4s; 21.7 percent were academic 3s; 12.3 percent were academic 2s; and a whopping 9.9 percent were academic 1s, of whom Dartmouth accepted one student. (As you will see in chapters 11 through 16, this student would have had to have been in a special category.)

This means a full 44 percent of the applicants were only academic 3s and 4s—very few of whom were admitted. Dartmouth considers the average (in its pool) applicant to be an academic 5, and even in this group, the acceptance rate is only 25 percent. The most numerous group is that of the academic 4s, of whom only 11 percent are accepted. I can say without a doubt that academic 4s are usually not weak students—typically an academic 4 has solid 600 scores all around and is ranked in the lower part of the first decile. The overwhelming impression is usually one of solidity—a solid but not exceptional student with particular strengths in one or more subjects, some decent leadership abilities, and strong recommendations. The average AI for the matriculating members of the class of 2000 at Dartmouth was 211. Of the 11,389 students who applied, the average AI was 200.

By now, you should have a sense of just how competitive it is at the most selective schools and how a few extra points in the CRS, and therefore the AI, can turn a marginal candidate into an easy admit. Guidance counselors should be aware that

---

*These stanines reflect the adjusted AI assignations, so if an officer bumped a stanine up or down because of an inequity in the CRS, those adjustments are reflected in these figures.

how they report students' ranking can make the difference between acceptance and rejection. The AI is the crucial number, since it affects the academic ranking. As we have seen throughout this chapter, the difference between an exact rank and a decile rank, or between a straight GPA and an exact rank, can result in a CRS difference (hence, an AI difference) of as many as twelve to fourteen points. Looking at the distributions above, even a twelve-point difference in AI can be the difference between an academic 8 (admitted at a 92 percent rate) and an academic 5 (admitted at only 25 percent). This difference cannot be understated. An academic 8 will almost always be accepted, while an academic 5 will probably not be accepted.

Many people assume that being valedictorian will virtually guarantee acceptance into any Ivy League school, but that is just not the case. Although typically 40 percent or so of the freshman class at Dartmouth is ranked either number one or number two in high school, each year Dartmouth rejects almost as many number ones and number twos as it accepts. Look at Princeton's class of 1999: Princeton received 1,534 applications from those who were ranked number one in their high schools, out of which only 495, or 32 percent, were accepted.

I can also tell you that after decision letters are mailed out, colleges get several weeks worth of "Why R" calls ("Why did you reject my child?") and they almost always come from the academic 4 or 5 group. From the parents' point of view, their child has nearly all *A*'s, highish test scores, and a fair amount of leadership ability. But, as you can see from the averages, the average SAT scores are over 1,415, the average SAT IIs are usually in the high 600s to mid 700s, and roughly 40 percent of the admitted class is ranked number one or number two in their high school class. The competition is indeed fierce, and most academic 4s, although not at all weak, will not make it into the class. In fact, almost 90 percent of them will be rejected, and of the 10 percent that are accepted, it is fairly certain they will have something very strong going for them in another area, which might not be entirely merit-based. Note also that together academic 1s and 2s comprise about 22 percent of all applicants, but most of these are low enough in the pool that they warrant only a cursory read by two readers. When people ask me, "Well, doesn't everyone look strong?" I have to answer no, because academic 1s and 2s really do look significantly lower, particularly in testing, which tends to be in the 400 to 500 range.

WHAT TO DO IF YOU ARE AN ACADEMIC 1, 2, OR 3

A full 44 percent of all applicants at Dartmouth (and by extension, a very similar percentage at the other highly selective colleges) fall into the academic 1, 2, or 3 category, of which not very many are accepted. If you fall into this category, what are some of the compelling reasons admissions officers might find to admit you and what can you do to strengthen your case despite the long odds?

- Some students accepted in this category come from extremely disadvantaged backgrounds. Usually neither parent will have graduated from college. Sometimes, the student is the first in his family even to graduate from high school. A student in this category, despite low test scores, would have to show exceptional academic promise and proof that he went beyond his immediate surroundings to seek challenges.
- Some of these students will fall into one or more of the special categories to which I devote the last few chapters. For example, the number-one-rated male ice hockey recruit might fall into this category, but he still must show some academic signs of life.
- Students in this category will need truly inspirational

recommendations from teachers and guidance counselors. They will also need some evidence (a regional science competition, research out of school) of exceptional academic achievements outside of high school, even if high school rank and scores are not top-notch.

- Students will need to write a truly extraordinary essay. Sometimes students will elaborate on their humble family backgrounds. Love of learning must come across.
- Grades must be improving dramatically and the student must be taking a challenging course load. Sometimes a student's CRS will be low because he had a weak ninth-grade year. Admissions officers will look closely at junior and senior grades.
- Students should have significant leadership and extracurricular involvement either in school or out of school. The colleges must be able to say to themselves, "This student would be a significant addition to our campus."
- Some students in this category will have tremendous talents, probably national-level, in a particular field—an Olympic athlete, a musician involved in a nationally ranked orchestra, a Westinghouse science winner.

Students in this low academic category are somewhat of a long shot for Ivy League schools, but there is always the possibility of making oneself stand out enough to warrant admission.

WHAT TO DO IF YOU ARE AN ACADEMIC 4, 5, OR 6

Forty-two percent of Dartmouth's applicants fall into one of these three categories. Though I will group them all together in order to make some general suggestions, note that academic 6s have roughly twice the admission rate of 5s, so there is probably a subgrouping here of academic 6s, and then academic 4s and 5s.

- All the essays and other written information should showcase the student's academic strengths and intellectual ability.
- Teacher recommendations and guidance counselor recommendations should be outstanding. They should give specific examples of how the student has been a high-impact player in high school and how they think the student will continue to be. Many of the students in this category who are rejected tend to be very diligent students who show no real academic spark. Again, students should make sure they are vocal members of their classes.
- Students should make sure their grades are going up and that they are taking the most challenging courses. Sometimes students in these categories will be turned down because officers note that they are taking fewer challenging classes than their classmates.
- Students should show some degree of academic initiative—summer programs, independent research, regional awards, awards in the high school, and so on.
- Love of learning and intellectual potential should be evident throughout the application.
- Significant in-school or out-of-school leadership or talents such as sports or music should be evident. One reason students in this category get turned down is that they have no leadership ability at all (member of three sports teams, but never captain), no work experience, or no real talents to add to the class.
- Students should have strong character and personality. Teachers should comment favorably on a student's personal attributes. Remember, though, academics still account for about 70 to 75 percent of the admissions decision, but students in this category need strong extras

and personal strengths in order to stand out from the pack.

- More than any other group, students in this category are aided by being in one of the special categories that will be discussed in chapters 11–16, because they are all "admissible," and in close cases, a tip factor could really shift the balance to an "accept."

If you fall into this academic group, you more than anyone need to focus on the following chapters so you can make sure you do everything in your power to put together the strongest possible application in every respect. Cases in this category can go either way, so the more you know about how to present yourself, the better your chances will be. Students in this category will be the ones who benefit the most from this book.

WHAT TO DO IF YOU ARE AN ACADEMIC 7, 8, OR 9

Most of the students (only 10 percent of the overall applicant pool) who fall into one of these academic categories will be accepted to any or all highly selective colleges they apply to. As general advice, students in this category should follow the advice for 4s, 5s, and 6s. The important thing to remember is not to rock the boat. You will be accepted unless you do something dramatically wrong on your application. For this reason, I have included specific reasons why a student in this high academic category might get turned down by a top college.

- The student shows signs of intolerance or bigotry.
- The student gets very negative character assessments (more in chapter 9) from one or more teachers.

- The student does absolutely nothing or the bare minimum outside of high school. There is no evidence that the student would add to any part of campus life other than the classroom.
- The student has some kind of honor violation or serious disciplinary problem.
- The student's essay and supplementary written material is poorly done and shows lack of academic strength.
- The student gets extremely low interview ratings on either his on-campus interview or alumni interview.
- The student is described by all as extremely diligent but not very interested in learning for learning's sake.

For the most part, students in this category should be accepted to many top colleges unless something is amiss. These students also will benefit from learning in depth about the reading process so that they will better understand what can go wrong in the reading of their applications.

Before concluding this important chapter, I want to mention an almost philosophical point about reading files. Much like using a particular method of literary criticism method to read "against" the fabric of a book, admissions officers see the AI (or if they don't see the actual AI, they see the GPA, rank, and test scores) and read against it. For example, if they pick up a folder that has a 230 AI, they have certain expectations: This student should show a love for learning, be exceptionally bright, have very high grades, write very well, and have extremely supportive teacher recommendations. At the same time, the readers are distrustful of the AI. Is the converted rank score overinflated? When officers see a very low AI, they will look closely for mitigating factors, such as poor background, exceptional hardship, or any other information that could boost the student despite a low AI.

Even if the Ivies were to abolish the AI formula someday, they will still use basically the same process for determining academic merit. Scores and class rank will still be paramount, as will intellectual curiosity and love of learning. The AI is only a vehicle for evaluating underlying academic qualities. Knowing your AI and approximate academic ranking will give you an idea of what your chances are of being accepted to the most highly selective colleges, and what concrete steps you can take to improve those chances.

7

Advanced Placement and International Baccalaureate Scores

———◆———

Perhaps the easiest and most effective way to override a mediocre AI and to stand out academically is to score well on Advanced Placement or International Baccalaureate exams. Even though these AP and IB tests are not factored into the AI formula (they are not offered by all high schools and therefore cannot be required by colleges), they are in many ways more useful for the highly selective colleges than SAT II scores.

Unlike AP courses, the IB offers not only individual courses, but also a comprehensive course of study that culminates in a full international diploma recognized by all the finest universities around the world. All the highly selective colleges I mention in the introduction recognize and give credit for IB course work. For example, a student who completes the full IB diploma could be accepted to Harvard with sophomore standing.

If your high school offers either AP or IB courses, you should be taking as many as possible so that it appears you are choosing the most challenging curriculum possible (more about this in chapter 9). Remember that these AP and IB tests are the only tests that are considered to be truly college-level—in fact, just about every highly selective college grants college credit for very high scores on these tests. In contrast, only rarely will college credit be awarded for SAT II tests.

AP tests are scored on a scale of 1 to 5, with 5 being the highest, and IB tests are scored on a scale of 1 to 7, with 7 being the highest. The IB program is not as common in the United States as it is overseas, so typically most highly selective colleges see many more AP scores than IB scores, although they are both treated the same. After taking an AP course (many high schools offer them as early as sophomore year), the College Board (the same folks who bring you the SAT Is and IIs) offers AP exams in May in a variety of subjects, the most common ones being AB calculus, BC calculus, biology, chemistry, physics (several different subconcentrations are offered), American history, European history, English (both language/grammar and literature), Latin (two levels), French (both language and literature) and Spanish (both language and literature).

Teachers who teach these courses follow the College Board Advanced Placement curriculum in order to be sure to cover all the topics that will be included on the test. Before the May test, some teachers will give their students practice tests so they can familiarize themselves with the topics covered. How are these AP tests different from the SAT IIs? In short, they are much more similar to college-level tests. That is, they are *not* primarily multiple-choice tests; they are writing-based, or problem-based in the science and math area. In the calculus tests, the student is asked to solve real calculus problems, showing all intermediary work, which is then graded. In history tests, students have to evaluate actual historical documents and extract meaningful conclusions in the form of coherent essays (these tests do have some multiple-choice sections, but not nearly as many as the SAT IIs). For students who are at an advanced level, these tests can be easier than SAT IIs because those who are good writers and thinkers can excel without necessarily having to memorize large quantities of seemingly irrelevant information.

So what effect can these AP or IB scores have on your application? A big one. Let's say I'm reading a student in the 5 or 6 range who has mid-600 SAT II scores (let's say a 670 biology, a 650 math level 1, and a 660 Spanish listening comprehension), which are certainly not weak, but as is, the student does not stand out academically. Then I turn to the student's AP scores and I see that he has a 5 on the AP biology exam, a 5 on the BC calculus exam, and a 4 on the Spanish literature exam. Let's look at each area individually. In the case of Spanish, I know that the listening comprehension test score is hard to judge, since a student has to listen to a tape of a native speaker and answer questions, which is not necessarily an indication of how smart the student is, but rather of how well he hears and how good he is at one small part of language comprehension. But to score a 4 on the AP exam, a student actually has to have read and comprehended literature by five major authors (Ana María Matute, Pablo Neruda, Jorge Luis Borges, Miguel Unamuno, and Federico García Lorca) and then has to be able to write at length *in Spanish* about various works of literature by these authors. Clearly the 4 is more indicative of ability to do strong college work than the SAT II listening test.

Looking at math ability, admissions officers know that the SAT II math level 1 test is basically geometry and algebra, and fairly low level at that. A score of 650 is not great, but if I see that the student has reached the second year of calculus study (AB calculus refers to the first year and BC to the second year) and scores a 5 on that AP test, I immediately know that the student is very strong in math and has reached a level few high school students in the United States ever reach. Most high schools in the United States do not even offer the BC calculus curriculum. At Dartmouth, this exam is the one you can get the most credits for out of all the AP exams—a 5 on the BC exam earns entering students two full credits (which is equal to two full classes), an award that allows them to take an extra term off and save a third of the year's tuition and room and board—not bad for an afternoon's work taking the AP exam.

Finally, an SAT II score of 670 on the biology exam is strong, although not exceptional in the Ivy pool. But the 5 on the AP exam represents a strong grasp of college-level biology, not the high school level reflected by the SAT II test. So in the example discussed here, even if the student's AI placed him in the academic 5 or 6 category, the officer would probably boost the academic rating to a 7 because of excellent AP scores. In addition, if the student didn't seem to be that exceptional academically, a number of high AP scores could suddenly change the picture dramatically.

Remember, it is even more remarkable to have a few strong IB/AP scores, because it means that the student took these exams as a sophomore or a junior, not a senior, since the application is read by offices in the fall of the senior year, well before May IB/AP exams. In many high schools, it is impossible even to take IB/AP classes until senior year, so the scores would be too late to be helpful for admissions purposes (although you still might be awarded credit once you are admitted to the school and colleges will see that you are taking a challenging course load). All the more impressive, then, to see a string of high IB/AP scores. I recall some of the strong magnet high schools and excellent private high schools in Florida, one of my regions, from which I'd see students with solid SAT II scores, but then as many as four to eight AP scores in the 4 to 5 range. If you score three or more APs over 3, you are designated an AP scholar by the College Board, a meaningful academic award for any highly selective admissions committee.

Needless to say, if you score 1s, 2s, and 3s on the majority of the tests, the scores can be used against you, even though they are not required. In most cases, low AP scores reflect low SAT II scores, since it is unusual to do extremely well in one area and horribly on the same subject at the next-higher level. All of what I have said for AP scores is valid for IB scores: 6s and 7s are all considered excellent scores on these tests.

Now that you are intimately familiar with the Ivy League formulas for calculating the AI, how AP and IB tests are used, and the implications of these different areas on admissions, you are ready for a full discussion of how a folder is actually read by a highly selective admissions committee and how the office divides the daunting task of reading several thousand folders.

8

The Reading Process

───◆───

Before we embark on the step-by-step process of evaluating applications, let me reveal how files get to be files in the first place, and then how they are divided up in most Ivy League offices. Let's trace the mysterious journey a folder takes from the applicant's house to the admissions officer's hands.

Once the applicant finally finishes his part of the application (form 1, usually mailed a few months earlier, and later, form 2), he usually panics because the deadline is nearing, and he pays an exorbitant amount to send the material via overnight delivery. Most people assume that there is a band of mail receivers waiting on January second for all mail to arrive so they can sort it out and divide it up immediately. If you stop to think about it, most schools get over ten thousand applicants a year. The applicant sends in forms 1 and 2, the high school sends in form 3, two different teachers mail in their recommendations under separate cover, and sometimes a peer sends in the peer recommendation. To add to all this, some students will also have alumni interviews mailed separately. Thus, for every applicant, between four and six different pieces of mail must be opened, stamped with the date, sorted alphabetically, and put into folders—roughly fifty to sixty thousand separate pieces of mail.

Most offices have only around ten or so people who do all this work, so it takes *weeks*, not a day, to open and sort the mail. In all likelihood, your FedEx package will be sitting in a huge bucket in a mailroom for at least two weeks, so it is never necessary to send anything overnight mail. The truth is, admissions offices cannot even tell if you mailed in your material late, as long as you were within one or two weeks of the deadline. Schools want their total number of applications to be as high as possible so they will appear to be more selective. As a consequence, many will accept applications received as late as March!

Here is a step-by-step list of how a folder gets put together:

1. Buckets of mail are delivered each day to the admissions office by the post office and other mail carriers.
2. Secretaries, systems workers, and sometimes the officers themselves sit around big tables, open the mail, stamp it with the date, and sort it in alphabetical order.
3. These alphabetized piles are delivered to systems technicians, each of whom is responsible for a certain section of the alphabet. In between hours of opening mail, they would spend a few hours each day processing and filing paperwork, sometimes entering the data into the computer system. This process takes over a month.
4. Once the bulk of the mail is opened, systems technicians work full-time to collect all the information about each applicant and place it in an individual folder. They go through each form 3 and calculate a CRS for every single student, following the rules set out in the Ivy League Blue Book.
5. Once the appropriate information is input into the computer (standardized testing and CRS calculations), an AI is calculated in those Ivies that use this measure.
6. At each school, as much statistical information as possible is printed out—at Dartmouth, it is produced on what is called a "master card," which contains many vital statistics for each applicant.
7. Finally, at least two or three weeks after the mail started coming in, complete folders are produced, with the

master card on top of the folder. As these folders are completed, they are sent to the appropriate regional officer for a first reading. After that officer has completed the read, the folder is sent back to systems, where it sits for a few weeks waiting for new information and is then updated and sent back for a second read.

The world is divided up into regions that each admissions officer covers. As I have mentioned, while I was at Dartmouth, my regions included Westchester and Rockland counties in New York, and the states of Florida, Ohio, Indiana, Kentucky, and Michigan, plus the People's Republic of China. In Ivy League offices, officers generally travel from four to six weeks every fall to visit their regions. These visits include travel to high schools, evening presentations, and meetings with local alumni of the college. The purpose of this travel is twofold: for the officer to get acquainted with as many high schools as possible and to spread the word about the college to people who might be less familiar with it. School visits are generally quite short—officers typically visit four or five high schools during the day. Later that day, they do a public presentation for parents and students, during which they give a longer version of the short presentations done in each high school.

Typically, high schools will post a sign for each visit so interested students can meet with an officer for twenty or thirty minutes, hear a brief presentation, get on the mailing list, and ask questions about the college. As an added benefit, especially if the group is small, the officer might really get a chance to talk to students. If impressed by a particular student, officers would usually write his name down so that months later when they read the file, they would remember who the student was. The general (and understandable) public perception is that this contact is very important, but I would disagree. The truth is that officers meet too many people too quickly on the road to record a lasting and meaningful impression. Imagine a two-week trip where you visit four to five high schools Monday to Friday and drive to three major cities. When people come up to you at an evening presentation attended by eighty people, introduce themselves, and ask a few questions, you are unlikely to remember talking to them at all. In addition, many of these students will not ultimately become applicants, so even if you did remember them, the information would not be particularly helpful.

During their brief stay at a high school, officers usually make contact with the guidance counselor, request a high school profile so they can gather information about the high school, and record their impressions of the visit in a folder they keep during travel season. Sometimes it is possible to learn interesting things that would not be immediately obvious by just reading about a high school in the profile. Students might tell you that because of double periods, the high school allows only a maximum of three AP classes. Oftentimes, the students volunteer helpful facts, such as, "Even though Mr. Nespoli's class isn't an Advanced Placement class, he is considered the hardest teacher in the high school and only the top kids take his class." This is the kind of comment officers would record so that when they eventually came across an applicant from that high school, they would give the student credit for taking a difficult course, even if it was not marked "AP" on the transcript.

Students might also tell you that in a given year they will have twenty-one valedictorians in the class, since the high school policy is to assign a number-one rank to anyone with over a 4.0 weighted GPA. As I mentioned before, this is not a helpful policy as far as colleges are concerned, because once officers find out how many number ones there are in a high school, they knock down the AI and look even more closely at such things as test scores and teacher recommendations. In other words, it usually works against the students, not for them.

My personal opinion is that high school visits are largely a waste of time and resources. With the exception of visits to less affluent or high-minority-concentration areas, the high school visit is becoming obsolete. It costs thousands of dollars for each admissions person to travel (airfare, hotels, gas, rental car, three meals a day), when actually many people can take advantage of all the information available about a college through books, the Internet, or a campus visit. The visits I do find extremely meaningful are those to inner-city or poor areas, where the applicants do not have the money or resources to visit or to use high-tech computer software to gather information. Many of them only consider applying once they get on the mailing list after a visit and receive literature about the college.

Regional officer visits do more to make alumni (they feel neglected if you do not visit their region, somehow assuming that if you don't visit, you won't take anyone from their area) and college counselors happy. Certain private high schools feel snubbed if they are not visited every year, even though their students are more than familiar with most highly selective colleges. In an ideal world, I'd say high school visits do influence the students, but practically speaking, it becomes almost a personality contest among admissions people.

Many times students have said to me, "You were so much better than the Harvard officer" (and a significant part of that was because I am young and used to teaching students that age and thus have an easier time relating to them). While flattering, it pains me to think that students would choose one college over another based on the affability of the admissions person; it is even worse when you remember that that person is probably not even a graduate of that particular college, and even if he is an alumnus, the sales ability of that person is not necessarily indicative of the strength of the academic program at the college. For these reasons, I think resources would be better spent doing much less travel and instead targeting less affluent areas and doing evening programs (rather than individual high school visits) both at public libraries and local churches or synagogues.

Once officers return from their travels, they have about a week before files for early decision come rolling in. By the time admissions officers get to see your folder, much of the personal data is recorded on a computer printout called a master card. All students have a master card (of course, each office has its own analogue for this summary of major information) in their file that summarizes all the numbers-oriented data: all testing, address, high school and Social Security number, legacy status, parents' occupations, rank in class (or GPA), languages other than English spoken at home, strength of course load, and so on. Behind each master card is a blank sheet of lined paper called a "ready sheet" (these terms probably vary for each Ivy League office, but the process is essentially the same), where the readers summarize the contents of your folder in a write-up of approximately half a page. On this sheet and on the front of the master card, the reader would enter both an academic and personal ranking as a fraction, academic over personal/extracurricular. A 6/5 rating would mean the student was an academic 6 and a personal/extracurricular 5.*

How does reading the folder work? Once a folder has been completed (which means that most, but not all, of the information is in—one missing recommendation would not hold up the reading, since after the first person reads it, it goes back down to the systems area to get updated), it makes its way up into the regional person's file drawer. When officers pick up their daily quota of from twenty-five to thirty folders, the folders are all mixed up, so they would never sit down and read all the folders from one high school. Since the regular-decision reading process drags out over months, it would be impossible to remember all the different applicants. So when parents ask, "Are students from our high school compared di-

---

*Again, each Ivy has a slightly different system. In addition, at some schools, professors have input in the process, but this is the exception, not the rule. The only school I know of that does this is Cornell.

rectly to one another?" the answer is no—they are read against the standard of the region first, then the whole country.

The regional readers on the admissions staff would be the first evaluators. They are expected to be familiar with the high schools, so if they have anything to add that would help the next readers, they would add it on the ready sheet in their write-up—for example, "The guidance counselor told me that this year's class is the strongest they've had in years," or "This high school has strict grading policies, so an 88 percent average is actually very close to the top." Even if regional readers did not know the high school very well, they would spend time reading the high school profile to decipher how a student stacked up against the rest of the class. As they read, they would summarize certain data (such as a list of extracurricular activities and parents' occupations) onto the master card and would take notes for about half a page on the ready sheet. Finally, after thinking about the whole folder, they would assign both an academic and personal/extracurricular ranking and then take all the folders back to the systems people, who would keep them for about a week to update them. In fact, folders usually stay with the systems people for several weeks because it takes quite a while to finish all the first readings.

There is one exception to this procedure. If the regional reader is amazed by how strong a student is (typically an academic 8 or 9), he might recommend what is sometimes called a "one-reader A" (meaning that it will take only one reader to determine that this person is a winner and therefore an acceptance) and put this folder directly into the director of admissions' file drawer. Then the director would read the folder to see if he agreed. The director has the option of writing a green A on the folder (just what it sounds like—he takes his special green pen and writes the final decision) and sending it to systems, where it will sit until final letters go out, or deciding that the regional reader was too optimistic and sending it along for a second read. In total, roughly 5 to 7 percent of all applicants in a given year would fall into the "one-reader A" category.

Conversely, if a folder is so weak that the regional reader realizes that the applicant has no chance of admission (usually academic 1s and 2s), he would put it directly into the associate director's drawer, where she would have the same options as the director. If she reads the folder and agrees that the applicant has no chance, she would write a red R on the folder and it would go downstairs to the "R" pile ("rejection letter"), or if she thought the regional reader was too hasty, she'd send it back to get a second read. Typically between 15 and 25 percent of applicants fall into this "one-reader R" category.

When most of the regional reads are completed, the systems people would input all the new data, update the folders, and dump them all into a "second read" drawer. Second reads are a bit less tedious, since the second reader does not have to fill in the biographical data or the other information on the master card. No record keeping is necessary because the first reader has already done that work. Basically, you can sit back in a chair, read the whole application, and then evaluate the applicant in a more holistic way.

Incidentally, the master card and ready sheet are tucked in the back of the folder, so the second reader would not see what the first reader wrote until after he'd read the whole folder and developed his own opinion. The second reader would write a half page or so and then read the first reader's comments (especially in case he had anything helpful to say about a high school) and assign a separate rating. By the way, at Dartmouth, the possible votes, which are written next to the rankings, are "A" (accept), "R" (reject), "P" (possible), and then different gradations, such as "P+" (almost an "A") and "P-" (closer to an "R"). Each college has its own variation on these votes.

Once the folder has had a second read, the second reader would look at the votes. If both readers agree that the applicant should be rejected, the file would go back to the associate director for a quick third read. Most of the time, she would concur and put the final "R" on the file and send it downstairs, but occasionally, she could find that the first two readers missed something or were too tough; then she could send the folder on to the committee. For any other combination of votes, the folders would be put into the director's drawer. If he decided that two "A" votes were enough to admit, he would put a green A on the folder and send it back to systems; if not, he would either vote or add his own comments and send the folder on to the committee. Since the director has the benefit of reading folders from every region as well as those from around the world, he has a good global perspective. Sometimes he might take a folder with two "A's" on it and decide that the first two readers were too optimistic. Maybe that applicant is slightly less strong than they thought. It is his job to serve as a safeguard to make sure the rest of the staff is being consistent.

Some schools have slight variations on the process I have just outlined. At Princeton, for example, the files are passed along, starting with the least-experienced members of the staff and ending with the member of the staff who has the most experience. All files are eventually seen by the director, so at least three people have a chance to review the applicant's file.

The process I have just described takes about two to two and a half months for regular decision. In March, once all the files have gone through these three readings (or at the minimum, two, in the case of a "one-reader A" or a "one-reader R"), the office would count the total number of "A's" and the total number of "R's," and then all the votes that average out to some gradation of "P." Then the committee would spend about five days with all the "P" folders. Depending upon how many people had already been selected for the incoming class, the director would decide how many people to accept from committee. Some colleges meet with professors and admissions staff in committee, some break down into small groups, and some meet as one large group. Dartmouth generally breaks down into three committees of four or five people.

Usually, committees are told that of the three-hundred-fifty or so cases they have, roughly one-sixth can be accepted. Thus, the committee process is very tough and many bright kids don't get picked because they simply do not stand out enough to be chosen above others in this brutal competition. Typically, about 1,000 students at Dartmouth are sent to the committee, while only around 170 are accepted.

The reading and committee process can differ at other highly selective schools. At Brown University, for example, it is the regional officer's job to present all applicants from each school in his region to the entire committee for a vote. The officer might briefly summarize the five applicants from one school and then say, "I recommend we take the valedictorian and the chess player and reject the other three." This process takes weeks and includes very little debate among committee members since they rely on the regional officer's summary.

In Dartmouth's system, the very strongest candidates (and the very weakest) do not have to go to committee. In fact, all the "one-reader A" applications that have been completed by a certain date are gathered and the applicants are mailed what is known in the Ivies as a "likely letter," which basically says that although the college can't come right out and admit the person (by Ivy League regulation), it is likely that he will be admitted when acceptance letters are mailed in April. (Actually, the Dartmouth letter, in effect, states that the applicant will undoubtedly be accepted in April.) There are some "one-reader A" applications that will be read late in the process (basically due to volume or the fact that these files were missing something), and these applicants won't get a "likely letter," even though they would have if their file had been read earlier. So not receiving one is not bad; it simply depends upon when the folder is read.

The first wave of "likely letters" at Dartmouth gets mailed out in early February and the second wave in early March. The parameters for a "likely letter" can vary a little by college and by year, but usually at Dartmouth they include one-reader academic 7s, 8s, and 9s, minority applicants who receive one-reader 5s and 6s, and a handful of students with maybe a 4, 5, or 6 academic rating but an extremely high extracurricular/personal rating, typically for some extraordinary accomplishments. In 1996, Dartmouth mailed out roughly 600 "likely letters," while in 1997 it mailed out over a thousand.

What is the purpose of sending out these letters? The Ivies and other selective schools feel that they might be able to gain an edge with an exceptional student if they are able to tell him ahead of time that he will be admitted. After all, if you were a top student and your mind was set on Yale but on February tenth you received a warm letter from the director of admissions at Dartmouth saying that you were one of the top applicants in the entire pool and that you will most likely be accepted in April (barring any major grade drops or disciplinary action), you might be tempted to go to Dartmouth, especially if Yale didn't notify you until the April deadline, several months later. The Dartmouth letter even says that one of its purposes is to take the pressure off the applicant. The letter encourages the student to relax and reflect upon his future plans and goals. Such a letter is a tool for yielding the very top students, the 7s, 8s, and 9s, who are likely to be accepted by many different selective colleges, not just one or two. The colleges fight over these top students, since having them on campus will serve the dual purpose of raising the intellectual and academic level overall and increasing the numerical advantages that college will have when calculating its testing averages and other academic measures of strength for college guides.

This, in short, is how each file goes through the reading process. The process may vary slightly in each Ivy League office, and each office may use different rankings, but basically the process is quite similar. There are many checks and balances built into the system. The director of admissions is the major check, since he can overrule a regional person or at least send a folder to the committee. As a point of fact, he rarely just decides himself—if he doesn't agree with the first two readers, he'd write down his reasons on the ready sheet and send the folder to the committee.

The process is really quite democratic. All the voting is done by majority rule. In committee, usually you would need a unanimous vote for an "A"; anything else would either be wait list or rejection. Any close committee vote would be double-checked by the director, who would go through each file separately. In my experience, the truly extraordinary students really do stand out in the process (mostly 7s, 8s, and 9s) and the more borderline cases (4s, 5s, and 6s) end up in committee. Even in committee, the most interesting students stand out and are chosen over those who are less exciting.

9

A Step-by-Step Look at How Your Application Is Read and a Brief Look at the Common Application

———◆———

In this chapter, I intend to shed light on the thoughtfulness of the reading process by giving a blow-by-blow account of how a file is read. Rather than trying to create an amalgam of a student, I have brought up the issues that come up in most files so that you can get an idea of how your folder will be read. I will use the Dartmouth application as my primary example, but before getting to this specific application, I wanted to say a few words regarding the "common application."

The common application is a recent development (within the last five years or so), aimed at making the college application process less tedious and more accessible to a wider variety of students. As its name implies, it is a general application (available in every college guidance office in the country) that can be copied and used for many different colleges, thus obviating the need to fill out ten different applications if you are applying to ten colleges.

Let's say a poor student in rural Arkansas wanted to apply to several highly selective eastern colleges but could not afford to call long distance to request applications. Thanks to the common application, this student can simply fill out one application and mail it to all the colleges that accept this type of application. The number of colleges that do accept the common application grows each year. Check with your guidance counselor to get an updated listing or look on the actual common application for a complete listing.

What are the fundamental differences between the common application and the college's own? First, the common application has only one essay question, while many colleges ask several questions. Initially, this might seem like a positive point, since you do not have to write as much, but upon further reflection it seems obvious that admissions officers end up finding out much more about students who use the college's application than about those who use the common application. Often I felt frustrated reading the common application because the main essay was the only sample of student writing in the entire application and the student had to follow the guidelines, which asked that the applicant pick one of three rather bland topics, instead of the more open-ended Dartmouth question, which was: "Write your own ideal question and answer it."

Second, the common application does not have a space to list IB/AP scores, so many students unknowingly forget to list them. I have stressed earlier how important these scores can be, but if a student does not tell the college his scores, the colleges will not be able to use them in order to help his chance of admission.

Finally, the common application has the information required by most colleges, although in a slightly different format. While this does not sound like a major point, it can be extremely annoying for the reader trying to get through from twenty-five to thirty applications a day if he cannot find the information he needs in a readily accessible format.

If you ask any college that accepts the common application, it will tell you that it treats the common application *exactly* as it would its own application. In theory, this is true, but in practice, almost every admissions officer I've ever met complained incessantly about the common application. I myself grew to despise it for the reasons I've mentioned. I tried not to hold my feelings against the student, but sometimes just the fact that I didn't find out the information I was looking for hurt the student, however unintentionally.

In order to give you the most realistic picture possible, officers also consider the applicant's background. If they are reading the file of an applicant from a very poor rural background, or that of a minority student from an inner city, they will understand that the student was using the common application as it was intended to be used—to make an Ivy League or highly selective college more accessible and to avoid the cost of requesting applications. In this case, the application will be treated exactly as the college's own application. However, if an officer sees a well-off student from the Collegiate School in New York City applying via the common application, he might just think the student was too lazy to request the college's own application or that the student used the individual applications for those colleges that were really important to him and then threw in a few less important ones using the common application. In my experience, I have found that very few officers will admit to these subtle biases, but in the examples I have just cited, using the common application could hurt your chances for admission.

In short, my suggestion to most applicants is to go the extra mile for all colleges you are really interested in and use that college's own application form. Very low-income applicants, applicants of non-college-educated parents, and disadvantaged minority applicants should feel free to use the common application, but they may want to supplement it by adding the extra essays included in other applications, listing their AP scores, and describing any or all part-time jobs they have had during the school year.

Now that we have discussed the pros and cons of using the common application, let us turn to the Dartmouth application as a representative example of a college's own application.

FORM 1

When we open the folder (we keep the master card right next to it so we can record key information on it, and we keep the ready sheet nearby so we can take notes as we flip through the folder), we come to form 1, which basically is a list of information, including name, address, Social Security number, other siblings and where they go to college, parents and their respective educational backgrounds and occupations, and test scores. This form really takes only one to two minutes to look over. We would manually record the parents' education level and occupations on the master card and make sure the student's self-reported test scores match the official test tape scores sent directly from the Education Testing Service in Princeton, New Jersey (they are input into the computer and printed on the front of the master card). As I mentioned earlier, we look at parents' information to get a general sense of background so we can see test scores in an approximate context.

For academic 1s, 2s, and 3s to have any chance of admission, there should be some indication of educational disadvantage or economic disadvantage. Privileged students who fall into this academic category stand little chance of admission. Most 4s, 5s, and 6s will not be admitted unless we see a similar example of a student rising beyond his modest circumstances. Some 6s will be admitted based purely on academic strength, regardless of background. Most academic 7s, 8s, and 9s will be admitted, so parental background is not quite as important here as in those cases where we have to excuse low scores because of socioeconomic circumstance.

So in our two-minute reading of your form 1, we are just getting a snapshot impression. We might think, Even though she comes from a well-educated and well-off family, she looks like a standout, with her mid-700 scores on both the SAT I and II, or, He comes from an extremely disadvantaged background but still has decent 600 scores, or, modest background, modest scores—we'll have to see more before making any kind of judgment. All scores, particularly those for the SAT I, are examined in the context of your family's economic and educational background.

FORM 2

Even before we turn to the all-important form 2, we have some idea of the kind of background you are from. Form 2 is the section where the student has to do a significant amount of writing. It is here where we start to flesh out the initial impressions we took from form 1.

Many students ask, "Should I type my form two, or can I write it by hand?" For 99 percent of the population, I would suggest typing it on a word processor or typewriter unless you have absolutely perfect block handwriting. Keep in mind your exhausted audience—officers spend up to ten hours a day reading applications and will be slowed down by really poor handwriting. If it looks sloppy, they might equate the writing with a weak effort on the student's part. I am referring mainly to the big essay question, but I think it is worth typing the other ones, too. No need to try to fit or paste your answers in the little spaces provided; just use separate pieces of paper and tuck them all inside form 2 so that the information is easy to find. If you have good handwriting, you can fill in the activity chart by hand and some really short-answer questions such as scores and jobs, but anything that is longer than a few sentences should be typed. The only exceptions I would mention would be for very low-income-background applicants who do not have access to a computer or typewriter. Obviously, the student's background will be apparent, so officers will not hold it against this student if the form is handwritten, but it is still important to show time and effort so that the answers are legible.

The first question—requiring a very short essay—is "What is your most meaningful academic subject and why?" Although the response is only four to five sentences, we can still get some idea as to your intellectual enthusiasm. For example, the student who writes, "Math, because it comes easily to me and always has an exact answer," submits a weak response because it doesn't show love for the subject and it doesn't show a deep conceptual understanding of math, which, as you get beyond the basics, rarely has only one answer. Compare that response to something like the following: "I fell in love with languages ever since my first day in French class, when I was transfixed by the sounds of a strange tongue. In fact, I picked up Spanish last year and started teaching myself Latin and studying with a tutor so I could have a better background in how Romance languages evolved. I'm looking forward to college so I can continue my language study and learn other languages that are not available in my high school." This short response really tells us quite a lot about the applicant. He or she seems genuinely excited about the study of languages and has shown a certain degree of initiative in pursuing the study of Latin independently. Needless to say, we would look for substantiation in the rest of the file. After reading this and then finding out that the student had a C- average in French or a 450 SAT II score on the French subject test, we might conclude that although the student has enthusiasm, he or she doesn't seem to have a very high ability level.

Here is an example of what I would call an excellent response to the academic question. Notice how the student's enthusiasm and intellectual curiosity shine through.

We are sitting in Mrs. Matusow's class, talking about Louis XIV as if we knew him. He is alive! "*L'état, c' est moi.*" Oh, really? We are not impressed, Louis. You revoked the Edict of Nantes! On the board is Hegel's dialectic. We absorb it, fascinated. What words, *thesis, antithesis*! Mrs. Matusow moves on to Marx. However, the lesson is halted by a heated exchange of ideas between two classmates. Class continues in this vein: almost everyone adds a new idea. I glance at Mrs. Matusow—she is both annoyed because we are behind in the syllabus and happy because she sees we are learning. She knows we are thinkers. She does not do anything to stop our thought flow. We are a democracy. We look down on democracy. It breeds chaos. But we *love* the chaos! We are in a twentieth-century salon. We study the winners and losers of history. We study politics, history, philosophy. We study history, but we are also a part of history. I wonder where I fit into this and what legacy I will leave. I love this teacher. I love these students. I love history.

Though a bit longer than the usual response, and perhaps overexuberant at times, it is still a very strong response, one that avoids the usual "I love history because I learned that unless we study the mistakes of the past, we are doomed to repeat them." (Fill in your version of Santayana's much-overused quote.)

Next comes a chart where the student lists his activities in and out of school (in order of importance), complete with grade participation (9-12, 10-12, 9-10, etc.), leadership positions, and hours per week. Here we are looking for depth of commitment and leadership. We are not looking for a laundry list of every club you have ever joined. In fact, when we copy the list onto the front of the master card in abbreviated form (that is, soccer 9-12, captain; part-time job fifteen hours/week; paper EIC 12), we usually leave out clubs that you were just a member of and that did not occupy more than one hour per week of your time.

I would *not* recommend including a résumé for several reasons, the most important of which is that it is much harder to compile a quick list from a detailed résumé. In addition, it seems somewhat presumptuous for an eighteen-year-old to have a real résumé. What I would suggest is to follow the chart format and then on a separate sheet of paper, give a *brief* explanation of each activity, one or two sentences at the most. For example:

Key Club: three hours of community service a week at a local children's hospital.
Voices: the high school literary magazine, which is published twice a year.

A short explanation is helpful if the item is not immediately obvious. However, there is no need to explain something like "Varsity baseball, 9-12, catcher," because it requires no explanation unless there were notable achievements, awards, or leadership shown.

Parents often ask about the importance of doing community-service work. I think many students are convinced that if they do one mission trip to Ecuador, they will be immediately accepted because of their ability to help change the world and make it a better place. The problem is that many high schools require community service, so officers are not going to be impressed that the student was forced to commit a certain number of hours to helping the community. The other problem is, I'd estimate that 85 percent of all the applications I read for Dartmouth in a given year indicated the applicant had done some kind of community service, so in and of itself, community service does nothing to enhance an application.

Having said this, an *extraordinary* dedication to community service (just like any in-depth commitment the student may have) would count just like any other activity that showed either incredible initiative or an unusual level of dedication. Usually, the trend is fairly obvious—that is, not only does the student list a few organizations for which he has volunteered over four years (a one- or two-year commitment is less impressive) but also he talks about this commitment in one of the short essays, teachers and guidance counselors refer to this extraordinary commitment, and local papers might even have featured a story on the student. One church-mission trip or serving soup to the homeless for an hour on Fridays is not going to help your chance for admission. One would hope that students would continue to serve the community for personal and moral reasons, rather than helping others only as a technique for getting into college. The mere thought is discouraging. Thank goodness there are many things in life that are of supreme importance but will not help you get into the college of your choice.

As mentioned earlier, Dartmouth uses the same 1-9 rating system to evaluate personal and extracurricular involvement, as well. Colleges usually use the same ranking system they use for academics for personal and extracurricular involvement. The reader's evaluation and final decision are based on the academic stanine (roughly 70 to 85 percent of the decision) and the extracurricular/personal stanine. As you might imagine, a high extracurricular/personal rating is the most crucial for academic 4s, 5s, and 6s. For academic 1s, 2s, and 3s, even a high personal stanine won't make a big difference, and for academic 7s, 8s, and 9s, as long as the applicant is a personal 5 or above, they will be helped, not hurt, by that rating. Naturally, an applicant rated 9/9, 9/8, 9/7, 8/9, 8/8, 8/7, et cetera, will have almost a 100 percent chance of being admitted.

Dartmouth gives a 5 rating for the average applicant, who is usually someone who is quite involved—let's say a cocaptain of one or two sports, Eagle Scout rank in Boy Scouts, and editor in chief of the high school paper. As impressive as that sounds, it would probably merit a rating of 5. A 4 rating would be good involvement but not any significant leadership (for example, a member of three varsity teams and some club memberships). A 3 rating would be not much involvement, and a rating of 2 or 1 would either be very little of anything or a negative personal trait (such as dishonesty or extreme arrogance), which would lower the ranking for personal reasons.

On the opposite end of the spectrum, an extracurricular/personal 6 or 7 is someone who demonstrates a significant commitment to one or more activities, usually with some level of regional or national recognition, leadership, or dedication. Typically, an extracurricular 6 or 7 would perhaps be an individual of truly impressive athletic accomplishment (captain of three sports/all-American athlete/MVP), or a nearly professional musician who might be the lead clarinet in the county orchestra and play in three other major music groups, or a nationally ranked debater, or the president of the regional office of a church or synagogue, or someone who shows significant leadership in high school, plus a twenty-hour-a-week job in the local supermarket.

Ratings of 8 and 9 are usually reserved for extraordinary students who have overcome extreme hardship to attain a high level of leadership and involvement, or just have truly extraordinary accomplishments for a senior in high school. As in the case of a very low ranking, a very high ranking usually mixes in a personal component. An extracurricular/personal 8 or 9 might be someone who escaped from the former Yugoslavia during the war there, lost much of his family, but who learned English and demonstrated leadership and academic achievement in a short span of three or four years in this country. Or perhaps a student who has overcome a major disability, either physical or mental (possibly a learning disability), and ended up being a nationally ranked debater, a chess player, a president of the class, or a talented jazz musician.

For the sake of comparison, let's look at Princeton's 1-5 (1 being the highest) ranking for extracurricular and personal areas as described by its admissions director, Fred Hargadon. The highest score of 1 is reserved for truly exceptional accomplishments, such as swimming at the Olympics, playing the violin at Carnegie Hall, patenting a product, writing a book, and so on. A 2 would usually reflect state or regional levels of accomplishment in a field such as music or sports. A 3 would be the norm in the Princeton pool, captain of a team or two, concert mistress of an orchestra, president of the senior class, et cetera. In the 4 category would be active students who are involved in many different areas but show no leadership or particular distinction, while 5s show little or no achievement.*

In any case, this extracurricular/personal rating is only about a third or less of the total vote, but in those borderline cases, especially with academic 4s, 5s, and 6s, it can really make a difference.

The truth is, if you are an academic 9 (now we are back to Dartmouth's 1-9 scale) and the most tremendous student in your high school, as long as you do a few interesting things outside of class, you'll probably be accepted on academics alone, but if you are in that tough middle range of an academic 4, 5, or 6, you will really need to show significant leadership and involvement either in school or out of school. As you might guess, the Ivies all differ in their emphasis on extracurricular activities. Some will have more academic focus and not care as much about extracurricular activities or leadership, while others will be extremely impressed by out-of-school activities and will be more inclined to take a risk. I'd say Dartmouth falls somewhere in the middle of these two poles, but leans toward the academic side.

To give you a better perspective on this, Dartmouth is more interested in seeing what the applicant does besides study in class. Someone who just does his homework but not much else is not someone who promises to add a lot to campus life at a college. The Ivies are not necessarily looking for any particular talent like sports or music. Instead, they are looking to

*See Bill Paul, "Getting In: An Inside Look at Admissions and Its Dean, Fred Hargadon," *Princeton Alumni Magazine*, November 22, 1995.

see what excites or motivates you. They'd just as soon see that you spend twenty hours a week writing software programs for a local computer company as see that you spend the same twenty hours a week as captain of your football team. Follow your interests. If you claim you are interested in medicine, the Ivies would be impressed if you took a class at a local community college and worked fifteen hours per week in a hospital, shadowing a doctor or doing volunteer work. If editing the high school paper is your forte, they'd be impressed to see that you went to a journalist camp in the summer where you refined your skills and brought them back to your high school. If you love math, they'd be impressed if you worked with your teacher independently on a special research project. In short, they don't value one activity over another—they look for patterns, academic interest, leadership ability, in-depth involvement, dedication to one or more activities, and, above all, a real passion for something.

If you go home and watch TV every day after school, or churn out six hours of homework a night, you will not really stand out in an Ivy League pool of very bright and motivated students. Contrary to what people may think, a tremendous amount of weight is given to the responsibility of having a job, even if you are not very involved in high school. If you held down a twenty-hour-a-week job and did a few high school activities, you would be seen in a very positive light. In fact, this has the additional benefit of making you look less sheltered.

The best thing you can do if you come from a privileged background is deemphasize it as best you can. For example, if you and your family took a ten-thousand-dollar vacation to Africa to go on safari, it would probably be best not to write about it on your application. First of all, it does not show much about what kind of student or person you are, since the fact that you were able to go has much more to do with your parents and their high income rather than with your own academic interests, and second of all, it may rub admissions people the wrong way, since most do not have the money and resources to take such an exotic trip.

There is a big difference between travel for pleasure and travel for personal enrichment. (The aforementioned safari would be an almost certain turnoff for an admissions person, but if you applied for a Rotary scholarship so you could spend three months in Costa Rica working on an ecology project you had designed with a teacher from your high school, that would show academic motivation and initiative in finding funding.) In conclusion, regarding travel, if it is purely for personal pleasure, don't bother talking about it on form 2, but if it has a significant educational component and it doesn't make you come off as privileged, definitely discuss it.

The next short essay is entitled "Your most meaningful activity and why." This is the time to flesh out one of your activities that shows your level of dedication. A good answer would be something such as this: "For the debate team, we practically live together while researching a topic for the national tournament. Last year, our team went to nationals and I won third place for my efforts. After spending an average of twenty-five hours a week discussing the assigned topic with the brightest people from my high school, how can I not call it my most meaningful subject?" A weak answer might read as follows: "I like ice hockey because of the camaraderie. I feel really close to the people on the team, since we've been through so much together. I hope to play in college." The latter response does not show much about how the student would add to the college, and the way it is written makes the person sound cookie-cutter-ordinary.

Next comes a brief query as to what college level courses you have taken, so if you haven't taken any community college classes or local college classes, list your AP classes. Many people leave out their AP or IB classes because they think such classes have to be taken at a college. This is not true.

After this, there is another short question that asks you to list prizes or academic honors you have won. Some honors are so commonplace that it is really not necessary to list them, such as mention in *Who's Who*. The company that produces *Who's Who* merely wants to sell as many books as possible. Such a wide range of students is included that the honor at the Ivy League level is meaningless.

What you should definitely emphasize are any legitimate prizes you have won while in high school. If you debate, list the results of major contests. If you scored well on the American High School Math Exam, list your score. If you graduated in the top 10 percent of your class and made cum laude, list that. If you have won a NCTE (National Council of Teachers of English) writing award, list it. Other legitimate awards would include any you have won for scientific experiments or research (that is, a Westinghouse, which would carry a lot of weight, or publishing an academic paper with someone), a National Merit semifinalist or finalist (the Ivies get so many "commended" students that it doesn't carry much weight*), American Legion Boy's State or Girl's State (for leadership), a Rotary scholar, AP Scholar, and department awards within your high school. If you go to the kind of high school that doesn't give academic awards, you should state that in the space provided: "Because of the intense competition at my high school, the administration does not assign any academic awards within the school." You would still be free to list any awards you won out of class. These awards and special honors are listed right on the master card.

What effect does this section have and why do we ask you? The answer is twofold. First, we get to see not just if you stand out in your high school but how you stand out in the national pool with some of the bigger awards. For example, if you were

*The index for determining whether you are a National Merit semifinalist or "commended" (ie., runner-up) student varies by state. Some states double your verbal and add the math; some treat them both the same—obviously in states like New York and Connecticut, it will be much harder to become a semifinalist because of the high concentration of excellent schools and talented students than it would somewhere like Montana or Idaho, where there are many fewer students and schools to compete with. The Ivies are aware of the high-competition states, so they may give some weight to a "commended" student from a very competitive area.

a Westinghouse semifinalist for a science project, we would have some verification for your avowed interest in science. If your paper is really interesting or involves a good deal of research, send a copy to the appropriate academic department at the college. If those in the department are favorably impressed, they would write us a brief letter telling us what they think of your work. Obviously, we would rate a professor's opinion quite strongly. Second, we can see if you are a standout within the confines of your high school. If you win three departmental awards (for example, AP European history award, best math student award, et cetera), we have additional confirmation that you stand out in your high school and that you are accorded high respect by the teachers.

Next you have to list any jobs you've had while in high school. This is the place to show that you're not a prince or princess who has never had to work. Be sure to include any entrepreneurial or research experience here, such as contracting yourself out to your high school to set up the new computer system, or working in a lab for three summers doing cancer research. Following this list (feel free to elaborate on an extra sheet of paper if anything you did requires further explanation and would add to our appreciation of how hard the task was) is the last short essay, which is entitled "What did you do last summer?" I trust I have made quite clear that you don't want to elaborate on your jet-set life.

As you might guess, we are impressed by significant commitments to summer programs, especially because many of them provide financial aid to needy students, so you don't need money to be able to take advantage. What we are not impressed by is your parents forcing you to take summer classes because they think it will look good for college. We would look for patterns and confirmation by teachers that you really do enjoy learning. Many of our applicants spend parts of several summers in educational programs pursuant to their academic interests. It is even more impressive if there is a sense of continuity for one or more summers. A one-week program wouldn't be as impressive as an eight-week intensive summer program. If you are thinking to yourself, But I'd hate to go to school all summer, too—I can't wait for high school to end, you might want to reevaluate your reasons for applying to a highly selective college. If you don't enjoy intellectual experiences and you don't get a rush from spending time with intelligent and interesting people, you might think twice about the colleges you are applying to.

THE ESSAY

The last and most important part of form 2 is your essay. I have a fair amount to say about this. I always get a kick out of the publication *Essays That Worked: Fifty Essays from Successful Applications to the Nation's Top Colleges.** (The same publisher also produces a similar book for law school and business school.) The problem with this publication is that it doesn't seem to admit that the essay is only one of many factors that determines an applicant's admission. In some cases, a student with a weak essay will be admitted for a multitude of other reasons. The book's implication is that all the essays contained within are excellent and would guarantee admission. This is not at all true. The essay by itself will not get you into college. If you are an academic 1, 2, 3, or even 4 and write a great essay, it won't make much difference, and if you are an academic 7, 8, or 9 and write a solid but not inspired essay, you will probably get in anyway. It makes the biggest difference for all the students in the middle range (4s, 5s, and 6s,), for whom the essay provides the best chance to stand out. Dartmouth's question is about as open-ended as it gets: "Write your ideal question and answer it."

*Boykin Curry and Brian Kasbar, eds., *Essays That Worked: Fifty Essays from Successful Applications to the Nation's Top Colleges* (Baltimore: Ballantine, 1990).

It will probably come as a shock to find out that more than 90 percent of the essays I read are weak and/or not notable. I'd say for the average essay, I spend roughly two to three minutes reading it through, sometimes less. The sad truth is that most essays, even those that strive to be original, are so clichéd that they barely warrant attention. If you want to read an excellent book on the subject that is short, hilarious, and informative, dig out a copy of Harry Bauld's *On Writing the College Application Essay*.* He worked in the Brown admissions office for many years (and, like me, he is an English teacher) and in his irreverent way, he groups *all* weak essays into nine clichéd categories.

My favorite is the "Outward Bound" (or substitute another name here, be it NOLS or the Sierra Club) essay, which usually starts with an enthralling description of the elements ("The icy wind bit into our limbs as we struggled desperately to reach the peak") and concludes with something incisive such as, "And I learned that no matter how hard it is, if you really push yourself, you are sure to succeed." Probably 20 percent of all essays in a given year at Dartmouth are a variation on that theme.

Another common category is the "community service" (or "how I helped mankind") essay, in which you describe how you went to El Salvador to build houses for Habitat for Humanity and were shocked at how primitive conditions were. But you learned that people everywhere are basically the same, you got along well with them, and were sad to leave. Another hackneyed topic is a kind of eulogy either to a deceased grandparent or a relative who meant a lot to you ("I remember sitting on Gramp's lap as he'd tell me how hard he had to work when he came to this country after escaping terrible persecution").

Now that you have a sense of how bad most essays are, how

*Harry Bauld, *On Writing the College Application Essay: The Key to Acceptance at the College of Your Choice* (New York: Harper Collins, 1987).

do you make yours less pedestrian? After all, this is an opportunity to shine. Easier said than done. Put yourself in the admissions officers' shoes for a moment. They want to find out what makes you tick, what kind of person you are, how much intellectual promise you have, and how well you write and think. If you write a silly essay on your teddy bear or your favorite pet, you are not helping your case. Quite the contrary—instead of showing your intellectual side, you come across as an immature student who can think of nothing more interesting than stuffed animals.

The best general advice I can give without writing a whole book on the topic is that the finest essays I have read are really slice-of-life essays that show what you are really like. Let me try to explain what I mean exactly by a slice-of-life essay. Rather than trying to fit everything about yourself into one small category, concentrate on one incident that sheds light on your personality. This does not have to be on a grand scale. The most effective essays take a small, seemingly insignificant incident and elaborate upon it. Don't try to fit your whole life into one short essay; instead, focus on just one experience in your life and make it come alive. The best essays are ones that help admissions officers understand your character better and/or shed light on any factors in your background that have influenced what kind of person you are.

If you come from a troubled background, you may want to use that as the subject for a moving personal essay. If you've done something truly distinctive, you may choose to write about that experience so that we can get an idea of the level of commitment you have. For example, if you have spent the last four years training six hours a day to make the U.S. Olympic rhythmic gymnastics team, write about the dedication it has taken. Like the activity list, this kind of essay will give us a better idea about how committed you are and what you would offer the college. These kinds of topics are helpful because they are truly interesting to read (unlike the majority of essays), they give us special insight into your personality, and they make you seem like a real person.

Some of the best essays I have read defy categorization, except that they fall into the aforementioned slice-of-life category. To give you a more concrete idea of what I mean, let me describe two of the best essays I've read in the thousands of files I've seen. The first one was from a boy from the South who happened to write in a beautiful southern style. He narrated a story about how when he was a boy he fixated on the idea of having an air rifle because he thought it would make him a man. ("I do not remember the maker of my first pellet gun. You could see the pellet fly out of the muzzle and come down in a long arch, not too far away. The gun's range and speed were deceptive, because it is just this kind of gun that is most responsible for taking a kid's eye out and putting fear into many a mother's heart.") He conjured up images of himself prowling around the family farm and protecting his family. He decided that for his birthday, he had to have a .22-caliber rifle as a rite of passage. After he begged and begged, his family relented and gave him a used .22 single-shot rifle, insisting that he enroll in a Hunter Safety Course. ("My father could not understand why I insisted so much on having a rifle. He never owned a gun and the thought of tracking down prey and killing it was the furthest thing from his mind. He is a quiet man who loves to read and work in the yard.") This young man was absolutely thrilled and spent the next day hiding in a tree so he could kill a squirrel and take it home to his family.

After many hours and several failed attempts, he finally shot one, only he didn't kill it—rather, he wounded it. This student skillfully narrated how he jumped down to see what he had done and then stared with horror at the suffering animal, who was twitching violently and bleeding. To put it out of its misery, he had to club it with the butt of the rifle. Even though his parents were not hunters, they felt that part of the responsibility of killing was to use what you killed, so his mother skinned and gutted the animal. He concluded:

> She served an oily, slick portion of the squirrel to me for supper. I pulled the stringy meat from the bones as best I could. Everyone else ate spaghetti and meatballs. I could not finish my serving. After supper, I felt tired and fell into a deep sleep. I woke up close to midnight and cried out. My grandmother rushed into my room and my parents came in soon after, just in time to see me vomit. My father walked me outside to get some air. I heaved and sobbed for what seemed a very long time. I think it was guilt that I was trying to expel from my body. My father put his arm around my shoulders and held me close to his side. I was a hunter for one day and on that day I had killed a squirrel. That day was also the last time I held a gun in my hands. Dad did not say anything that night, but he understood. I, too, am a gentle man.

In this short but touching essay, we find out about what kind of person the applicant is, as well as how he thinks and writes. He took a seemingly insignificant episode from his childhood and turned it into a moving story that opened a window into his personality. He told us about himself in a unique and moving way. He stood out from the crowd—he was the only one who had this particular experience, and he made it work for him, while at the same time showing his character and individuality.

Another great essay from a recent applicant started out by describing how this girl's family watched *Jeopardy* together and how she competed with her dad to get the answers first. How can you not laugh at an opening gambit like hers: "García Márquez! It has to be García Márquez. García Márquez, you idiots!" She describes with pride how her father always used to lead the family while at the same time encouraging his daughter to acquire a broad base of knowledge. As the essay proceeds, we find that this *Jeopardy* game was a way of showing how her father's battle with cancer was slowing him down to the point where he could no longer blurt out the answers. ("My father doesn't shout out his answers anymore. He no longer jumps up on his seat or throws his head back in disbelief when he finds out the right answer. The contestants do not bother him as much as they used to and he finds Alex Trebek a lot less amusing. He whispers the answer to the 'Final Jeopardy' question because breathing is difficult for him.") Even so, he was happy to see that his daughter was acquiring the requisite knowledge and the passion for learning that obviously was a driving force in his life.

The essay ends with her dancing around the hospital room in her "winning jig" because she got the final question right: " 'Richard Burton! I know this one! No, not the actor. I'm serious. I really know this one! He was the first European to visit Mecca!' My father is not as surprised as the nurse about my sudden outburst. As the answer is revealed, I proceed to dance the winning jig around the bed, chanting, 'Ms. Abt's AP European history class, eleventh grade, I can't believe it.' " As a postscript, she added that a few weeks after she finished this essay, really a moving tribute to her father, he succumbed to the cancer, but he had been happy knowing that his daughter loved learning as much as he had and was following in his footsteps.

Granted, not everyone has this kind of dramatic incident to write about, but the beauty of this essay was that the writer did not set out to write a maudlin essay so we would feel sorry for her. By describing the relationship she had with her father, she showed what kind of person she was and how much she loved learning and acquiring knowledge. Although the essay turned into a eulogy for her father, it was very upbeat and subtly done. It even contained humor. Every time I think of the essay, it brings tears to my eyes and makes me want to meet the writer. This is the kind of effect you hope for in the best of cases. If the reader wants to drop everything and meet you in person, you have written an extraordinary essay.

I hope you can contrast these slice-of-life essays with more mundane topics, such as the five-sentence essay that answers the question "Why do you think you'd make a good Dartmouth student?" with such trite conclusions as, "I'm a student leader and a strong athlete and I like the outdoors, so I think I'd really fit in." I'm sure you think I'm exaggerating, but I can testify that many more students than you would think write variations on this theme. It's probably always better to observe Hemingway's "Show, don't tell!" technique of writing. Rather than describing what you are like ("I'm a leader, athlete, and all-around great guy"), let it come across in your essay.

Finally, have a literate friend read your essay and ask him what he would think about the kind of person you were *just* by reading your essay. If your true personality does not come across or your friend cannot think of a single reason why your essay would make an admissions person say, "We want this student at our college," it's back to the drawing board. I say show it to a friend and not your guidance counselor or parents for several reasons. Most importantly, there is nothing more discouraging than an overprocessed and overedited essay. Most alert readers can actually pick out where adults have edited an essay and added more sophisticated words that don't quite fit in. In their effort to try to think like an admissions person, or like an adult, they take away all the vitality and freshness of an essay and leave it sterile and well groomed.

I'd much rather read a slightly rougher essay that had real feeling in it than a dry but perfectly crafted one. In addition, some of the best essays are actually about your family life, or your parents, or are very personal, so it might be harmful to show it to your parents. They might think that there is no need to air dirty laundry to total strangers. By having a friend read your essay, you will be able to fix the egregious errors (of course, it does help to use the spell-checker on the computer to avoid embarrassing typos) and keep your personal thoughts and style intact. If you don't get across some aspect of your personality, you have not written a successful essay. I'm sure you could describe to a friend what makes you special (and I'm sure that friend could tell you why he thinks you are special), so think of your task as coming up with a creative way to express your unique qualities. The best way to do this is through some variation on the slice-of-life idea. Avoid trite or puerile topics like the amazing spirit your basketball team has, your success making chocolate chip cookies, how you pulled a muscle but managed to recover due to your dedication to rehabilitating yourself, the diving play you made in the play-off game, or how you always manage to cheer your friends up when they are feeling down. None of these will add to your academic or personal side enough to aid admissions officers in their decision-making process. Especially for academic 4s, 5s, and 6s, the essay is crucial.

Now that we've gone through form 2, which is the student-controlled part of the application, let's take a step-by-step look at form 3, which is presented by the high school.

FORM 3

After you fill in on the front of form 3 what your senior courses will be, the guidance counselor takes over and fills out some of the short-answer questions. If the high school ranks, what is your rank? Is it weighted or unweighted? What is the GPA (weighted or unweighted), or what is your decile ranking? Right next to rank, most forms now ask, "Shared by how many students?" so the guidance counselor can no longer simply write down "number one" without mentioning whether this rank is unshared or shared by twenty people. It is dishonest not to fill this part out thoroughly.

The other important piece of information the guidance counselor must provide is the comparative level of difficulty of your course load: "less demanding than average"; "average college-bound program"; "more demanding than average"; "most demanding available." Officers summarize this information on the master card (using Dartmouth's system—other schools use their own designations) by circling the number 1, 2, 3, or 4 (4 being the hardest load possible) that corresponds to your course load. Of course, they would also read your transcript carefully to see if they agree with the counselor. For example, if the counselor checked off a "track 3" load because you took five AP classes, while some classmates took six APs, they'd probably call it a "track 4," since that is still considered a very difficult course load for any high school in the country. Before looking at your transcript, officers try to get a sense of where you stand in your high school and how hard your courses have been. If you have a 4.0 unweighted GPA and a high rank but have taken only a "track 2" load, you will not be a competitive applicant, nor will you if you have the hardest load but a C average.

You *always* want to take the hardest courses available to you, since that shows a love of learning and the desire to face challenges. Parents always ask, "Is it better for my child to get a B or a C in an IB/AP course or an A in an honors or slightly less difficult class?" The easy answer to this query is that it is better to get an A in the IB/AP class; that is the reality of the situation. Always take the most challenging classes when given a choice. One low grade will not finish you off—the real question is where do you stand in comparison to your classmates who are taking a similarly difficult course load. If you can only manage C's in IB/AP classes while several others get A's in those same classes, you probably will not get accepted to highly selective colleges, but you still wouldn't, even if you had gotten A's in easier classes. The worst thing you can do is to drop a class because it is difficult and opt for the A in a less challenging class to save your GPA. Although it might raise your AI, any officer would notice the change and knock your AI down manually, so it's not worth the risk.

Schools also ask what percentage of the senior class usually attends a four-year college. This number is very useful in determining how strong or weak your high school is. If only 10 percent go on to four-year colleges, clearly you have attended a very weak high school. Rather than hold it against you, officers adapt their expectations to the opportunities that were afforded to you. If they were wondering why you took so few IB/AP classes even though the guidance counselor checked off "most demanding available," they would realize that your high school did not have extensive offerings, but that you were taking the hardest classes possible. Finally, officers would be able to be a bit more lenient on SAT II test results, since your classes were probably not very competitive on a national scale.

Of course, they adjust their expectations accordingly if 100 percent of the students usually attend four-year colleges. Clearly, this would represent a more affluent community with a high emphasis on education (or a strong private high school) and with many upper-level course offerings. If you were number one in a class where everyone went on to college, you would definitely stand out and would stand a better chance of having high SAT II scores. In reality, this percentage is used along with other factors, such as parental occupation, level of education, money spent per student in the school district (usually from the high school's profile), to determine what obstacles the student may have faced growing up in that particular area.

After filling out a series of boxes about your academic and personal profile (again, officers look for patterns—if the counselor checked off very low-level boxes, they would worry, but if he checked off lots of "the finest I've seen in my career" and you're in the third decile of your class, they would not believe him), the guidance counselor must check off whether he has any personal reservations about your character. Ninety-eight percent of the time, counselors would check off "no," indicating that they have every personal faith in your integrity. When they do have reservations, they usually do one of four things:

(1) check "yes" and give a brief explanation; (2) check "yes" with no written explanation; (3) leave it blank; (4) write "call me," with no further comment.

Every time an officer sees options 2-4, he calls the guidance counselor personally. In this age of lawsuits and aggressive parents, counselors are sometimes unwilling to put anything down in writing in case the parents try to subpoena the records if a child is not accepted. In one year, I made four personal calls, and in every single case, there was a major problem. The gravest problem would be an academic violation like cheating, copying, stealing notes, or plagiarizing. In one particular case I had an academic 9 with suspiciously low check marks by the guidance counselor. When I called, it turned out that the student was not only arrogant and haughty but also the leader of a cheating ring at the high school. This student would make copies of her exams for later classes and sell them for profit. When she was caught, her parents threatened the high school with lawsuits, so everyone was afraid to put anything in writing. In addition, the high school was terrorized into not punishing her, so there was nothing on her transcript to indicate a suspension.

The guidance counselor was too scared to say anything, but once I promised I would not pinpoint where the information had come from, she told me how this girl had no moral principles. Despite her academic rating, we of course denied her admission, but the alarming thing is that not every reader would necessarily take the time to call the counselor. My personal opinion is that it is the counselor's professional responsibility to reveal any personal reservations, since colleges have no other way of knowing. At Dartmouth, there is a strict academic honor code—tests are not proctored, many exams are take-home, and students must take positive action if they see any evidence of cheating. Especially at a school that gives students lots of academic freedom, there is no way that the college would admit anyone who showed signs of dishonesty.

The other major problem would be one where the candidate displays a lack of personal integrity. In 1995, there was the famous Harvard case where someone who had been admitted early action was found later to have murdered her mother. All the Ivy League schools reserve the right to rescind admission if there is a drop in academic performance or a major violation of some sort. Interestingly, although Harvard rescinded its acceptance, she was accepted by Tufts.

The best course of action that the counselor and the student can take is to be honest. There are many cases where officers might read about a suspension or disciplinary action but would not be concerned. Officers use their best judgment in evaluating violations. In a recent case, a student wrote a brief note that she had been suspended for an alcohol violation. The details were as follows: She went to a boarding school and a friend's family took her out to dinner and bought her a bottle of Kahlúa for her birthday. She took it home and put it in her dorm room. Although the bottle was not even opened, she was suspended when the dorm parent found the bottle there. Even though the high school took disciplinary action, we deemed this a very minor infraction and ignored it. It worked in her favor that she was up-front about the suspension and offered a brief explanation.

Another student was expelled from high school because he had brought in an antique pistol for a special school game of Clue that was to be played that day. The headmaster panicked and expelled him because the high school had a strict law forbidding possession of firearms. It helped that this student had an on-campus interview and made a very good impression by telling the interviewer about the incident. In fact, the interviewer found him very appealing, open, and straightforward. Rather than being defiant, he was extremely repentant for having been so naïve and for doing such a stupid thing, even though he didn't think it warranted expulsion. In this student's case, the committee discounted the high school's expulsion and judged him strictly on academics and extracurricular/personal qualities.

In yet another case, the student was less fortunate. This student attended a military academy and because of its strict moral code, he felt compelled to explain an event that had happened the summer after his junior year, at summer school. A girlfriend of his had turned him in for having a beer with an older friend's family (that by itself did not bother anyone). Since this particular summer school had very strict alcohol rules, it was about to expel him for this minor infraction. Again, that would not have bothered anyone. But what did send out warning signals was the fact that he got angry with the girl, showed up in her dorm room to accuse her of turning him in, and then proceeded to throw a bottle at the wall (not near her, so it was not a life-threatening situation) as hard as he could.

This event was bothersome because it made the whole office worry about his rash reaction. What would he be like to have as a roommate? If his temper could flare up so easily, the next time he might throw the bottle at someone and injure him. Of course there was the gender issue, as well—both the men and woman on the committee felt that he had used force to intimidate a female student, and it doesn't take much imagination to see how this pattern could lead to more serious offenses. One officer wondered aloud if he would be the kind of person to get drunk at a party, try to make a pass at a girl, and use force if necessary to get her to have sex with him. The committee thought a lot about this case before deciding unanimously to deny him admission, even though he was a fairly strong candidate.

The last part of form 3 is the guidance counselor's letter of recommendation. In some of the high schools, each counselor is responsible for hundreds of students and does not know each student well enough to be of significant help. In cases such as these, officers do not hold an overly general letter against the applicant, since it has nothing to do with his academic potential. This lack of knowledge on a counselor's part is fairly apparent to colleges if they know the high school has one thousand students in each class and only three or four guidance counselors. The length of the recommendation is not proportional to quality. Officers would much rather see a short but descriptive letter than a long and formulaic one. It is dismaying to see how some counselors, even at strong high schools, ramble on and on for pages about a student without saying anything substantive. I'm sure it makes them feel they've done their job to the utmost, but from the college's point of view, they are not helping in the decision-making process. In fact, if the letter is that long, officers usually skim for main points anyway. Since officers come to know many of the counselors in their areas, they usually have a good idea of who is on target, who writes concisely, and who blathers on endlessly.

Remember, officers are looking for confirmation of what they have already found out about the student. If they have gotten this far and find an academic 8 or 9 who has tons of academic awards and honors and is the best student in the high school, all that is needed is a brief confirmation. In this case, all that is necessary is a letter that is short and to the point: "Of the ninety-five seniors in the class, Brad is head and shoulders above the rest. He has superior cognitive abilities, has impressed all of his teachers, is generally considered the strongest student in the last five years, and has an impeccable character to boot." What else needs to be said? Why waste pages and pages when it's clear that this student blows everyone else out of the water?

Sometimes counselors alert officers to a student's weakness by writing a standard recommendation but assigning lower check evaluations in the boxes. What is meant by a standard recommendation? Typically, officers would get a page full of comments about how nice the student is, all the great clubs and leadership activities he participates in, how very fond teachers are of him, but nothing much about the student's academic performance. This is usually because the student is the proverbial "great kid"—loved by all, a leader, but an average or just hardworking student who is not going to stand out enough in the Ivy pool of applicants. Many of these students fall into the academic 2 to 5 category.

Should a guidance counselor lie or exaggerate in an attempt to get a borderline case in? In a word, no. For example, the exuberant counselor who checks off "one of the most outstanding in my career" and writes a strong letter in the case of a student with mid-500 to low-600 scores with a third decile ranking in a "track 3" course load ("more demanding than average" but not "most demanding available") is going to undermine his credibility completely. Officers would think to themselves, This high school must be terrible if this student is the best in this counselor's career, or, The counselor must be totally out of touch with reality, or, The counselor must be related to the applicant or the applicant's family.

Many admissions officers might jot down a note about the credibility of a particular counselor in their notebook, especially if a pattern emerges over time. For example, the private high school counselor who writes a strong but almost identical letter for ten students is not helping to distinguish between the merely good and the excellent. In the case of the totally off-base counselor, an officer might write down in his notebook, "Watch out for apps from X high school; the counselor pushed all the kids, even the ones in the lower deciles." The regional reader would probably make a brief comment for the record on the ready sheet. Remember, the counselor letter alone is not going to get a student accepted at the college of his choice. The student's own accomplishments are what lead to acceptance and should be supported by the counselor, rather than invented or exaggerated.

As mentioned in chapter 6, the most helpful information a counselor can give is an overview of where a student stands in the senior class, especially if the high school does not rank. It is not necessary to quote from six different teacher opinions, although it is helpful to get specific information from one or two teachers. There are many other helpful comments a counselor can make that help colleges get a better idea of where a student really stands in his class.

Let's take a case in which the student has very high test scores but a disappointing second-decile rank. The counselor could really make or break this kind of case if certain things were true. If the letter starts, "Although it is surprising that Jane is ranked in the second decile, she is taking the hardest course load of any senior this year (six AP classes), but our high school does not weight grades. If we did, Jane would be number three out of two hundred students," this is helpful information. It assuages doubts as to why Jane's rank was so low even though she seemed to be very bright. Once officers are able to confirm that many above her had much lighter course loads, they could give her the credit she deserves by boosting her AI and her academic ranking.

In conclusion, the guidance counselor can either have no effect (that is, if he has such a big caseload that he barely knows the student) or a huge effect in confirming what is expected from the rest of the folder, or explaining why something is not as it would at first seem. In the best letters, officers get a much better picture of what the applicant is like as a student and where he falls in his class relative to the difficulty of his course load. Oftentimes, the briefest letters are the strongest. The most savvy counselors know how to write a short but effective letter telling colleges what they need to know. After all, applicants are not judged by the writing ability of the guidance counselor. What colleges are looking for is information that will help them put this student in the context of the entire senior class.

THE HIGH SCHOOL TRANSCRIPT

If academics are two-thirds of the admissions decision, the high school transcript probably accounts for roughly 60 percent of the academic determination, even though as we have seen the AI formula does not accurately reflect this emphasis. The transcript is the single–most–important piece of the whole puzzle. Students with very high standardized test scores and C grades are routinely turned down by most highly selective colleges. They understand that the student is smart, but they are not impressed with the fact that he is not working up to potential. Most highly selective colleges would rather have a student with slightly lower scores but still high enough to be competitive in the larger applicant pool who is top in his class and is a force to be reckoned with in class discussions. There are several key components to reading a transcript. On the whole, officers spend more time on this part of your application than on just about anything else.

The first thing they look at, of course, is rigor of course load. Officers always consider a student against the context of what has been available to him. They are very aware of non-privileged students who, because of lack of monetary resources, live in an area where the high school is weak and does not offer much either academically or in the area of extracurricular activities. If your high school offers only two AP classes and you have taken them both, officers will look for how you have tried to deal with the situation. Usually, students with true academic motivation stand out. In many cases, they will have taken summer classes on scholarship at a good program or have gone to a local college in the afternoons or evenings to follow up on something their high school might not offer, or have done independent research projects with faculty members. On the other hand, if your high school offers APs in twelve different subject areas and you are taking all average college-prep courses (usually considered "track 2," or two levels lower than AP and honors classes), your rank and grades will be irrelevant, since you have not sought out academic challenges.

Once officers get a sense of the rigor of your course load (it will either confirm what your guidance counselor checked off or modify it), they look at grade trend. Is your rank lower than it should be because you had a *C* and a *B* freshman year but all *A*'s after that? Some colleges do not even count your ninth-grade grades when computing your GPA (Princeton uses only tenth- , eleventh- , and twelfth-grade grades for every student in its recomputation of GPA, which is put on a 4.0 scale), but your grades would still affect your rank. Colleges would much prefer to see an upward trend in grades, especially as the course work becomes more challenging. The very worst thing that they could see would be declining grades in the junior and senior years, when you are likely to be taking mostly AP and honors classes. Almost always on the ready sheet is a comment about grade trend: "*A*'s in ninth and tenth grade, but downward trend in eleventh with four APs."

A good guidance counselor will append any helpful information about extenuating circumstances that might have affected grades, such as, "The only quarter Mindy ever got *B*'s was the two-month period where she was in and out of school with a serious case of strep throat."

Officers check to see if grades are weighted, and they are, what your actual grades are, compared to what the weighted grades are. This is the time where the regional reader will add personal comments to the ready sheet about the high school. There are certain high schools in my area, for example, that I know to be very tough in terms of grading scale. In one high school in Ohio, most students have grades in the high 70s and low 80s, and good grades are 88 to 93, with hardly anyone scoring higher. Therefore, I always make a special note on the ready sheet regarding where I would place this student in the context of the class. Conversely, if grading is very inflated, I would make a note of that. I would also give my sense of how many APs would be a competitive load in that high school. Some high schools allow students to take only three AP classes, since those classes are considered very intensive, while others allow up to six. The admissions officer's personal knowledge of a high school can be very helpful in interpreting the transcript. When the officer is unfamiliar with a high school, he spends a few minutes perusing the profile for relevant information.

FORM 4A AND 4B: TEACHER RECOMMENDATIONS

Almost every comment I have made about the guidance counselor's letter holds true for the teacher recommendation, as well. Admissions officers would much prefer a concise but helpful recommendation ("In thirty years, I have never met a student with such a brilliant facility for math") to a rambling tome. Most colleges ask for two teacher recommendations (Dartmouth calls them form 4A and 4B), although in some cases students might want to provide one extra letter, but they should be careful not to go overboard.

These letters are extremely important because they let colleges see the student behind the grades and numbers. Officers always ask themselves, What would this student add to the classroom? If you have high scores and a top rank but both teacher recommendations say that you don't work up to potential, you are done for. Many students are rejected because they are merely diligent but do not show that extra spark that sets them apart from their classmates.

Besides form 2 and the guidance counselor's letter, officers get the best sense of this spark from the teachers' letters. In probably half of the letters, it is obvious from the boxes and the comments that the student is fine but not a standout. Once again, officers would write on the ready sheet, "Standard rec," meaning that the teacher is quite fond of you and you work hard, but you are not the driving force behind class discussions.

For some reason, many teachers feel the need to downplay academic achievements in favor of character by saying such things as, "I'm sure you can see Eric's academic side from the rest of his application, so let me concentrate on his personal side." This is usually a *mistake*. The truth is that officers almost always get an excellent sense of the candidate's personal side from the rest of the application, whereas they are counting on the teacher recommendations to give a sense of the student's academic side and intellectual potential. The main purpose of the teacher recommendations is to give a snapshot of the student's participation in class, interest in learning, level of achievement relative to other students, and overall academic ability compared to students over the years. They are also used to confirm or deny academic trends seen in other parts of the application, such as testing, grades, rank, and other recommendations.

I would encourage teachers to be honest. If you have any reservations about a student, now is not the time to hide them. Your credibility is on the line. It is helpful to keep in mind that negative comments do not automatically diminish a student's chances. They are taken into context along with all the other information in the file.

Before concluding this section, I want to add a note about teachers who use words like *diligent* and *conscientious*. Though often teachers are trying to say something positive by commenting thus on a student's work ethic, admissions officers at highly selective colleges tend to interpret words like these to mean that the student is merely a hard worker, or a grind, but not a very insightful or naturally bright student. *Diligent* implies that a student dutifully plows through assignment after assignment without ever reaching any deep insight or adding to the class in any way. I think teachers are trying to say that the student can handle the workload, but that is something that is evident from the rest of the student's application. If a student has SAT Is and IIs in the low 500s, it is already obvious that he would have trouble with the workload at an Ivy League school.

In any case, roughly *75 to 85 percent* of all the applicants who apply are perfectly capable of doing the work at an Ivy League school. Fred Hargadon of Princeton asserts that 80 to 90 percent are qualified to do the work, so high grades and high testing are not enough. Remember, what the highly selective colleges are looking for are students who will light up the classroom, those who will make a significant contribution to their classes and to scholarship. Diligence alone is seen in a negative light—a plugger who will always hand work in on time but will never contribute to the academic life of the college in a significant way.

In short, the teacher recommendations can make or break a close case. If up to this point you have not shown much spark or academic intensity and both your teacher recommendations are positive but not exceptional, you will probably fade out like the many academic 4s, 5s, and 6s who are strong all around but are truly not standouts in the overall applicant pool. The well-rounded student often fades out because he is good at a little bit of everything, but where it really counts, in the academic arena, he is a good student, studious and diligent, but nothing beyond. Conversely, if you have made a fairly strong overall impression by this point and your teachers say that you light up the classroom, you do extra research, and you are the one who stimulates all class discussion, you will be considered a high-impact admit who will bring these talents to the Ivy League classroom.

FORM 4C: THE PEER RECOMMENDATION

I do not want to devote much time to the peer recommendation, since it is a very minor part of the application. Besides, Dartmouth is the only Ivy League college that I know of that even asks for a peer letter. Its sole function is to bring out parts of your personality and character that might not be apparent from the rest of the application. If your closest friend says that you are such a brilliant student that the whole high school is in awe of you, he would be helping an admissions officer to get a better sense of your academic strength. A peer might also confirm your avowed major interests. If you spend most of form 2 talking about your involvement with debating and your friend mentions that you are a debate nut who spends forty hours a week preparing and researching, his comments will confirm what has already been seen. For the most part, officers are trying to give the applicant every chance to shine—in the case of the peer letter, sometimes officers can find out things about you that might make you look more attractive. However, a peer letter will rarely swing a vote one way or another or change a decision.

I can only think of one case out of the thousands of applications I have seen where the peer recommendation changed a final decision. The case was an extreme one—a "friend" writing that the student was a cheater who was hated by the whole school and even got himself elected to honor council so he could exonerate his guilty friends. The letter ended by saying, ". . . is so arrogant that he does not have any idea who his friends really are, as you can probably see by this letter." Just so you don't fret unnecessarily, an officer would never react to this kind of letter without doing his own investigation. The first thing he would check would be whether the friend had also applied (in this case, he had not), in case it was a jealous attempt to sink his friend's application. Next, our office called the high school and spoke to the guidance counselor and the principal. As it turned out, every accusation the friend had made was true. The tricky part is that our office could not reveal where we had received that information, because we would never reveal anything specific from a file, for fear of lawsuit.

In this one isolated case, we rejected the applicant because of the damning peer letter. I blame the high school for withholding this kind of important information, and to this day, I remember which high school it is. Admissions people share this kind of knowledge with one another, so it is just not worth the risk to protect a student in order to get him into college. Once the word gets out that your high school covers up major incidents, it reflects badly on the high school's reputation and on all the applicants applying from that high school.

THE PERSONAL INTERVIEW

In my opinion, the importance of the interview is overrated. It may turn out to be a cause of extreme anxiety in many cases, and for no valid reason. Remember, the interview is seen in perspective, against the background of the entire application. A negative interview will not necessarily sink an applicant, just as a positive interview will not guarantee admission. Like the peer recommendation, the interview gives officers either a confirmation of what they have seen or a contradiction. Many highly selective colleges have both on-campus interviews, conducted by either an admissions officer or a senior interviewer, and alumni interviews, conducted by local alumni. Since it is problematic to require an on-campus interview (that would assume that the applicant had enough disposable income to fly to your college), the general policy of highly selective colleges is to use it if it is there but not to hold it against the applicant if it is absent. At Dartmouth, there is also the option of an alumni interview (if there are alumni who live in the student's area), but not all colleges offer this option.

Students usually, then, have four choices: an on-campus interview, an alumni interview, both, or neither. Statistically, the acceptance rate is a few percentage points higher for students who have had two interviews than for those who have had one, and slightly higher for those who have had one than for those who have had none, but I think it's safe to say that the primary reason for this small statistical difference lies in the self-selective process. Some of the strongest applicants are bit-ing at the bit to show their stuff during an interview. More modest applicants might not want to interview at all for fear that they will come across as they are—merely solid, well-rounded students with no special talents or attributes. In addition, with two interviews, both of which are extremely strong, officers definitely get a better sense about what the applicant is like and where his strengths lie. If the applicant has not done a thorough job on form 2 and the high school personnel have not given the colleges much information, an interview definitely helps the college to get a more complete picture of the applicant.

What do interviewers, either alumni or on-campus, look for and what is the point of having one? Following Dartmouth's selection criteria for admissions, the interviewer divides the write-up into "academic," "extracurricular," "personal," and "overall," usually writing a few short sentences for each. The rating scale is much like the boxes on the teacher recommendations, ranging from "below average" to "brilliant—one in a hundred." Since there are five distinct categories, Dartmouth matches them to its 1-9 ranking scale, using the odd numbers. Alumni interviewers give only one overall rating, whereas on-campus interviewers give a rating in the four areas I just mentioned, plus an overall rating. The overall rating is the one that is reported on the master card. For Dartmouth, the following descriptions are used as guidelines for the interviewer. These would be similar at all highly selective colleges that grant interviews.

A 9. Outstanding: Superior in nearly all respects; the one-in-a-hundred applicant; a rare individual.

A 7. Highly desirable: A very appealing candidate with either great academic strength, great extracurricular/personal strength (and very positive academic strength), or both academic and personal strengths; one who possesses talent in one or more areas and who will contribute greatly to the life of the college.

A 5. Desirable: A generally strong candidate whom the college should be glad to have in the student body and who should make a contribution to the life of the college.

A 3. Acceptable: Has no significant weaknesses and has promise of academic success and personal development; like many others.

A 1. Recommended with reservations: Possesses strength in some area(s), but the interviewer has expressed reservations (write down your reservations).

A 0. Not recommended: Does not possess the overall academic promise or personal strengths expected of competitive students, for the expressed reasons (write down your reasons).

The interviewer is trying to get a sense of what makes you tick, where your passions lie, how much of an impact you would have at the college, and how sharp you are academically—exactly the same information that officers are looking for throughout the whole application.

The purpose of the interview is twofold: to get an impression of the applicant and at the same time to answer questions about the college for the benefit of the applicant. Don't forget, the interview serves as much as a recruiting tool as a basis for selection. Dartmouth hires and trains a small core of seniors who work during the summer and fall doing interviews just as officers do. It is neither advantageous nor disadvantageous to have a student interviewer instead of an officer. Ivy League offices give the same weight to any interview, whether it is done by an officer, a graduate of the college, or a senior interviewer.

Some parents are convinced that they should pull every possible string to arrange an interview with the director of admissions. I would not recommend this path, because in general, Ivy officers frown on the idea of any student having an unfair advantage in the admissions process, especially based on wealth or status of a parent. In fact, you will most probably end up annoying the director, who is extremely busy and might not want to take time out of his day to interview your child. Plus, what if the student does not make a favorable impression on the director? I cannot think of a more certain way to ruin your child's chances of being accepted than to have a weak interview with the head of admissions.

Having said this, I think the interview can be helpful, because it is the only piece of information in the folder that is done by someone who does not know anything about the applicant prior to meeting him. Thus, officers find an unjaded opinion of the applicant. For this reason, the interview has a role in the process and is used in the same way as recommendations and the guidance counselor's letter—to confirm what officers already have seen or to cast doubt. For example, if officers got through the whole application and thought that a particular applicant was fairly strong (let's say she was an academic 6 with strong teacher recommendations and lots of interesting involvement in and out of school but was still not an obvious standout) and then the alumni group that interviewed the applicant said that they were tremendously impressed and rated her "one in a hundred—outstanding," the admissions office would probably lean toward "A," an acceptance.

In the opposite scenario, if the interviewer rated "recommended with reservations" and said the person could barely articulate a sentence, didn't make eye contact, and had nothing to say, the officers would probably lean toward "R," a rejection.

As you might guess, the interview has the greatest effect on the middle of the pool—academic 4s, 5s, and 6s. If the student is an academic 9, unless the interviewer says something horrible (usually a rating of 1 or 0), officers won't be as critical, especially if this is out of line with all the other information. It could just be that a brilliant student comes across as slightly nerdy, although interesting nonetheless. However, if the interview was truly negative, officers would think twice, sometimes even calling the school to ask more questions, especially if there were any serious reservations based on comments brought out by the interview. In the same vein, if the student is an academic 1, 2, or 3, even an exceptional interview probably would not make a difference, since it goes against all the other information in the folder.

When reading alumni interviews, all admissions officers are careful about taking what they read in context. For example, officers do not use "desire to attend this college" as a factor in admissions. But alumni take it personally if a student has not done the research before going to an interview. Thus, they might say, "Ellen seemed qualified and was very articulate, but she didn't seem to know much about Dartmouth." If the comments were all positive but the interviewers gave a lower rating based on desire to attend a particular college, officers would most likely use the comments but not the rating. Many alumni are overly positive about the applicant because often-times they are trying to compete with other areas by getting as many students admitted from their area as they can. For this reason, alumni ratings are taken into consideration with a small grain of salt. Most offices keep track of each interviewing area and calculate an average rating. If the alumni in a specific area assign high ratings to every student, those ratings will not be as helpful as those of more discriminating interviewers. Of course, officers typically get to know many of the alumni over the years, and in the cases of the ones they have grown to respect, they trust them 100 percent. Again, officers are looking for consistency. If alumni rave about an academic 2, the interview will not be given much weight.

Incidentally, officers would consider their interviews in the same way. Since during the interview, many of the observations are based on first impressions and personality, officers don't take it personally when they are wrong. I can think of many students I have interviewed who had great, outgoing personalities and seemed interested in their academic work, so I gave them a high rating and a positive write-up, but then when the applications came in, I would see that they were ranked thirtieth out of one hundred students in the class and had low scores and a weak academic schedule. At least I found out more about the student and was able to give him the benefit of the doubt until I could consider the interview in the context of the entire application. Remember, the interview is the very last piece of information read in the file. By that time, officers usually have a fairly accurate picture of what the applicant is like, so if the interview is entirely off-base, it can be pushed aside.

My general advice would be that if you are very interested in a particular college and know you come across as an interesting person and are able to talk about your interests, by all means try to schedule an on-campus interview, or accept an alumni interview if you are not able to visit. It definitely shows interest if you arrange an interview at the college, but, as I have said, since many are unable to afford a campus visit, its presence is seen as positive, but its absence is not seen as negative. Do a little bit of research beforehand so you have some sincere and well-thought-out questions to ask during the interview. Every interviewer leaves time for questions, so if you say, "I don't have any," you will not make a very good impression. Think of how to get across your love of learning. At some point, the interviewer will ask you about your high school and your classes, so take the opportunity to discuss in depth what it is you like about your classes. If you just list them without giving any specific information, you are not going to get any points for academic motivation and intellectual curiosity. If you are a voracious reader, talk about what you like to read. Even if you have a great extracurricular talent, don't spend the entire interview talking about it at the expense of academics. The interviewer is judging you two-thirds on your academics and one-third on everything else, so if you are intense or academically focused, make sure that comes across, followed by a discussion of your extracurricular talents.

I was always impressed by students who seemed genuinely interested in what they were doing. For me, it was easy to tell that a student was just a grade grubber by the way he described classes and teachers. True passion for acquiring knowledge is easy to detect, and it's not necessarily proportional to charisma. I met lots of quiet students who were tremendously impressive when you really got to know them, just as I met lots of charismatic and socially polished students who were vacuous—all style and no substance. The bottom line is that highly selective colleges are looking for substance. You don't have to be flashy; just be yourself and let your true passions shine through. Fascination is contagious.

I would much prefer that a student be natural and relaxed instead of artificially animated. I feel sorry for students who have bland personalities, so their parents pay for consultants who try to prep them for the interview. The problem is that those students come across as packaged or processed (like a piece of Velveeta cheese). It takes about two seconds to detect this artificiality. Style will only get you to a certain point, but without substance, it just won't be enough. If you know you are quiet, no problem; just be prepared to give detailed answers about your classes, your academic pursuits, and what you do out of class. Bring questions and write them down, so if you get nervous, you can refer to them. Try to look your interviewer in the eye instead of staring off into space. Don't worry so much about how to impress the interviewer. Interviewers are just people who are trying to get to know you and find out what is special about you. Try to find a common bond. If when you start talking about your passion for detective books, your interviewer's eyes light up because he, too, loves detective books, stay on this topic for a while and share your ideas. Feel free to ask the interviewer questions about his interests. Pretend you are just having a conversation with a friend. When you are done, ask for the interviewer's card (if he doesn't offer it first) so that you can write a brief thank-you note, a nice gesture.

It is not a bad idea to pause for a moment to think about a question, rather than just blurting out the first thing that comes into your head. A thoughtful response is much more helpful than a hastily concocted opinion. Many questions will be open-ended, so if you have an idea before the interview of some things you want to emphasize or get across, you will feel more confident and be better prepared. I have included some common interviewing questions used by highly selective colleges. You will notice that they are not trick questions, just conduits to allow you to express your passions and interests.

- Tell me about your family.
- Tell me about your high school, some strengths and weaknesses.
- How many people are in the senior class?
- Why are you interested in applying to this college?
- What are the subjects you enjoy most? (Elaborate.)
- Tell me about your junior-year classes.
- Tell me about any academic pursuits outside the classroom.
- If you could change something about your high school, what would you change?
- What activities are the most important to you?
- What have been the biggest disappointments or failures in your high school career?
- What did you do this summer?
- Do you have any interesting hobbies, outside interests?
- What teacher has had the biggest influence on you?
- If you could take a year off between high school and college, what would you do?
- If you had an entirely free day, how would you choose to fill the time?
- How would your friends describe you, your strengths and weaknesses?
- Are there any accomplishments you are particularly proud of, and why?
- Have you read any interesting books lately?
- What current event has sparked your interest?

In summary, the interview can be very important for those applications that read well but for one reason or another don't come across as truly exceptional. After reading that type of application, I used to think to myself, An interview would really be helpful in this case, because I feel as if I still don't have a good sense of what makes this student tick. Suppose that the alumni interviewer or the officer who interviewed this student was wowed by his intellectual curiosity, passion for history, interesting hobbies (that the student failed to mention in his application), and his ability to make a positive difference on a campus. In this case, the interview would be a crucial piece of the application and would probably tilt the scales in favor of the applicant.

Let's take the same case of the student who came across as solid but not exceptional and suppose that the alumni group or officer who interviewed him thought that he showed little interest in academics, spent most of the interview talking about his baseball team, and could not answer basic questions about current events because he had no idea what was going on in the world outside of his high school. In addition, suppose the interviewer found him to be arrogant and overconfident. In this case, the interview would be crucial and would probably cause the student to be rejected. My general suggestion is to try to schedule an interview if possible, unless you are trying to hide something like extreme shyness, lack of interest in academic subjects, or a strong personality problem. Remember that the interview is meant to help the applicant and the interviewers are trained to look for substance over style. Just because you are quiet does not mean you will have a weak interview; the important part is to have substantive topics to discuss that will show your academic strengths.

The interview is the last piece in the admissions folder. On the average, officers spend from fifteen to twenty-five minutes on each applicant's file, looking for patterns and overall trends. Admissions officers generally write between a quarter and a half a page of summary about your file. When you look over your part of the application, ask yourself if your real intellectual passions come across. If not, keep working at it. You must be your own best spokesman. Make sure you don't leave any important information out, because if you do, officers are unlikely to find out about it if no one else brings it up. You don't have to be egotistical, but don't sell yourself short. If you have devoted nine years to soccer and are all-American, do not leave this information out. Check the balance of your application. If you have devoted 75 percent of form 2 to sailing, you have not successfully showed your intellectual side.

10
A Brief Trip to
the Committee

———◆———

A great many files will not make it to the committee process at all because they are either very strong or very weak. In order to select folders that will go to the committee, any "one-reader A's" (typically 8s and 9s) or "one-reader R's" (typically academic 1s, 2s, and 3s) are omitted. In those cases, the decisions are final already. Then, the director would look at all folders (he does this continually during the process as the officers complete their reading of a folder) and if the readers' votes were still undecided, he would either make the decision himself or decide that the folder should go to the committee. In many offices, Dartmouth's included, the regional officer would review all the folders from his region and add any further comments or recommendations.

The director would decide by himself only if he read the comments of all the readers and they seemed to push in a particular direction. For example, if the first reader rated an applicant a "P+" and the second reader rated a "P++" and both their comments were extremely positive, he might look over the folder (remember, he sees applicants from the entire pool, so he is better able to compare the overall quality and to enforce a constant standard) and decide to put the "green A" on the folder and accept that student. On the other side of the coin, he could read negative write-ups with "R" and "P-" ratings and decide that student just was not up to par. Unlike the officers who sometimes hesitate to reject a student, the director usually feels no such compunction about doing so.

The only folders that would not be included in the committee process besides "the one-reader R's and A's" are recruited athletes (after going through the regular process, the athletic liaison and the director would decide on those applicants), VIP cases (these also go through the regular reading process, but the ultimate decision lies with the director), and high-need (in terms of financial aid) international applicants, since even totally need-blind offices are not need-blind with regard to international students.

In the case of international students, applications go through the regular reading process and the no-need ones can go to the committee, but the high-need ones go to a special small committee with the international officer and the director, who have to select the "A's" while taking financial need into account.

Minority-student applications, after going through the regular reading process, are usually voted on by those officers assigned to these cases, subject to approval by the director. Even so, many borderline minority cases will go to the committee, as well. These special cases are discussed in the following chapters, so I won't go into more detail now other than to say that every other special case except the ones I just mentioned would go to the committee.*

Once the majority of folders made it through the whole reading process (around mid-March), the director would calculate how many admits there were so far, how many rejects, and then how many "possibles." From these numbers, he would be able to tell the committee, for example, that there would be six hundred cases for consideration but that out of those six hundred, the college would be able to admit only

---

*As I mentioned earlier, a few schools (Brown is one example) do things differently and make nearly all decisions through committee vote.

one hundred applicants, one out of every six. At Dartmouth, this is usually the ratio officers are allowed to accept during committee sessions. Then the director breaks up the staff of from thirteen to fifteen officers into three or four committees of four people and divides up the folders evenly among them.

The responsibility for methodology lies within the individual committee. Some committees will decide to rotate readers and have one person read the master card and the ready sheet out loud, discuss the candidate, and then vote to accept, reject, or put the applicant on the wait list. Other committees will decide that rather than reading the master card out loud, they will all huddle together, look at the master card silently, and then read the ready sheet out loud, discuss the case, and vote.

The surprising fact is that committees will rarely read beyond the master card, which contains a summary of all the basics, and the ready sheet, which contains the comments of all the individual readers, unless new information has arrived, such as an interview summary, which would be right at the front of the folder. Only in cases of severe disagreement would the committee members decide to refer back to an actual document in the folder. I think this is a tribute to the thorough write-ups done by officers while reading and voting on a student's file. Officers depend upon one another's write-ups, especially considering the fact that it is possible that none of the committee members was one of the original readers of that applicant's folder, although sometimes one or more of the readers might be present.

The committee process tends to be fair, if strict (in that the committee has to eliminate five out of every six applicants), since there is very little pressure from regional officers (they are not necessarily present).* If an officer felt very strongly one

---

*In 1997 at Dartmouth, only one out of eight or nine students, out of roughly a thousand who reached committee, was accepted.

way or another when he was reading an applicant's folder, that fact should be reflected in the rating and the write-up. In this way, the reader's opinions and insights are represented through his own writing, whether he is present or not in the actual committee deliberation.

Now that you know the basic committee process, let me take you inside of some imaginary, though typical, conversations that might take place during committee review. I will take a representative four committee members and reconstruct some typical dialogues. You should assume that one person already read the master card and ready sheet out loud, so now you are becoming a fly on the wall right after the basic information has been read.

CASE NUMBER ONE

MIKE: You know, those activities are so typical. How many yearbook editors have we read about already today? Josh is a member of three varsity teams, but notice that he has no leadership anywhere.

JANINE: Yeah, neither teacher rec makes any mention of Josh's leadership role in the school. I get the feeling from the four B that Josh gets good grades and is dependable but that he rarely contributes in class. In fact, the four B rates only a three in "participation in class."

TERRY: I liked the fact that he spent part of his summer working on an Indian reservation in Arizona.

JOHN: That's true, but he did no community service at all for three years of high school, and then suddenly he decided the summer before applying to college that it would look good to do a program. Besides, it was only a one-week program, so I'm not overly impressed that his represents a deep commitment.

TERRY: He *is* ranked three out of two hundred in his high

school. I wonder why he's only taking three courses his senior year. I know for this high school, that is a light course load.

JANINE: His rank is excellent, but he comes across as a plugger who gets the job done. He went to a strong public high school and has two very educated parents, yet his standardized test scores are only mid-six hundreds and he only got a three on the AP bio exam and a two on the AP English.

JOHN: Okay, are we ready to vote? All in favor? [All four vote to reject.]

Analysis: In many ways, Josh represents the typical academic 5 or 6 who is pretty strong on paper but ultimately does not get accepted. What hurt him the most was the perception that he was just not serious about learning, despite a high rank. For example, why such a light senior course load? Why didn't teachers rave about him? How come his AP tests were so unimpressive? The fact is, those scores made him seem slightly below average in the applicant pool, even though his rank was high and he had some decent extracurricular involvement.

CASE NUMBER TWO

TERRY: A young African-American woman with scores in the mid-five hundreds and a high school rank of twenty-five out of a hundred. She grew up in Brooklyn, went to a magnet high school. Single-parent household—mom went to college and works in an insurance company.

JOHN: I don't mean to be cynical, but I don't see the disadvantage factor.

JANINE: Her scores are pretty strong in our overall African-American pool. My problem is that her teacher checks off only a "track two" course load and she's taking only three classes this year—that's kind of light, don't you think?

MIKE: Now that you mention it, her rank is unweighted, so with the easier classes she is taking, her real rank might even be lower than twenty-five. She's taken only two AP classes in four years. In this magnet high school, there are over twenty AP classes offered. Plus, she has no work experience and very few extracurricular activities. I can't see what she would add to this campus.

JOHN: Vote? [Three vote to reject; one votes to accept because minority numbers are not great this year. The final vote is to reject.]

Analysis: One reader voted to accept because he was concerned that if they held up such a high standard, they would come up short in terms of minority numbers. But, as one reader pointed out, this student had no real economic disadvantage, although she did come from a single-parent home (not that uncommon these days). What really finished her off was not her mediocre rank but the fact that she had made such a weak effort to take challenging courses. This college might have been too challenging academically for her based on her average grades in fairly easy courses. Finally, she had nothing interesting by the way of extras—how would she add to the life of the college? This committee could not think of any reason at all—hence the "R" vote.

CASE NUMBER THREE

MIKE: Jesse strikes me as somewhat unusual. I know his rank is only so-so—forty-five out of four hundred—but all his teachers stress that he is so interested in class that he does extra projects on his own and then shares them with the class. The four A said that he spent three weeks programming the graphing calculator to compute every concept in the first half of the textbook so other students could use the calculator to review for the final.

JANINE: That's right, and even the four C says that Jesse once stayed up all night doing background reading on the philosophers they were studying in European history so he could give a presentation the next day that tied together all the existentialist philosophers with the unit they were studying. His friend said that the teacher still talks about Jesse's incredible enthusiasm.

JOHN: You know, he's not a leader in the traditional sense, but he has followed his interest in computer programming by working ten hours a week for the last two academic years for a local programming company. One of his games turned into a big seller for the company. The last two summers, he has taken classes at Cornell summer school.

TERRY: He just seems like a cool kid, the kind I'd like to room with. I can envision him jumping up in class and adding his two cents.

JANINE: Vote? [Three vote to accept; one votes wait list. He is an admit.]

Analysis: Jesse is your typical neat kid who doesn't have the highest rank or numbers (probably an academic 4 or 5), but he comes across as extremely interesting to be around. He had pursued his love of math and science in two consecutive summer programs (continuity), as well as holding down a part-time job in his field of interest for two solid years. He obviously is stimulated by learning and often follows a project well beyond the obvious conclusion. Teachers loved having Jesse around in high school and there's no reason to think that his college teachers would not feel the same. Even the peer rec showed Jesse's intellectual side. A student with a rank as low as Jesse's (below the top 10 percent) would need exceptional recommendations and extras to get in, given the fact that over 90 percent of all the students at this college are ranked in the top 10 percent of their high school classes. Jesse would be one of a handful of exceptions, especially since most exceptions fall into one of the special categories to be discussed in subsequent chapters.

CASE NUMBER FOUR

TERRY: He's number one—shared by only two others—in his class of two hundred students. You'd never know it from the teachers' comments. They don't seem very impressed by him. In fact, four B says that he's a hard worker, but it shows lower check ratings for "written expression." Four A shows only threes, even though the write-up seems fairly positive.

JANINE: It's hard to say no when his math SAT One is eight hundred and his SAT Two chemistry score is seven fifty.

MIKE: Not really. Look at his verbal score—only six hundred; that's a hundred and ten points below our average. And his writing SAT Two of five ninety—that's just not impressive.

JOHN: This is the tenth or so applicant we've seen today with strong math/science skills but low verbal/writing ability.

JANINE: His senior course load is very strong—five AP classes.

TERRY: I'm not excited by him, but he's captain of two varsity sports teams, vice president of the senior class, and editor of the literary magazine. And an Eagle Scout to boot!

MIKE: Come on, though, what is he going to add to life here? He's not a strong enough athlete to play sports, we have zillions of editors, and he just doesn't come across as anything but a dutiful student. His essay was just the typical "Outward Bound" adventure story. I guess he survived or he wouldn't be applying.

TERRY: Okay, let's vote. [One votes to reject; three vote wait list. This student will be added to the wait list.]

Analysis: This is a typical wait-list candidate—high rank, high scores (at least in math/science), lots of leadership, but in many ways, the typical applicant. Remember, the Ivies receive countless applications from strong math/science students with high ranks but lower scores in the verbal/writing area. He would have had a much better chance had his essay been more compelling or his teacher recs stronger, or even if he'd held down a major part-time job, but he just came across as dutiful, not intellectual. This particular kind of wait-list candidate really has very little chance for admission. In this case, he was put on the wait list so that the high school would not be upset. After all, his numbers were impressive and he had significant high school leadership and high visibility in the high school, but there was not much substance on the intellectual side.

CASE NUMBER FIVE

JOHN: Korean-American girl from a strong public school. Parents are both college-educated professionals. She's ranked top ten percent in her high school in a class of three hundred and fifty, has scores all in high six hundreds, low seven hundreds, two solid AP tests—four on AP bio, three on art history—and good recommendations. She's a cellist in the school's orchestra and the county's symphony orchestra—over twenty hours a week of music.

TERRY: The recs all talk about her musical prowess—apparently, she's one of the strongest musicians in the school. Notice that she also does a lot of activities with the Korean church group on weekends. She's president of the French Honor Society and the Multicultural Club. These last two leadership roles don't take up much time, though—only one or two hours a week.

MIKE: I wish the guidance counselor's letter was more helpful. It's impossible to tell from her transcript if she's closer to number one or to number thirty-five in the top ten percent.

Her recs are positive but not really glowing. Her essays and the recs together paint a picture of a dutiful girl who spends hours doing her work but doesn't seem that excited by any of it.

JANINE: I'd be more excited if she had a stronger interview, but the student who interviewed her described her as quiet, smart, but not that accomplished except for music. The interviewer did not make any special notes about her academics except to say she was very devoted to her work.

JOHN: Ready to vote? [Three vote to reject; one votes wait list. This student was rejected.]

Analysis: This applicant was certainly strong all around, probably an academic 6 or 7 (notice that she would have been an 8 or 9 if the school had given an exact rank and if that exact rank had been in the very top part of the class—the top 10 percent ranking hurt her, since the readers could not tell if she was nearer to the top or to the bottom of the top 10 percent) with some leadership capability and tremendous music ability. The problem is, she didn't stand out from the pack, especially in terms of intellectual power.

Unfortunately, neither her recs nor her own part of the application gave any indication of a true love of learning. More than anything, she came across as a typically strong Asian-American applicant, good student, excellent musician, but with nothing to set her apart. As we will see in chapter 16, Asian-Americans are not one of the targeted affirmative-action minority groups, so this candidate did not get any extra consideration because of her minority status.

If this applicant had come from a more disadvantaged background (recent immigrants, poor neighborhood, non-college-educated background) she would have stood a much better chance, since her accomplishments would have been seen against a different background. Even though she wouldn't have been given an advantage because of her status as an Asian-American, she would have been given the general benefit of a lower income, more modest background, with some degree of disadvantage. However, as is, she fell short because she came across as a student like many others, with nothing to set her apart from the hundreds of other very qualified applicants. The committee members saw her as someone who would do well at the school but who would be the kind of student who gave all the right answers, not the kind who asked all the best questions. The latter is the type of student the Ivies and highly selective schools are looking for—students who will shake things up on campus, not just blindly follow the lead of others.

This represents a day in the life of committee deliberations, except for the fact that I have shown only five cases out of some seventy to one hundred covered in a day. It is a very difficult and time-consuming process. The most interesting students tend to stand out, while the more average (in the overall pool, that is) candidates tend to fade away. Every college has its own version of committee. Some colleges meet as one large committee; some have the regional officers represent their top cases to a committee that decides the cases by region. This general description of the process is fairly typical. All committee processes share the task of choosing the most highly qualified students out of a much larger pool of applicants.

11

Flags and Tags:
Athletic Recruiting at the
Ivy League Schools

———◆———

Since all the Ivy League schools are part of the same athletic league and all use the AI for sports purposes, a similar process is used for athletic recruiting.* As mentioned earlier, except for football, which is Division I-AA, the Ivy League varsity teams are Division I, as opposed to smaller colleges, such as Amherst or Williams, which are Division III. The recruiting of athletes is definitely allowed; however, paying for them is most definitely not. None of the Ivy League schools are allowed to give athletic scholarships.

Why is the AI so important for athletics? First of all, it was *invented* precisely because of athletics, and second, for athletic purposes, there is an AI cutoff for Ivy League athletes (it is the same for all the Ivies)—approximately 169.† A student with an AI in this low range would have to have a particularly low rank (third decile or below) or very low scores, or perhaps both. An AI of 169 is not very impressive when you consider that Dartmouth's average AI is around 212. If a college wants

---

*As I mentioned earlier, not all the Ivies use the AI to guide their academic rankings, but they usually generate an AI for every student, which *must* be used for recruited athletes in order to uphold Ivy League athletic regulations.

† The number will vary a little by year, but this is what it was set at for the class of 2001.

to take an athlete who is below the minimum AI, it must present that candidate's file to an all Ivy meeting and provide an explanation that must be approved by the Ivy League deans of admissions.

The major "money teams" (that is, football, men's basketball, and ice hockey—so called because tickets cost money and the teams bring in tremendous amounts of money through alumni donations) must keep an average AI that is no less than one standard deviation away from that college's average AI. Therefore, the University of Pennsylvania (because of its size, diversity, and slightly less selective admissions) can accept lower AI athletes in these sports that can most of the other Ivies, which is probably why they field so many powerhouse teams. Have you ever wondered why you'll see a really brilliant student sitting on the bench but not seeing much playing time? Basically, that student's AI is balancing out some of the lower students on the team, who may be better players. The other teams are not bound by Ivy regulations to be within one standard deviation of the average AI, but each individual college can enforce its own in-house regulations to maintain high-quality student athletes.

Football is in a category by itself, since it requires many more recruits than any other team. It has different "bands" (or ranges of AI athletes it can accept), which are related to the individual college's average AI. The rules are very complicated and very regimented, but the basic result is that lower AI colleges can usually take some lower AI athletes as long as they stay within the Ivy League football regulations.

Let me explain how the recruiting process works from the admissions side of things. I'll use the Dartmouth office as an example, but the process is very similar at all the Ivies. Coaches spend many months each year traveling around the country, reading local newspapers, sending out letters, and trying to find the best athletes in their particular sport. For some sports, there are designations that can be used, such as all-American, or high-visibility teams, such as competitive summer baseball leagues, which are good grounds for recruiting. Coaches make contact with students and try to get a sense of whether their AI would put them within the reach of an Ivy League school.

If these athletes haven't taken the appropriate standardized tests, coaches might encourage them to do so in the hopes that they might qualify for Ivy admission. If these students have an AI of 140 or so, they stand absolutely no chance of admission at any Ivy, no matter how great they are as athletes. Coaches face the extremely difficult task of finding top athletes whose academics put them into an acceptable range. In some sports, this is nearly impossible. Take squash, for example. Thanks to national ratings, a coach can easily find out who the top twenty men and twenty women high school squash players are, but of these forty people, maybe only six will have AIs anywhere near Ivy level, so every college ends up fighting over the eligible players.

Starting with early decision or early action in the fall, coaches will compile lists for their sports to aid their athletic liaison in the admissions office. I served as an athletic liaison for from six to eight different sports, both men's and women's, so I am intimately familiar with the process. Each team has a target number of admits, which would vary for each college and for each sport. These numbers are top secret, even between coaches. Obviously, a sport like football would have a higher target number, whereas a sport with fewer players, like basketball, would have a lower target number. Money sports, like football, basketball, and ice hockey, are higher priority than nonmoney sports, like swimming and field hockey.

Plus, each college has its particular history with each sport. Squash has traditionally been a strong area for Harvard and Yale, so it has a higher priority than it does for a college like Dartmouth. Princeton has had one of the top women's softball teams in the country for several years, so I would imagine that it has a higher priority than some of Princeton's other sports. At Dartmouth, the women's lacrosse team was recently ranked as high as number three in the country, so because of its winning record and strong coaching, it has become a high-priority sport.

Once the admissions officers get the coaches' list of recruits, the systems workers take small round purple tags (hence my chapter title, "Flags and Tags") and stick them right on the front of the master card, entering the appropriate sport code into the computer.* Once the folders are tagged, they are usually sent directly to the athletic liaison, who may also want to consult with the regional reader, especially if he is not familiar with the high school an athlete attends.

How much of a factor is the purple tag? In some cases, it will be an enormous factor, and in some cases, it won't make any difference. It depends on how important the sport is, how high an athlete is ranked on the coach's list, how low the AI is, and how well the officers think the student would be able to handle the rigors of an Ivy League program.

There are many athletes with relatively high AIs, but because they are taking only track 2 programs (that is, college prep or below), their AIs are inflated and do not reflect their academic ability. There are also many athletes with slightly lower AIs who have taken an entirely Advanced Placement course load and therefore are more ready to face the challenge of classwork at an Ivy League school. Many times, low AI athletes are accepted because they come from modest backgrounds (one or both parents did not attend college and/or are blue-collar workers) and have done well in high school, even if their scores are not very high. Clearly, if the coaches rate an athlete number one or number two, that athlete is given a higher priority than if he was ranked lower on the list. It should come as no surprise that the top picks for most of the major sports tend to be very low AI students compared to the rest of the pool.

Not all the Ivies are as discriminating as Dartmouth is with

---

*These tags are the convention that Dartmouth uses. The other Ivies identify the particular folders by some kind of code, although not necessarily with Dartmouth's color-coded tag system.

its athletic recruits. I say that because at Dartmouth the coaches tend to criticize the admissions office for rejecting many athletes who are ultimately accepted by Harvard or Yale but not by Dartmouth. I would attribute this stringent admissions policy to the director himself. The director felt that as numbers went up and the average AI of the pool went up, the caliber of the athletes should go up as well. He also believed that Dartmouth should accept no student who could not handle the workload. While you would think his policy would be wholeheartedly embraced by other directors, this is sadly not the case.

Many Ivy directors are big sports fans and would take almost any athlete who qualified in terms of a minimum AI, especially for sports they were fond of, regardless of the athlete's true academic ability. At Dartmouth, all the members of athletic teams maintain average AIs well over the required "less than one standard deviation away from the average AI." In addition, Dartmouth's varsity athletes have a higher overall graduation rate in four years than do its nonathletes, even if only by two or three percentage points. Dartmouth will not accept any athlete it feels will not be able to handle the workload—period.

Can coaches make promises of admission to prospective players? Technically, no, but in some cases they do, even though they ultimately are not the ones empowered to make the final decision. Sometimes students falsely interpret a coach's optimism as a guarantee for admission. What coaches do know is where they have placed you on their recruiting list, so they can make a rough guess as to whether or not you will be admitted, but the athletic liaison has to present the case to the director of admissions before the athlete can be accepted.

What if a coach tells you what number you are on the list? I would be distrustful. Even if he is not lying, he submits several lists, one every three weeks or so; therefore, the numbers can change quite a bit. Once a coach gets feedback from the admissions office that his number-one recruit is too low and will not get in, he might drop that player and place someone else in the number-one slot. Thus, even if the coach said you were number one, that could change at any point. Also, if a coach talks to a student and finds out that the student really isn't interested in attending, he will in all likelihood drop this athlete from the list so as not to waste the number-one or number-two slot on a long shot.

Every time liaisons get a list, they read the files, take into account comments by other officers who may look at the file (often they will ask for the input of the regional officer), and give early feedback to the coaches in the form of "likely," "unlikely," or "possible." Coaches take this feedback, talk to players, adjust their lists, and submit new ones. The process is long and tiresome, both for the coaches and the athletes. Most coaches are extremely honest, but you always hear of abuses of trust where coaches make false promises to students, or where families hear what they want to hear and draw erroneous conclusions. At Dartmouth at least, the process is fair, if a bit harsh, on particular sports teams, which usually don't get anywhere near their full list admitted.

New coaches who are not accustomed to Ivy League standards submit low AI lists and are shocked to find that most of their athletes are rejected. Once they learn the ropes, they submit more realistic lists and build their teams player by player. Keep in mind that most teams have fairly short lists, between six and fifteen, so if you are near the bottom, the purple tag will not have a huge effect on your chances of admission. However, if you fulfill a big priority, like goalkeeper or pitcher, you might end up being a top recruit at several colleges, which would have a significant effect on your chances for admission.

It is interesting to note that recruited athletes comprise only 2.5 percent of the entire applicant pool at Dartmouth (287/11,400 in 1996), but they are accepted at a roughly 62 percent rate—*much* higher than the overall acceptance rate of 22 percent. Therefore, since Dartmouth has a comparatively small freshman class (usually around 1,100), recruited athletes for the approximately forty sports teams make up about 15 to 16 percent of the incoming class. Princeton, very similar in size to Dartmouth, historically admits 60 to 70 percent of its recruited athletes (1979-1994). Except for football, most coaches at Princeton are limited to ten or so on their lists, since Fred Hargadon has cut back the number of athletes in an effort to keep the academic standard high. Twenty-five percent of the freshman class at Princeton participate at the varsity level, although probably not all 25 percent were recruited athletes.

At a larger college, the actual number of recruited athletes might be higher, even if they make up a lesser percentage of the freshman class. Is it a bad thing to have such a high percentage of recruited athletes? I don't think so, except in a few isolated cases. Many of these athletes are strong enough to get in without the push of the purple tag. I remember the recent case of high AI twins who were ranked number one and number two in their high school (with roughly 220 AIs) and were top field hockey recruits. Not only were they a huge boost to the team; they were easy admits because of their academic prowess. The truth is, only a few sports have "deadweight" athletes, meaning that they only deserve admission based on their athletic skills.

The lowest AI sports are football and ice hockey, by far. At least many of these applicants come from modest blue-collar backgrounds. Again, because of biases against well-off students, the recruited athlete who stands the lowest chance of admissions is a prep school athlete who has a C/B average, no work experience, and wealthy parents. This athlete will not get the sympathetic eye of the admissions committee.

A very basic and substantive difference with regard to athletes is that, unlike the process of reading other applications, when you try to find a weakness, you tend to look for strengths once you see the purple tag. Instead of asking yourself, What kind of impact would this student have, you ask yourself, Would he be able to keep up with a rigorous course load? The best thing for prospective recruited athletes to do is to take the most demanding course load possible so colleges know that they are looking at a serious student. The reason I support accepting low AI athletes, at least in a handful of cases, is the same reason I would give for supporting other applicants who are talented in one particular area: They have achieved Division I–level distinction in their sport through countless hours of dedication, practice, games, training, and so on. These hours can take their toll on academics. Most (but of course not all) serious athletes don't have the luxury of a lot of free time to prepare for standardized tests, to put that finishing touch on their research paper, or to get straight A's in high school. For anyone who has been a serious athlete, you know how much time goes into reaching a high enough level to be considered a viable candidate for a Division I college.

I am always amazed by the fact that Ivy League schools achieve national rankings in sports when they compete against colleges such as Stanford that are not restricted by AI cutoffs and that are allowed to give athletic scholarships. For example, Dartmouth always has several teams with a high national ranking, even though the competition includes all Division I colleges throughout the country, many of which can lure athletes with money. Dartmouth's ski teams, downhill and cross-country, are almost always in the top five nationwide and have had many Olympic medal winners over the years; women's lacrosse was number three in the country in 1996; men's and women's soccer are usually top twenty nationwide; men's lacrosse top twenty, et cetera. Remember, the Ivy League cannot give any athletic scholarships, so unless an athlete is very financially needy, he will get no money, whereas at a less competitive college, he might very well get a full scholarship because of his athletic prowess.

The Ivy League loses many great athletes to larger and less selective universities that can pay for their athletes. Of course, that scholarship is usually tied to continuing success at the sport, so if the athlete developed an injury, in many cases he would lose that college's financial support. It's true that at an

Ivy League school, you are not bound to play, although I and many coaches consider it a major breach of honor to use your athletic talents to get accepted if you do not intend to play. To me, this is the lowest form of underhanded dealing. Coaches have very short lists, and I don't think it's fair to take up one of these coveted spaces unless you really want to play. Because there are no athletic scholarships at the Ivies, you cannot have your financial aid taken away if your athletic performance is not up to par.

If you prefer not to commit, be up-front with the coach. The healthiest student-coach relations are based on honesty and integrity, not willful deceit. The coaches I have worked with have my utmost respect. It is an incredibly difficult job to come up with a realistic list of athletes who qualify for Ivy League admission and possess a certain academic spark, as well. Many times, coaches are disappointed when admissions offices turn down their athletes, even after an athlete has orally committed to accepting the offer of admission. Imagine finding out after all that hard work that the admissions office finds only four out of your nine athletes acceptable, and of those four accepts, you may get only two, since the others may choose a scholarship school or another Ivy League school.

In most cases, the athletes who get accepted are fine students who end up doing quite well. In rare cases, they really have to struggle with the academics, but thanks to intensive academic support and the discipline they have developed because of their dedication to athletics, they come through with shining colors.

"SQUEEZE PLAYS"

What happens if you are a top recruited athlete applying to several colleges, Ivy League and others, and one of those other colleges tells you over the phone that they will definitely accept you but that you must commit yourself to attending?

This kind of offer sets into motion what is known as a "squeeze play."

Let's play out the scenario. Stanford University calls you January twenty-fifth (only twenty-five days or so after your application was handed in) and tells you that they will give you a full scholarship for four years and guaranteed admission if you agree in writing to attend. The problem is, you have also applied to Harvard, Brown, and Dartmouth, but you know that you will not hear from these colleges until mid-April.

What you need to do is immediately notify the coaches at the Ivies and fax them the offer from the first college, including the financial-aid package, if there is one. The coaches will then fill out an Ivy "squeeze play" form, have the athletic liaison immediately evaluate your file (probably sharing the folder with either the regional person or the admissions person in charge of coordinating the liaisons), and have the financial-aid office do an early read on the possible financial-aid package. One fact that bears repeating: the Ivies cannot compete financially with colleges that are not prohibited from awarding athletic scholarships. So your scholarship at Stanford might be based entirely on your athletic ability. Your estimated *Ivy* financial-aid package will be based entirely on need, so if you do not qualify for aid, you will not be granted any.

Once the various Ivies complete the squeeze play (a day or two later), they will be able to tell you whether you will be accepted and roughly what your financial-aid package will look like. For the sake of argument, let's say that Dartmouth and Harvard say yes but Brown says no. Now you have an accurate picture of your various options and must decide which college you want to attend. The moment you tell Dartmouth that you choose to attend, you will receive an official letter (this does not violate any Ivy League athletic rules) saying that you are accepted into the class. You must also tell the other colleges that you are going to Dartmouth so that they can

cross you off their lists and fill in your spot with another recruit.

The obvious advantage of doing a squeeze play is that you
can have your final decision as early as January, rather than
waiting until April. In terms of risk, there is not a huge one.
If the Ivies are able to accept you, and you are a very high-
priority athlete, they will do everything they can to accept
you. If they can see that the other college that originated the
squeeze is not competitive academically and that you do not
look very promising on the academic front, they might say no
on your squeeze, but in all likelihood, that is probably what
would have happened had you waited until April. If they see
that a strong academic institution like Stanford admitted you,
they will most probably decide to admit you as long as you are
over the minimum AI cutoff.* In short, a squeeze play will
not get you more money, but it will get you a prompt decision and, if you are admitted, a guaranteed acceptance.

Now that we have looked at how athletic recruiting works,
let's examine the other areas where "flags and tags" carry
weight in the admissions process.

---

*Again, since Stanford is not part of the Ivy League, they do not have any AI cutoff, because
the AI is strictly used for Ivy League schools.

12

Flags and Tags: Legacies

———————

As noted in the previous chapter, recruited athletes at Dartmouth are given round purple tags on their master cards to set them apart. For legacies, green tags are administered. What exactly is a legacy? At most of the highly selective colleges, it is defined as the son or daughter of a graduate from that undergraduate institution. In other words, if either of your parents attended Dartmouth College, you would be considered a legacy there. Many people mistakenly think that grandparents or great-grandparents count—they do not. Nor do siblings who attend, nor do relatives who attended any of a college's professional schools. For all intents and purposes, a *parent* has to have attended Dartmouth College, or the respective Ivy League school to which the student is applying, in order to be considered a legacy.

What effect does the green tag have? Basically, at all the Ivies, legacies are accepted at *twice* the rate that everyone else is (not as high as athletes, I might add). At Dartmouth, the legacy acceptance rate is around 40 percent, as compared to the overall rate of 22 percent. So, in a close case, legacies are given the benefit of the doubt. At Princeton, the legacy acceptance rate is over 40 percent, as compared to its usual low acceptance rate of 14 percent. This means that many academic 4s and 5s who would normally be overlooked get in because they are legacies. It does not mean that academic 1s, 2s, and 3s get in. Remember that Dartmouth and Princeton (most of the other Ivies have very similar legacy numbers) still reject 60 percent of all legacies, a statistic that does not make the alumni very happy. As any Ivy League school will report, it makes good economic sense to accept legacies at a slightly higher rate, since many of the biggest donors come from this group of loyal alumni. However, sending a yearly donation of even several thousand dollars to your alma mater will not make much difference. Anything under hundreds of thousands of dollars is too low for development purposes (see chapter 14). Keep in mind that legacies are not accepted because of their potential as full-paying students—the Ivies are completely need-blind in terms of financial aid. It is the long-term gain, not the short-term gain, of building loyalty to the institution. Accepting legacies is one of the most effective ways to accomplish this task.

At Yale, legacies comprise a full 15 percent of the student body; at Princeton, legacies comprise 12 percent; whereas at Dartmouth, the figure is about 7 percent. I have no problem with legacy admits, since many are highly qualified and all the borderline cases are still strong relative to the overall applicant pool. To put things in perspective, a low AI legacy admit might be a 202, while a low AI recruited athlete for a major money sport might be 170. Is it fair to give legacies a leg up? In my opinion, yes, since it is good for the long-term health of the college both monetarily and in terms of school spirit. Plus, it is not necessary to stretch very far for more than 95 percent of the legacy applicants. When applying to colleges, be aware of what colleges consider you a legacy and use their policies to your advantage.

13
Flags and Tags:
Special Talents

———◆———

The Ivies also consider any special talents that a student might bring to the class, and they use a rating scale that varies from college to college. The most common special-talent flags are for music, dance, and art/photography.

If a student sends in a musical tape, the officers would send it to the music department, which can send back a ranking on a scale of 1-9 (9 being the highest) of how good it thinks the student really is in that area. Again, using Dartmouth's scale, a 9 would mean that the department really wants this student to attend so he would be able to participate in its musical ensemble. If you are an artist, you could send slides of your work, which officers would then forward to the appropriate department.

My general recommendation is *not* to send additional materials unless you are extremely talented and are planning to use that talent on campus. For example, if you are a serious cellist, submit a tape only if you want to continue playing in college. If a professor of music goes out of the way to recommend you, he will be very disappointed if you get accepted and then decide not to participate in his group. As you might imagine, these departments get tons of supplementary materials and have very little patience for inferior work. If you are a weekend pianist with mediocre skills, do not waste time sending a tape, because you will be judged against serious musicians, some of whom have been performing for years.

Remember, the admissions staff is not usually qualified to judge your artistic talents. Sometimes it is easier to send your materials directly to the specific department. Be sure to make it clear that you are applying for admission and would appreciate a letter of support if the department is impressed with your work. Make sure you put your name and Social Security number in a very obvious place so if your materials do get separated from your application, the office can figure out to whom they belong.

If you are lucky enough to get a special-talent ranking, it will make your application stronger, either to a small degree or a large degree, depending on the comments. If a professor writes, "This is the best oboe player I have heard in the last ten years and I could really use her for the symphony," you might get a big push, as opposed to someone who gets a 5 rating with a comment like this: "Good piano player but won't make much difference here." Of course, if you are already in a very high academic category (usually 7s, 8s, and 9s), a special talent ranking will just be hot fudge on the ice-cream sundae, but if you are somewhere in the middle (4s, 5s, and 6s), the rating might push you over the top. If you are an academic 1, 2, or 3, the rating probably will not be enough to make a difference.

State in your application what your special talents are and send additional materials if you think it will improve your chances. If you are strictly an amateur, just list your activity without sending supplementary materials. As a general rule, colleges will accept your word in good faith, even if you do not send supplementary materials. If you write that you are an experienced jazz trumpet player and play in an all-state/all-area band, they will believe you. Likewise, if your photos have won several major awards, just list those awards on your application under "Special honors or prizes." In the majority of cases, it is really not necessary to send the actual materials to the admissions office or the appropriate department.

14

Flags and Tags:
Development/VIP Cases

———•———

In plain English, *development* means "I will give vast fortunes of money to your college if my child gets accepted." This does not mean a few thousand dollars; typically, it means an amount in the millions. As mentioned earlier, sending in your yearly donation of one thousand dollars to your alma mater will not give your child a greater chance (that is, not greater than the already-high 40 percent legacy rate) of getting in.

If one of your parents is the CEO of a major company and makes it clear to the development or alumni affairs office that he plans to fund the new chemistry building, the alumni office would contact the admissions office. You would then receive a development flag, meaning that your folder would be encoded with a number that corresponds to a development case. Unlike the tags that are stuck right on the front of your master card, a flag is just a numerical code that gets entered on the master card, in essence flagging your file. The special-talent cases I mentioned in the previous chapter get a flag, not a tag. In rare cases, that flag would make a huge difference, but you'd still have to be in the right AI ballpark—that is a 4 or above.

I was surprised to find out that the real development list includes only *big* donors—of the almost 11,400 applications Dartmouth received in a recent year, only about thirty people were on the full development list, and of those roughly one-third were accepted. Thus, under 1 percent of incoming freshmen got in because of their parents. Part of this relatively low number again has to do with the director of admissions.

The number of development cases varies substantially from college to college. Dartmouth's director is very strict in that he does not believe in accepting subpar students because of their parents' giving potential. I saw only one case of a student who really did not deserve admission, but his family was one of the biggest donors in Dartmouth's history. Is it worth it to accept development/VIP cases? I'd argue that development cases make up such a small number that, yes, they do help the institution. It's not a big deal to accept one weak student if the other 4,200 students can enjoy a better library, for example.

I am convinced that most people think development or VIP cases make up a much greater percentage than they actually do. The vast majority of students do not fall into this category, so it's not very productive to devote much space to it. Yes, they exist, but only in a very limited number. The best thing to do would be to contact the alumni affairs/development office, since it puts together the official list and submits it to the admissions office. The director of admissions still has total autonomy over the admitted class, so the decision depends upon who the director is. I'm sure other Ivies take more development cases than does Dartmouth, but the total percentage pales next to the number of recruited athletes.

The VIP label (as opposed to strictly development) is reserved for celebrity applicants, such as the son or daughter of the President or Vice President of the United States or Arnold Schwarzenegger's offspring. Unless the student was a doorpost or fell way below the AI cutoff, most colleges would snap up the offspring of a major celebrity because it attracts money and the attention of the national press to the college.

This flag is relatively rare, though, and after the application goes through all the regular reading channels, the director would still have the final say.

15
Flags and Tags: Faculty and Trustee Recommendations

———•———

Another relatively rare flag is the faculty or trustee flag. If a faculty member writes a strong letter on your behalf or a trustee knows you and writes on your behalf, your folder would get some extra consideration, but unless you were relatively strong, it would not have a huge effect.

Again, some colleges take more of these cases, but Dartmouth is very stringent in this respect. It would be more impressed if you submitted a research paper to a professor who was so taken by your work that he said he would love to have you in his department than it would by a professor who said that you were a friend of the family. The president of the college can write or lobby on behalf of students, but most Ivy presidents do not try to exert influence on the admissions process.

Perhaps two or three students a year get in because they come strongly recommended by the president or an influential member of the board of trustees. It does not help the credibility of the recommenders if they pass on less-than- competitive candidates. If the student is borderline, it might make a difference, but if he has a very low AI, in all likelihood he will be rejected anyway.

A final warning here: Do not try to stuff your application with letters from important people who don't know you that well. If your parent's law partner is on the board of trustees but doesn't know you at all, the letter will in all likelihood rub admissions officers the wrong way. It just shows money and privilege, not talent on your part. The same would go for other letters from important people. A letter from the President of the United States that says that he met you or your parents or knows you does not reveal anything about you that was not already known. I would seriously caution applicants from trying to get letters from "big name" people.

Most of the time, the letters are brief and say such things as, "I've known Bobby's family for years and they are wonderful people. I'm sure Bobby would love Dartmouth." These kinds of letters make officers wonder why you feel so insecure in your own abilities that you have to try to get someone to go to bat for you. It is always better to trust your own academic achievements and let those speak for themselves. Name-dropping in most cases works against you, and the last thing you need when applying to highly selective colleges is a strike against you.

16

Flags and Tags:
Minority Recruiting

———•———

Minority recruiting is one of the most misunderstood aspects of the admissions process. My goal in this chapter is to explain exactly what a minority tag means and how much influence it has on your application.

As recently as thirty years ago, the Ivies were extremely homogeneous—most of the members of the population were affluent male white Anglo-Saxon Protestants. It was not uncommon for many students at prestigious northeastern preparatory schools to be accepted to an Ivy League school, even if they were not at the top of their class. As mentioned earlier, these high schools were called "feeder schools" because they fed their students mostly to Ivy League colleges. In those days, the Ivies drew a significant percentage of their classes directly from certain high schools, primarily on the basis of high school recommendations. No longer do true feeder schools exist. Nowadays at all the Ivies, about 60 to 75 percent of each entering class hails from public high schools. It seems the world has become a much more democratic place over time.

The Ivies, in their attempt to foster racial, ethnic, and economic diversity on their campuses, now consider each applicant in a socioeconomic context. In fact, contrary to what the chapter heading would suggest, white and other nonminority students also receive special consideration. For example,

Dartmouth has a special flag for "north country applicants"—applicants from Vermont, New Hampshire, and Maine whose parents did not attend a four-year college. These applicants are rural, less affluent, and white. They receive special consideration in the process. Their test scores are interpreted in light of possible deficiencies in their access to sophisticated educational resources, such as Advanced Placement courses, high-tech labs, and computers. Regardless of race, educational background, and family income, when admissions officers look at an applicant who is "first generation" college (that is, his parents did not graduate from college), they are more lenient with standardized test scores and try to evaluate the student's accomplishments against a background of what resources have been available to him.

Let's return to the subject of this chapter, minority recruiting. The term *minority* can be misleading. For admissions purposes at most Ivies, the term refers to traditionally "underrepresented" minorities (that is, underrepresented in the Ivy League applicant pool): black, Hispanic, and sometimes Native American, native Hawaiian, and Pacific Islander. These categories are problematic. For example, consider the category "black." This category encompasses U.S. citizens whose parents were born in Africa, U.S. citizens whose parents were born in the West Indies, and African-Americans, those of African descent whose parents were born in the United States. Those of African descent (including West Indians) without U.S. citizenship are supposed to be treated as international applicants. In point of fact, some colleges may include these students in their minority counts, even though they should be counted solely in the international category.

The term *Hispanic* encompasses Mexican-Americans, Cuban-Americans, Nicaraguan-Americans, and, in general, anyone from South or Central America who is a U.S. citizen. Again, any non-U.S. citizen from South or Central America, Spain, Cuba, the Dominican Republic, or Mexico is considered an international student. But Puerto Ricans, regardless of where they were born, are counted as Hispanics and thus receive special consideration. By now, you may appreciate the imprecise nature of these categories. Should a wealthy banker's daughter from Argentina who lives in the United States and is a U.S. citizen receive special consideration as a Hispanic? Should the daughter of a Nigerian diplomat who lives in Washington, D.C., be categorized as black? And what about the impoverished student from Calcutta or the Vietnamese boat refugee who does not fit into any of the official minority categories? How should these students be treated?

In my view, universities have conflated the rationale of three major goals: affirmative action, diversity, and equal opportunity. As a consequence, there is little principled application of these categories to students. One of the key objectives of affirmative action is to serve as a remedy for past or current discrimination against certain U.S.-born citizens. The historical rationale for affirmative action was based upon past discrimination against blacks, which placed them at an educational disadvantage and, as a consequence, at an economic disadvantage. Construed narrowly, even Hispanics and Native Americans would not fit under the rationale of the program (although Native Americans may have an equally compelling claim for recompense). Nevertheless, these two groups are treated as underrepresented minorities by the Ivy League.

But the problem gets more complicated because explicit race-based remedies often conflict with another compelling goal, that of ensuring equal opportunity for all U.S. citizens. If spaces in the class are limited and a poor white farmer's son from Kansas is competing against a black student whose father was the victim of discrimination, who wins? As if the tension between affirmative action and equal opportunity weren't enough, there is the university's attempt to realize an even broader objective—diversity.

Diversity is a catchall word that encompasses any trait, characteristic, or attribute that is different from the norm. One rationale for creating a diverse class seems to be that student learning is enhanced by a respect and understanding of differences. Unfortunately, our conception of difference depends upon the set of attributes that constitutes the norm.

My goal is not to indict the goals of affirmative action, equal opportunity, or diversity. However, it is imperative to distinguish the rhetoric of admissions literature on minority admissions and diversity from the practical implications for your chances of admission. In practice, at the end of the year, one set of numbers is reported to the public—the percentage of blacks, Hispanics, and Native Americans in the entering class. If these numbers are high, the minority-recruiting effort is deemed successful. But what happens if the numbers look a bit low at the end of the admissions season? Would it surprise you to learn that if the minority counts seem low, one way of boosting them is to give less weight to test scores and class rank than would be accorded to nonminority applicants? Some would maintain that what admissions officers have done is lower the standard applied to these students. Others would counter that at least one and possibly several of the three aforementioned goals has been satisfied. In the next section, I will take up these arguments in detail.

ADMISSIONS POLICIES AND MINORITY STUDENTS

At Dartmouth, minority-student status is designated by blue tags for black students, red tags for Hispanic students, and black tags for Native American students. At a very elementary level, the admissions procedures are the same for all students: All are required to complete an application and all are required to submit letters of recommendation. In addition, all applicants go through the regional reading process that I have already described in detail. So how does the admissions office know your ethnicity? It won't unless you check off one of the boxes for ethnicity on the application. (You don't have to, and some students don't.) Admissions officers don't ordinarily assume ethnicity from one's surname or geographic area, because they might easily be wrong and they respect the right of the student to have his application read without consideration of racial or ethnic background. If a student chooses to identify himself with a particular race or ethnicity on the application form, that information is used.

What about Asian-American applicants? For a school to receive federal aid, it must report the number of African-American students, Native American students, Hispanic students, and Asian-American students. However, for affirmative-action purposes, only the first three groups are counted. It's not that Asian-Americans are not a minority in the United States; it is just that they are not underrepresented in Ivy League applicant pools. In fact, the Ivies get many Asian-American applicants, so there is no problem with their being underrepresented, and for this reason, they do not receive a special minority tag. Even so, at Dartmouth their acceptance rate is usually a little bit higher than the overall rate of 22 percent. From the entering class of 1996 to the class of 2000, the acceptance rate for Asian-American applicants has ranged from a high of 35.5 percent to a low of 22.4 percent. I suspect that even if Asian-Americans were underrepresented, the Ivies would not make a special category for them. The general stereotype seems to be that even if they come from a poor background, at least it is one that emphasizes education.

This certainly may not be fair, but it is a reality at the Ivies. Of course, the applications of severely disadvantaged Asian-Americans are still read sympathetically, just as those of any disadvantaged student or student whose parents were not college-educated are, particularly in regard to standardized testing. Thus, in theory, there is no special minority category for Asian-American students, but in practice, the Vietnamese boat child or the single-parent, low-income Korean student might well be given a break, just not in the systematic way that the three major minority groups are treated.

Having said this, what's the real scoop behind minority admissions? Based on my experience during my four-year tenure at Dartmouth, while the application of the admissions procedures is the same, the tacit cutoffs for nonconsideration of a minority applicant and the interpretation of information provided by that applicant are viewed much differently. In the case of the minority applicant, there appears to be no hard-and-fast cutoff—in terms of class rank, test scores, or AI—that automatically disqualifies him from consideration.

But practically speaking, it is extremely unlikely that a minority candidate with any one SAT I score below 450 or SAT II score below 400 would be admitted to an Ivy. With respect to class rank, a minority student in the lowest half of the class would be a long shot. On the other hand, for a non-tagged white candidate (that is, not a legacy, recruited athlete, north country case, or any of the other categories I have discussed), the criteria for nonconsideration is different. This typical white candidate must have SAT I and II test scores that exceed 650 and a class rank near the top 10 percent of the class.*

In the case of a minority applicant, officers are willing to trade off test scores for class rank—that is, they are willing to accept lower test scores if accompanied by superior class standing, or higher test scores with inferior class standing. For white students without tags, modest test scores are not offset by superior class rank, except for cases involving extenuating socioeconomic circumstances. Both class rank and scores must simultaneously meet the tacit cutoffs for further consideration. When all is said and done, letters of recommendation, the interview, and other qualitative information are all factored into the decision, as I have already discussed in detail. Thus I must

*There are no strict cutoff points used in the Ivy League—the numbers I am using are rough guides to the unspoken cutoff. Below these scores, the applicant's admission is unlikely, although not impossible, if there are other mitigating factors.

emphasize that the decisions are far from mathematically pre-determined. But because the emphasis on quantitative consid-erations suggests some immutable standard (when indeed the process is not exclusively quantitative and the standard changes for white and black students depending upon a variety of cir-cumstances), I avoid the declaration that "standards are low-ered for minority students" in favor of the gentler and far more accurate statement that "they are merely different." For every accepted minority student with below-average test scores or lower than first-decile class rank, there is an accepted white recruited athlete or accepted legacy with equally low scores and rank.

To get a sense of how other qualitative factors can make a difference, consider the case of an applicant who notes that he is black and that his dad is a Harvard-trained lawyer and his mom is a graduate of Cornell Medical School. Furthermore, suppose that his SAT I and II scores are supe-rior (above 650) and yet his class rank is only top 30 percent. It is my experience that he will be admitted because he is ca-pable of doing the work, even though his class rank would cause one to pause and would probably have disqualified a nontagged white applicant. My guess is that you would probably not receive a clear explanation from an Ivy League officer as to why this student was admitted. If one was prof-fered, I doubt that the affirmative-action rationale would be invoked. Even if the candidate's family had been a victim of historical discrimination, it is unlikely that his file would be interpreted in this light, because the parental education and occupational information suggest that this discrimination is not continuing. Note how the admissions officer has altered the original intent of the affirmative-action edict to redress past discrimination by substituting the judgment that the discrimination must be continuing. My experience is that this candidate's "specialness" would probably be based largely on the diversity rationale and perhaps on the equal-opportunity rationale, although the internal case discussions are never this pointed.

Let's look at the case of a Native American applicant from a reservation in Oklahoma who has an AI of 175. For a non-tagged white student, this kind of AI alone would put him in the "one-reader R" category, but for a Native American applicant from this kind of background, a low AI alone would not eliminate him. Suppose the student has scores of 490V and 530M, no SAT II tests, and a class rank of 12/200. Even though these scores are very low in the Ivy applicant pool, if the student had strong recommendations and wrote fairly well, it is my experience that he would be admitted under the rationales of affirmative action and diversity (and probably historical discrimination, as well, since the student lives on the reservation and has to drive an hour each way to school).

To round out the picture, let's take the case of a Puerto Rican applicant from Brooklyn who attends a small Catholic boys high school. Furthermore, let's suppose that both parents are college-educated and that since they have lived in the United States for a long time, no Spanish is spoken at home. The father works for a small company and the mother teaches in a high school. Let's say the student is ranked first decile in his class and has scores of 600V, 660M, and SAT IIs of 550 Spanish, 640 math level I, and 490 physics. Recommendations are fairly strong, but they make it clear that the student is basically a hard worker, not particularly bright or insightful. He is involved in a few activities in high school, but nothing major.

One could argue that this student would not bring very much diversity to the campus because his "Puerto Ricanness" has been downplayed over the years, to the point where the family is very assimilated. Judging from the fact that Spanish is not spoken at home and the Spanish SAT II score is low, the student would not bring a second language to the table. In addition, the student is not disadvantaged, since mom and dad both went to college, have decent jobs, and were able to send their son to a private Catholic high school, even if perhaps there was some scholarship assistance from the school. Finally, the student is not extremely talented or interesting in terms of accomplishments, intellectual curiosity, or high scores. In fact, the 490 physics SAT II is frighteningly low. Despite all these concerns, in my experience I have found that this student would be accepted by the majority of Ivy League schools, depending on the total number of Hispanic applicants they received that year. Again, I don't think you would get a clear explanation of exactly why the student was accepted, but the reality is such that he most likely would be.

It is important to note that most of these students manage to do fairly well at Dartmouth and their respective colleges, even if they do not graduate at the top of their class. Keep in mind that at all of the Ivies, the retention rate from freshman to senior year is well over 90 percent, sometimes as high as 98 percent, so very few students drop out for academic reasons.

The bottom line is that the Ivies and highly selective colleges are very concerned that their minority numbers might go down, so they are always actively recruiting students from these three minority groups. All these colleges invite qualified minority students (the colleges screen them by looking at their transcripts and seeing if their AI or academic level is acceptable) to their campus on bus trips, invite them to campus after they are accepted, oftentimes paying for their transportation even if it means flying them to campus (Dartmouth in a typical year spends in excess of fifty thousand dollars to fly or bus accepted minority students to the campus in April so they can have the chance to experience a few days at the college), and do everything they can to matriculate these students so they are counted in the total minority numbers at the end of the year.

The difficulty is that many of the highly selective colleges end up fighting over a small number of qualified minority students, such that it becomes a Sisyphean task to enroll even a low number of minority students at each individual college. Every highly selective admissions office has a few staff members whose sole responsibility is minority recruitment. Even so, it is often an uphill battle to find the best minority students and get them to enroll in your college.

17

Summary of All Tip Factors and Geographic Diversity

———•———

If you look at the acceptance rates for specific groups, you will find that "tip factors" (that is, information in the application that may tip the admissions decision to the positive side) play a part across the entire spectrum of applicants, not just in minority cases.

At Dartmouth, legacies (sons and daughters of a Dartmouth-educated parent) are admitted at about a 40 percent rate (from the class of 1997 to the class of 2000, the acceptance rate has ranged from 40.8 percent to 46.1 percent) and their test scores and high school class rank are lower than the Dartmouth class average. Recruited athletes are admitted at about a 60 percent rate, while black students are admitted at about a 50 percent rate (from the class of 1997 to the class of 2000, the acceptance rate has ranged from 40.2 percent to 56.4 percent), Hispanics at about a 25 percent rate (from the class of 1997 to the class of 2000, the acceptance rate has ranged from 23.6 percent to 33.5 percent), and Native American students at a rate of about 30 percent (from the class of 1997 to the class of 2000, the acceptance rate has ranged from 27.8 percent to 39.3 percent). These numbers show that minority students are not the only students given preferential treatment in the admissions process in terms of tip factors.

It is true that a different selection process (not different in a procedural way, but, rather, in the way information is interpreted) is used to appraise the information provided by minority applicants, but it is wrong to suggest that nonminority applicants are placed at a competitive disadvantage. Minority applicants do not make up a large percentage of either the total number of applicants or of the freshman class. At Dartmouth, roughly 6 percent of all students enrolled are black, about 5 percent are Hispanic, and about 1 to 2 percent are Native American. (By comparison, at Princeton, roughly 8 percent are black, 6 percent Hispanic, and .5 percent are Native American.) Nearly 17 percent of the admitted freshmen are recruited athletes, and although some are minority students, these athletes are predominately white. Only 1 percent of the admitted freshmen are development cases and 7 to 8 percent are legacies.

Some of these categories overlap, but even if they didn't, that leaves at least 61 percent of the space in the freshman class that is used for nontagged applicants with no tip factors at all. If you are in one of these categories, I've tried to show accurately the implications your status has for the admissions decision. If you are not, my best advice is to focus on the factors that are under your control and aim to become one of the 60 percent of each year's freshman class that gets in entirely on their academic merit, without the benefit of tip factors.*

Before concluding this chapter, I want to address another area of major concern, one that I heard constantly while I was recruiting around the country for Dartmouth—that of geographic diversity. Isn't it true, parents wonder, that it would be easier for my child to get accepted to an Ivy League school if I lived in a state like Maine or Vermont or, say, South Dakota, rather than a highly competitive state like New York or Connecticut?

---

*Naturally, this percentage will vary by school.

To address this issue of geographic diversity, I would say that yes, selective colleges are interested in having students from all around the United States and all around the world, but believe it or not, those numbers (that is, the geographic distribution) work themselves out year after year without any tinkering or additional tip factors. Remember that regions are divided up in such a way that different states are mixed together, so at no time would an officer read one hundred applicants in a row from New York and then another seventy from California. In reality, an officer reads from *all* the states in his overall region, recommends a decision, and then that student is read by several other officers at random.

In other words, it is not possible until the end of the process even to figure out the acceptance rates from different states. After carefully analyzing Dartmouth's statistics and considering how regions are divided up, I can assert that the state the student applies from is *not* a factor in the admissions decision at all. Let's look at the examples I used above. The acceptance rate for Vermont applicants for the class of 2000 was 20 percent; from Maine, 23 percent; and from South Dakota, 0 percent. One would expect that any applicant from South Dakota would get accepted, since usually Dartmouth receives only from ten to fifteen applicants from there, but in reality, not one student was accepted, because the ones who did apply were not on an academic par with the rest of the applicant pool. The admission rates for Vermont and Maine were just about at the average for that year, 20 percent. If you want to see more examples, study the following list of the top ten states by number of applicants, followed by the acceptance rate for each of these states.*

1.	New York	22%
2.	California	18%
3.	Massachusetts	18%

*Again, all of these statistics are for the class of 2000 at Dartmouth College.

4. New Jersey	20%
5. Connecticut	19%
6. Pennsylvania	17%
7. Illinois	22%
8. Florida	25%
9. Texas	24%
10. Virginia	23%

You will notice that statistically there is not a very noticeable variance from the average of 20 percent in any of these states. If you want to convince yourself further, let's compare two very competitive areas, Washington, D.C. (32 percent) and Maryland (20 percent), with two states that are less competitive, such as New Hampshire (20 percent) and North Carolina (20 percent). Interestingly, in an area such as Washington, D.C., from which Dartmouth gets many very qualified applicants, it tends to admit more of them, although undoubtedly the high number in this class reflects the overall strength of the applicants from this area rather than the preferential treatment some people think they receive. Curiously, the rate of acceptance is exactly equal for New Hampshire, Maryland, and North Carolina, even though these states are not usually considered equal in terms of the number of highly qualified applicants.*

I hope you can see for yourself that where you apply from is not nearly as important as how strong an applicant you are. A top-notch student will stand out whether he is from New York City or North Dakota. The statistics show that where you apply from is not a significant consideration in the admissions process.

Another related question I used to hear a lot was, "Won't it hurt my child's chance of admission if many students from his

---

*There are a few exceptions to the neutrality rule. The most pointed: The director of admissions at Georgetown goes through every file and assigns several ratings to each student based on ethnicity, low socioeconomic background, and geographic desirability, among others. Thus, in this case, the geographic distribution would have some effect on admissions, although still not a tremendous one.

high school apply?" Again, the answer is *no*. As in the previous geographical examples, students are usually not read by high school group. In fact, such group demographics are not even examined until the very end of the reading process, once all the decisions are made. Thus, from high schools where Dartmouth gets many qualified applicants, it tends to admit many qualified applicants.

Keep in mind that even if the college does not read all applicants from one high school at the same time, admissions officers generally keep a record of relative rank by GPA within popular high schools. Some colleges are more meticulous about this record keeping than others. Georgetown, for example, has each officer enter every student's rank or GPA into the computer before files are even read. Then, when the officer has input all the applicants from his region, the students within each high school are placed in GPA or rank order so that at a glance (or a keystroke, since while reading any folder, they can access that student's rank among the current year's applicants) the officer can tell if the student is near the top of the year's pool or the bottom. Of course if several students were strong, they might accept as many as four out of five applicants, but at least they have an exact idea of where the student stands relative to his classmates who are applying.

Not all colleges are quite this rigorous, but from experience spanning the years, most officers have a good mental idea of what a good GPA is at most of the major high schools in their regions. A student with an 85 average at Stuyvesant High School will probably not be accepted to the most selective colleges because officers are aware that this student is really not near the top of the class, since the GPA distribution is fairly similar each year.

Here's a look at the top ten high schools that matriculate the highest number of students at Dartmouth in a given year and the acceptance rates from those high schools:

	Accepted Applicants	
	Percentage	Total
Stuyvesant High School (New York, NY)	33%	(37/111)
Phillips Exeter Academy (Exeter, NH)	25%	(16/64)
Phillips Academy (Andover, MA)	23%	(13/56)
Acton-Boxboro Regional High School (Acton, MA)	35%	(7/20)
Deerfield Academy (Deerfield, MA)	24%	(9/38)
Horace Mann School (Bronx, NY)	27%	(9/33)
T. Jefferson High School/Science and Technical (Alexandria, VA)	48%	(14/29)
Norfolk Academy (Norfolk, VA)	89%	(8/9)*
Harvard-Westlake School (North Hollywood, CA)	30%	(7/23)
Miramonte High School (Orinda, CA)	25%	(4/16)

It would seem that the reality is quite opposite to the public's perception: The admission rate at these very competitive high schools is higher, not lower, than the average in every case. In other words, it is *not* harder to get accepted from a strong high school like Stuyvesant because even though Dartmouth receives over one hundred applicants a year, it typically accepts 30 to 35 percent, since many are extremely qualified academically. You should also notice that of these top ten high schools, four are public and six are private.

The acceptance rate at private high schools versus public high schools is virtually identical at most highly selective colleges. Although, for example, Dartmouth's population has a much greater percentage of public school students (about 65 to 70 percent) than private school students (usually 20 to 25 percent), that simply reflects the overall number of applicants

*Unlike the other schools that send between 20 and 111 applicants to Dartmouth each year, Norfolk Academy only had 9 applicants, so the unusually high acceptance rate reflects the fact that their very top students applied and were accepted. The sample, however, is not comparable to the other schools in the top ten.

from each group, public and private. Dartmouth always receives more applications from public school students than from private school students, but the important fact to note is that the acceptance rate from both groups is almost identical year after year. Even if you look at the above list, many will be surprised that it is not the elite private high schools like Exeter and Andover that have the highest acceptance rates, but, rather, the big public high schools like Stuyvesant, Acton-Boxboro Regional, and Thomas Jefferson Science and Technical School. (I left out Norfolk Academy, since the number of applicants was significantly smaller than that of the other high schools on the list.)

But, parents ask, don't a higher percentage of students from elite prep schools attend Ivy League schools than do students from public schools? Not necessarily, and as we have seen, the actual acceptance rates are no higher. Why, then, do the prep schools themselves sell their schools to parents by asserting that a high percentage of the senior class attends Ivy League schools? What they are neglecting to mention is that admission to these high schools is highly selective in the first place, so the group applying to colleges is already self-selected to some extent and is going to be a much more college-bound group than the typical public high school class.

Let's examine two typical private schools: Phillips Academy in Andover (Massachusetts) and the Hotchkiss School (Connecticut). For its graduating classes of 1996, Andover admitted only 603 students out of the 2,276 who applied for admission. Thus, only 26 percent of the students who wanted to attend Andover were granted the opportunity. Of course, these students were judged primarily on academic ability, so what we have is an already very able academic group who are bound to be very competitive students and good candidates for highly selective colleges. In that Andover senior class, 112 out of 361 seniors, 31 percent of the class, were accepted to Ivy League schools.

These numbers are indeed high, but no higher than any

highly selective high school, public or private, which would include most competitive magnet schools like the Bronx High School of Science in New York, Stuyvesant High School in New York, or, for that matter, the magnet IB program in Coral Gables High School in Miami, Florida. In effect, the students have already been through a rigorous selection process just to get into high school, so naturally a high percentage are going to continue on to highly competitive colleges.

Note that the numbers in the preceding examples do not necessarily reflect the percentage of students accepted to each of these colleges. In fact, the actual acceptance rate from Andover was only 23 percent—that is, only thirteen out of fifty-six applicants were accepted to Dartmouth (the total is thirteen, not seven, because I have selected two different years of comparison—the totals would naturally vary a little bit by year). This rate is pretty close to Dartmouth's overall acceptance rate of 22 percent.

At the Hotchkiss School, 28 percent of a recent senior class was accepted to Ivy League schools. Out of 152 seniors, 12 were accepted to Brown, 5 to Columbia, 5 to Cornell, 3 to Dartmouth, 10 to Harvard, 3 to Princeton, 3 to the University of Pennsylvania, and 2 to Yale. Again, the same argument applies. The senior class at Hotchkiss already faced a rigorous selection process to get into Hotchkiss in the first place. These numbers do not reflect the individual acceptance rates to the Ivy League schools, only the total number of students accepted.

Thus, of all the tip factors, the ones that play the smallest—indeed, the most insignificant role—are geographic diversity and public versus private high school. This is as it should be, since a student should be neither handicapped nor aided by the strength of his high school, especially since more often than not, the student's choice is limited by financial means.

18
The Postgraduate Year

———◆———

What exactly is a postgraduate year? In short, it is an extra year of high school (thirteenth grade) before college. Why do a small handful of students decide to spend an extra year in high school? For some, the reason might be that they do not feel academically prepared by their current high school. For others, the reason might be because they are very young for their grade and do not feel psychologically ready for college. In some cases, a late-blooming student might realize that with his very mediocre grades in high school he is not going to qualify for admission to competitive colleges, so he might decide to spend a year at a top prep school to show that he can handle the challenge of college.

Very few, if any, public high schools provide for a PG year (as it is referred to in admissions circles), so in almost every case, students apply to private schools that have PG programs. Many of the top northeastern boarding schools have provisions for PG students and are a popular choice for students seeking a challenging program. Phillips Academy in Andover has about eighteen PG students in each senior class (roughly 5 percent of the class) and the Hotchkiss School has about ten, 8 percent of the senior class, to name two. At the high school where I used to teach, the Putney School in Putney, Vermont, we always had a few PG students. For the most part, private schools reap financial benefits by having PG students. Most of them do not get financial aid (although a few exceptional ones might qualify), so they help to generate income for the schools and to "fill beds," or spaces in the school, to keep enrollment numbers high.

To fully understand how the PG year is treated, we will have to examine three categories of students: Ivy League recruited athletes who chose a PG year, Ivy League applicants (that is, not recruited athletes) who chose a PG year, and applicants to highly selective colleges (but non-Ivy) who chose a PG year.

IVY LEAGUE–RECRUITED ATHLETES

As it happens, in a given year, many (if not most) of the PG applicants at the Ivies are recruited athletes who realized from talking to coaches that they were not going to qualify for Ivy admission because they were below the AI cutoff. Typically, these students will attend a strong private school with good athletic teams so they can continue to develop in their sport while trying to improve their academic record. The private school benefits by having a star athlete on its team and by having a student who has a good chance of getting accepted at a highly selective college as a recruit.

Let's say that a particular recruited athlete was a star ice hockey player with mid-500 scores and a *C* record in high school. Because of his low third decile ranking, his AI falls below the Ivy League cutoff for athletes. Then the student attends a private school, takes some advanced courses, and earns a 3.7 unweighted GPA. Logic would tell you that the Ivies, for purposes of computing the CRS, would count the PG year as one-fifth of the total CRS and calculate a weighted average so that the four-year high school record counted as four-fifths of the CRS. However, this is *not* what happens.

In fact, up until 1997 (for the class of 2001), for purposes of calculating the AI, the only year that counted at all for the computation of the CRS was the PG year. That means that up until 1997, a *C* record was effectively wiped out and replaced by one year of PG course work. Needless to say, this rule was invented to benefit recruited athletes so that more would be eligible for Ivy League admission. The rule was so unbalanced that in 1997 the Ivy League deans and athletic directors voted to change the rule so that CRS would be calculated by taking the CRS from four years of high school (however it might have been generated: rank, GPA, decile) and the CRS from the PG year (again, however it might have been generated), averaging the two CRSs, and then calculating the AI using this average CRS. As you can see, the "solution" is far from ideal, but at least it moved the process in the right direction.

If both CRSs were generated by different systems (that is, a rank-generated CRS from high school and then a GPA-generated GPA from the PG year), you can see that the average is not going to make much sense, since you are combining apples and oranges, but it still serves the purpose in most cases of raising the AI those few crucial points to qualify for Ivy admission. In short, if a recruited athlete gets good grades in a rigorous program during a PG year, he could stand a much better chance of admission.

IVY LEAGUE APPLICANTS WHO ARE NOT ATHLETES AND OTHER APPLICANTS TO HIGHLY SELECTIVE COLLEGES

Unfortunately, in these two cases, the same philosophy of wiping out or minimizing the damage of four years of high school will not apply. Don't forget that admissions officers at all highly selective colleges, Ivy or non-Ivy, see your four-year high school record *and* your PG year. If you had a *D/C* record in high school, usually one strong PG year will not be enough to convince an admissions team to admit you, since the obvious response is something like this: "Okay, the student did absolutely minimal work during four years of high school and then got *B*'s during the PG year—I don't think that one decent year erases such a weak high school record."

Granted, there could be special cases where a student had a solid record in high school and then showed signs of a real intellectual awakening, attended a strong private school, took five AP classes and got *A*'s in all of them, and garnered incredible recommendations that spoke to his incredible intellectual ability and passion for learning. These cases, however, are not the norm. What usually happens is that the student does solid, but not exceptional, work during the PG year and does not retake some of the tests that might do more to raise the overall academic level than the PG year would in the first place. When all is said and done, the scores are the same; only the grades have changed slightly.

Highly selective *non*-Ivy colleges do not use an AI at all, so you will not reap the benefit of raising your CRS in a PG year. You would have to rely on factors like those in the example I just cited. For those Ivies that calculate an AI for nonathletes and base their academic ranking directly on the AI, if there was a big disparity between your four years of high school and your PG year, they would see it immediately and manually readjust the stanine assignation. For those Ivies that do not use an AI-based scale, the readjusting of stanines would not be an issue—you would probably not rise very much in the academic rating, because you still have four weak years of high school and only one strong year in a PG program.

As you can see, the PG year has its use in Ivy League athletics and in genuine cases where a student has a good record in high school but wants to add to that before going to college for the reasons I mentioned at the beginning of the chapter. What the PG year does *not* do is salvage a disastrous four-year high school record so that colleges will want to look only at one year and omit the previous four. The process just does not work like that. I do think in many cases the PG year does benefit students and will help them get into a better college. The key part is understanding how the highly selective colleges look at a PG year so that you can make an educated choice (and a sound financial decision) about whether to add another year to your high school career before moving on to college.

19
Postacceptance and Beyond

What about once you are accepted to a highly selective college? Especially if you are accepted early decision, it is tempting to rest on your laurels and not do much work during the remainder of the senior year. This is a bad idea for several reasons. To me, the most important one is that you let down the very teachers who were your staunch supporters. You might notice that your teachers don't quit once they feel that they have covered all that is necessary for the AP exam.

Besides, you were accepted because of your perceived love of learning. How does going on sabbatical your senior year reflect this love of learning? It doesn't. In extreme cases, teachers become so enraged that they write to the colleges to tell them that they no longer want to be associated with the student or considered a supporter. This has happened. It is not what you'd call ending your high school career on a positive note.

How low can your grades drop before a college will decide to take back its acceptance? When I was a student, I didn't think Ivy League admissions officers took the time to monitor senior grades, but I was wrong. In fact, I was in charge of monitoring senior performance of our accepted students for four years, so I know exactly how this works and how many people it affects, at least at Dartmouth.

At the beginning of summer, well after high school has ended, I personally reviewed every file that had an AI or CRS drop of three points or more, and any file in which senior grades of *C*, *D*, or *F* were present. The systems technicians add all the senior grades and recalculate rank and grade point averages. If the CRS goes down, it will affect the AI. Once I collected all the folders in my office, I would exercise my personal judgment to see if the student was going to receive a warning letter.

When I examined the folders and the transcripts, I looked for grade trends and any extenuating circumstances. If the student's rank dropped unexpectedly with a corresponding drop in CRS because he got one *B*+, I would not take any further action, since obviously the high school had a very compressed GPA range. In this case, a small drop in GPA precipitated a significant drop in rank and, therefore, AI. Moreover, since so many people work hard and still receive a *C* in AP calculus, most offices more or less ignore a *C* in an advanced math class. However, if two or more grades dropped from *A*'s to *C*'s or *D*'s, you would receive one of the three versions of the letters sent out by Dartmouth (each college would have a slightly different system).

The first letter is for a significant drop in one class (usually from an *A* to a *C* or *D*, except in AP math); the second is for two grades; the third, for three or more grades. This last letter is very dire and starts by saying that your place in the class is in jeopardy. On the average, Dartmouth sends out about twenty such letters a year. Usually, the colleges will also send a copy to the student's guidance counselor. Once the student receives the letter, the college requires a written letter of explanation regarding the grade drop. In some cases, there is a credible reason, such as an illness or a death in the family. I personally reviewed all the letters to see if I thought the student was being honest and had a legitimate reason. I shared my thoughts with the director, who would be responsible for making the final decision. In very extreme cases, where the student had no compelling reason for a major drop in grades, he would be denied admission. Roughly from six to eight students a year are denied admission to Dartmouth based on an academic decline or a serious disciplinary infraction.

Even if the admissions office accepts your explanation, you start out your freshman fall under the surveillance of the first-year office, which would have your file, since all files are forwarded there. This office would monitor your first-term grades to see if the trend continued or reversed itself. This is not necessarily a bad thing if something really traumatic happened in your life, since the first-year office would be aware of the problem and would be there to offer help. In most cases there are reasonable explanations, but why risk getting put on academic probation before you even get to college?

It is easiest to avoid senior slump by staying engaged even after you are admitted to college. Besides, if you are taking AP/IB classes, there are plenty of reasons to keep working. At most of the Ivies, you will get college credit if you score a perfect 5 (sometimes a 4 or 3, depending on the test) on an AP exam or a 6 or a 7 on an IB exam. Why is this good? It can save you thousands of dollars. At Dartmouth, you need thirty-five credits (or classes) to graduate, but under the trimester system, you take nine classes a year. Thus, if you received two credits coming in, you could take an extra term off and save roughly ten thousand dollars, thanks to your IB/AP credit—just one more reason (besides your personal sense of pride) why it pays to continue working hard until the end of high school. It's not that you can't drop a little—if you go from five *A*'s to two *A*'s and three *B*'s, you will not receive a letter. This is considered a reasonable drop in grades. Usually, a greater drop than this is unacceptable.

After four long years of hard work, it does not pay to slack off during the homestretch. Think long and hard before you decide to let yourself, your family, your teachers, and your high school down by jeopardizing your college acceptance. Besides, you have all summer to celebrate.

20

The Wait List

So far, I've focused on the process of getting accepted to the college of your choice. However, what should you do if you end up being put on a college's waiting list? Every college uses its wait list in a slightly different way, so you should call the particular college that wait-listed you and find out its policies. The first thing you should do is decide whether you are still interested in remaining on the wait list.

Each year, Dartmouth wait-lists hundreds of very strong applicants because it simply runs out of spaces in the class. All candidates on the wait list receive a card that asks them whether they wish to remain active on the list. Once the candidate sends back the card saying yes, that person is considered a "hot" wait-list prospect. If the college receives a negative card or no response, it assumes that person does not want to remain on the wait list.

Every year, Dartmouth probably ends up with between two and five hundred "hot" wait-list candidates. How many do colleges accept from their wait list? That really depends on their yield in the first round of accepted students. For example, if a higher number of students than were expected accepted the offer of admission, a college might not even need to go to the wait list. There have even been some years when Dartmouth has taken no one from the wait list. The norm for Dartmouth is to accept between fifty and one hundred students from the wait list, because, like every college, it has to account for summer attrition. The class usually loses between ten and twenty students who decide to accept another college's offer, or who get accepted from the wait list at another college and decide to go there instead, or decide that they want to defer their admissions indefinitely because of health or personal reasons. It usually behooves a college to take at least a small number of applicants from the wait list if it looks as if there will be room in the class.

Princeton typically wait-lists from three to four hundred students a year to convey the message that they were too strong to be rejected. Unfortunately, the majority of these students won't be admitted, since Princeton accepts a mere handful each year from the wait list.

Who ends up on the wait list anyway? At Dartmouth, for example, if you refer to chapter 10, you will remember that some students get wait-listed for "political" reasons. In the case we saw in that chapter, Dartmouth chose to wait-list that candidate to soften the blow to the high school and to acknowledge that this student was close to being accepted. In committee, any applicant who has more acceptance or wait-list votes than reject votes would be placed on the wait list.

The director usually takes all the really close folders (ones that just missed being voted into the class by one committee member's vote) and keeps them in his office. As time passes, he eliminates the "cold" wait-list candidates, until he has a short list of maybe fifty or so superstrong applicants. For the most part, these are students who were voted almost unanimous "A" votes in committee and are usually nearly as strong, if not as strong, as the students who were admitted. In Dartmouth's case, it is forced to admit a small class, since it is one of the smallest of the Ivy League schools. Thus, many top candidates are put on the wait list for want of space in the freshman class.

If the college examines its overall yield and it does look as if it will be able to accept students from the wait list, the director first turns to his "hot" cases in his "close" pile and goes through them one by one, selecting whom he considers to be the most compelling applicants. Since Dartmouth is need-blind in terms of financial aid, all decisions are made without regard to financial need. This is not true for all the highly selective colleges, so in some cases, the college would be forced to pick full payers over financial-aid applicants in this part of the process. Again, check with the college to ascertain its policy.

Then the director will ask all the officers to go through the applications of all the "hot" wait-list candidates in their regions and make a list of their top picks, giving a one-sentence summary of why they think each student should be admitted. Depending on the year, each officer might select anywhere from five to twenty top students in his region and recommend them to the director. He would then read through all the suggestions and select those students he felt were the very top applicants across all regions. Once again, I would have to say that the very top applicants stand out, even in this wait-list process. The regional officer has the chance to pick out any standouts in his region.

As the student, should you send in lots of extra material if you are on the wait list? In a word, no. Many students flood offices with extra letters of recommendation and lists of insignificant awards. As you might guess, these tend to annoy officers, who then have to wade through lots of paperwork. It is much better to make sure that any truly powerful recommendations are already part of your file so that they are read by officers and then the whole committee during the regular reading process. It is too late if you try to catch up in the last stage of the game. It is much better to let your accomplishments stand for themselves.

If you have your heart set on getting off the wait list, the most I would suggest is asking your guidance counselor to call in order to see if he can get an accurate indication of where you stand. As you can see, most offices do not rank their wait-list candidates per se, so it is not easy to give feedback to a guidance counselor, but at least the counselor can stress to the regional person that Dartmouth is the student's top choice, and even though he was already accepted at Yale, he would pick Dartmouth if accepted. This is useful information to the regional officer, who could then select that student from his region if he felt so compelled.

Occasionally, parents call and explain an extenuating circumstance to the individual officer. Let's say that the student applied only to two or three colleges because he had an incompetent guidance counselor who didn't tell him that he should apply to some "safety" schools. Of course, if the student were from a well-educated family and/or a very good high school, officers would not be very sympathetic, but I can think of two or three cases where Dartmouth wait-listed a nonsophisticated student from a small town who ended up getting rejected or wait-listed at a few colleges but was not accepted at any. If the student was very strong, the regional officer could use his discretion and point out this kind of situation to the director. In some cases, the student would be accepted based on academic strength. In other cases, the director would decide that the particular student really wasn't enough of a superstar among those on the wait list.

I would caution parents against calling to harass regional officers. If you do not have any truly important information to relay, it is better to leave things to chance or, if you insist, have the guidance counselor call. In nine out of ten cases, officers go through the procedure exactly as I described above and select the crème de la crème of the "hot" wait-list applicants. Occasionally, some of the factors I just mentioned might have some influence over the officer's recommendation to the director, but ultimately, the director would have to see if he felt that the applicant was truly compelling compared to all the others on the wait list.

Most highly selective colleges tend to finish all wait-list deliberations as early as they can. It is rare to drag the wait-list period on past June fifteenth or so. In general, it is the less selective colleges that extend their wait-list times so they can pick up the "leftovers" of the highly selective colleges. At Dartmouth, wait-list acceptance letters are usually sent out before June first.

Sometimes, in the first round (if it is unsure of yield, the college might go through the process I outlined above two or three times over a period of two or three weeks), officers might call applicants personally to tell them that they are being offered admission. Usually, only those very top students who just missed being voted in by the committees would be called personally.

Remember, once you enroll the following fall, no one will know whether you were accepted in April or off the wait list in June, so you might as well keep that knowledge to yourself. If the college admitted you, it considers you a top candidate and you should be proud. Every year, I look at some of the students on the wait list and I am shocked that they were not admitted in the first round. I suppose this is one of the frustrations of very selective admissions—many great candidates are not accepted because of the very low acceptance rates at the nation's most competitive colleges.

21
Communication
Among Schools

———❖———

I remember when I was in high school that all my classmates and I thought admissions officers at highly selective colleges, particularly the Ivies, spent most of their time sitting around their offices talking to each other on the phone to see which students applied to each college, how many from each high school, which ones they were planning on accepting, and so on. I even imagined that some colleges tried to "bid" for the best students by bargaining, so that Brown, for example, would turn down a student that Princeton really wanted so that Princeton could get that student to come. It was my own personal version of an *X-Files*-like conspiracy theory that involved all highly selected colleges, but especially the Ivies.

I have to admit that when I started working in admissions, I was disappointed to be proven wrong. In fact, my conspiracy theory could not be further from the way things really happen. In actuality, I have had the chance to meet other Ivy League colleagues only during our annual Ivy League conference for admissions officers and on the rare occasions when I have called other colleagues to arrange joint travel for recruiting purposes. The only Ivy League personnel who see one another more often would be the Ivy League deans and directors, who meet several times a year (almost always to argue about athletics and AI rules affecting athletics).

During the annual Ivy League conference, it's not the case that every single officer sits in a big room and listens to speeches, votes on issues, and decides major policies. What really happens is this: There are several smaller meetings going on at the same time (about minority recruitment, athletics, travel strategies, new technology) and each officer decides which meetings he would like to attend.

During the whole two-day retreat, each officer would typically attend from three to five meetings. The meetings end on the early side, so there is plenty of time to tour the town (a few years ago it was in Newport Beach in Providence, Rhode Island), go out dancing with friends and colleagues, have dinner and drinks, take a boat cruise, or whatever. My overall impression from attending three conferences over the past few years was that we didn't really accomplish very much except to meet a few of our colleagues and have a minivacation. There is such a high turnover of Ivy League admissions officers that you could not keep track of all the new people from year to year. Most of the sessions were unhelpful or organized at the last minute, so they ended up being earnest discussions about issues but very little was actually accomplished. No one seemed to mind, though, since the point appeared to be to reward ourselves for a long and tiring reading season and to renew ourselves for the ardors of spring and summer work with the public.

So is there any news at all that is shared among colleges? Yes, there is some basic reporting: how many applicants total, the yield on applicants, how many early decision/early action, how many minority applicants, general trends, et cetera. But this is all ex post facto based on the class just admitted. As you can see, there is absolutely *no* time during the hectic reading season to be calling other colleges to find out who applied from where. In fact, until this spring conference, there is no communication at all among Ivy League schools or among other highly selective colleges, except for the one case I will mention shortly. The plain truth is that everyone is too busy trying to get thousands of applications processed, read, and decided upon before the April mail date.

The only information that is shared among all highly selective colleges is a list of those students accepted early decision or early action, because of the commitment on the student's part to honor the agreement. When Dartmouth finishes its final decisions for the early-decision applicants, it mails a list to the Ivies and several other highly selective colleges (most of the ones listed in the introduction, as well as others that have early-action or early-decision programs) so that systems technicians can run the names through the computer and check to see if anyone who is already committed to attending Dartmouth has applied early action or early decision somewhere else.* Most of the other colleges would do the same, thereby making sure that students follow the rules.

The moral of the story is that you should not be paranoid about communication among colleges, because it simply does not happen. You should be careful to follow the rules for early action or early decision. You cannot be accepted at two early-decision colleges and then weigh your best financial-aid offer. When the colleges find out, they might both decide to rescind their acceptance, so you would be left with no college. In some cases, you *can* apply early action and early decision, but if you are accepted to the early-decision college, you must immediately withdraw your application from the early-action college. If you do not, when the early-action college gets the list from the early-decision college, they will in all probability send you a letter saying that your file is now inactive, since you have already been accepted. One college would never try to "steal" a student from another college in an underhanded manner.

In a similar "conspiracy" vein, I used to imagine that the little Ivies (Amherst, Swarthmore, Williams, Wesleyan, and

---

*Surprisingly, almost all the Ivies operate on different computer systems, so no information is shared electronically. The lists have to be input manually so that they are intelligible to a particular school's system.

whatever others we could include) evaluated their applicants in relation to the probability of that applicant getting accepted into an Ivy League school. My idea was that if, for example, a Williams admissions officer was reading a tremendously strong application he might say to himself, "Why should we admit him when it seems certain that all the Ivies would probably accept him and then we'd waste a space in our class?"

As you can probably guess by now, this scenario never occurs, for several reasons. First, as I mentioned, no college has any idea to which other colleges the applicant has applied. In this case, officers would not know if the student had indeed applied to other Ivies. Second, even if Williams, for example, somehow knew that Yale was the student's first choice (sometimes an alum will find out that kind of information from an interview, or the applicant will mix up the essays and write about why he wants to go to Yale in the Williams application), that information would not be acted on. I know it is hard to believe, but let me explain the reasoning behind this.

All the highly selective colleges keep track of their yield, the percentage of students who accept their offer of admission. If you study the yield for the last few years for all the highly selective colleges, you would notice that yield stays relatively constant over the years. Dartmouth's yield has hovered around 50 percent for the last few years. This means that Dartmouth will always admit roughly twice as many students as it has spaces for in the class. For the class of 2000, 2,273 students were accepted and 1,095 matriculated. If the yield is slightly higher, there will be a few more students in the freshman class. If the yield is slightly lower, there will be a few less, causing the target number of admits to rise slightly for the next year's class.

Since all the highly selective colleges can count on a steady yield that does not vary much over the years, they make all decisions regardless of the applicant's desire to attend a particular college. Besides, what if at some point in the application process it is true that the applicant's first choice is one college but the next week he changes his mind? Also, what if the information from an outside source was incorrect, as in the case of a peer recommendation that tries to hurt a friend's chance of admission? Because of all these variable factors, especially the fickle mind of teenagers, officers do *not* take into account a student's desire to attend their particular college—they know that it might change. What would happen if that student who applied to Williams and Yale (and said that Yale was his first choice) got denied by Yale but accepted to Williams? In most cases, that student would happily go to Williams. The only way colleges take "desire to attend" into account is in the case of early decision, where the student is clearly signaling that the college is his first choice, since it is the only one he is applying to and he must attend if accepted.

All this means that not only is there little to no communication among highly selective colleges; these colleges do not try to second-guess a student's first choice and make decisions accordingly. Doing so smacks of "playing God," and it could have dire consequences for the student. So rest assured that your application will not be shared among colleges, colleges will not compare notes on where you apply, and they will not try to guess where you really want to go to college. Their main goal is to complete a tremendous amount of reading and evaluation in a relatively short period of time.

22

Financial-Aid Implications and International Students

———•———

I do not want to spend a great deal of time on financial aid, as it is a subject so complex as to merit a separate book. What concerns us here are the implications that applying for financial aid may have on a student's admission to the college of his choice. First, I will address the issue of financial aid for U.S. citizens (either natural-born or permanent residents with green cards) and then I will turn to the more complicated case of international students.

All the Ivy League schools are known as need-blind in terms of admissions for all but international students. This term means that admissions decisions are made without regard to financial need. In other words, if a college knows that you can afford to pay the full tuition and it decides to accept you over another, poorer student, it would be blatantly violating the need-blind rule. Not all the highly selective colleges are need-blind, so before applying, you need to check every college's policy, at least insofar as it concerns your chance for admission.

In addition to being need-blind, some of the Ivy League schools (but not all) guarantee 100 percent of financial need for all admitted students (except international ones). At Dartmouth, for example, if after doing a financial-aid "need analysis" the financial-aid office determines that you need twenty thousand dollars a year to be able to afford Dartmouth, it would come up with a combination of scholarship (if you qualified—the higher the need, the more scholarship dollars), work-study money (money that you have to earn over the year through work), parent contribution, and student contribution (if you had your own savings) to equal the full amount. What some colleges do is admit students on a need-blind basis but then resort to "gapping," which, as it sounds, means that if you need twenty thousand dollars, they might give you only ten thousand and expect you either to come up with the rest or go to another college.

Since all the Ivies are need-blind in terms of admission for all but international students, why should there be any effect on your chances for admission? After all, financial-aid offices are always separate from admissions offices in the Ivy League and there are strict rules prohibiting the sharing of information between the two offices. The answer is that even though the Ivy admissions officers cannot access specific financial-aid information, right on the front of every application form is this box: "Are you applying for financial aid, yes or no?" Thus, every Ivy League school will know whether or not you are applying for aid—at Dartmouth, this information is coded right on the front of the master card and is on the first page of form 1 in the application.

I have previously discussed the implications of parents' college background and occupations, explaining how if students come from very humble backgrounds, they might get a break on certain standardized test scores, whereas if their parents are supereducated and have high-paying jobs, they will be judged accordingly to stricter standards, especially regarding standardized tests. Well, what if after reading where your parents went to college and what jobs they have (manager, or director, or systems analyst), the officer reading the file can tell absolutely nothing about what kind of background you come from—a manager could mean the manager in a supermarket, who gets

222

paid very little, or the manager of a multimillion-dollar investment fund.

In these cases, all an officer needs to do is let his eye wander over to wherever on the application it asks whether or not you have applied for financial aid in order to give him a rough idea. At Dartmouth, a code "O" means the student checked off "no" to applying for financial aid, and a "2" means that they checked off "yes." So if the officer cannot tell what kind of manager your parent is but he notices that you are not applying for financial aid (which means that the family can afford the tuition and room and board, which will exceed thirty thousand dollars a year), he realizes that you are not disadvantaged economically and therefore do not deserve any breaks in terms of socioeconomic background.

The mere fact that a student checks "yes" with reference to financial aid does not in fact mean that he will qualify for financial aid or that he will even apply for it, so seeing a "2" (applying for financial aid) is more mysterious. In the aforementioned case, if the officer saw that the student was applying for financial aid and he still had no idea of educational background or income level, he would have to remain neutral in his reading regarding family background.

Again, I'm not suggesting that anyone subvert the system by checking off "yes" with regard to financial aid, because this is only one of the many factors involved. If officers suspect that you are trying to manipulate the system, it could obviously work against you. Even if you have little money but both parents attended Ivy League schools, no disadvantage would normally be assumed—the socioeconomic-disadvantage reading is meant to aid students who truly have grown up in areas where they have not been exposed to top-notch schools, high levels of education, or privileges such as traveling around the world. Remember, officers will see other factors than just a "yes" with reference to financial aid: they can see your parents' address, highest level of education and which colleges they attended, along with which high school you attend. In addition, many times guidance counselors or teachers will unknowingly reveal a student's level of economic background by a reference in a letter—such as, "She takes after her father, who is the highest-ranking federal judge in Ohio," or, "Tim has to work twenty-five hours a week to help his single-parent mom meet basic expenses."

The most needy students will apply for a fee waiver, as well—which is stamped right on the front of form 1 if it is approved by the officer who monitors fee-waiver requests. These students would be easy targets for finding out about economic disadvantage. Conversely, a student whose parents live on Fifth Avenue in New York City, went to Ivy League schools, work as doctors or lawyers, and whose child attends an expensive private school will come across as able to pay full tuition, whether or not the student checks off the "yes" or "no" box. In this case, checking off the "yes" box would be considered willful deceit.

I think the really surprising fact about all this is that people have assumed for years that being able to pay for college would actually help their child's chance for admission, but this is not necessarily so. At these colleges, unless you plan on donating a huge new building or making a very large-scale donation, being able to afford the full tuition will give you absolutely no advantage in the admissions process. I cannot go so far as to say that if you do not apply for financial aid, you have a lower chance for admission, because that is not true, either. It's just that you won't get any of the breaks or allowances that would be given to truly disadvantaged students. This is as it should be.

I think it is important to know all the facts about the implications of applying for financial aid, but the bottom line is that ethics and morals have a role, too—these facts are not here so one can try to cheat the system; they are here so one can make a fully informed decision about finances while upholding the moral and ethical standard that you would want your children to live up to.

INTERNATIONAL STUDENTS

Before examining the implications of financial aid for international students, we need to define what exactly an international student is. The most obvious example is a student who holds a passport from a foreign country and who has attended high school abroad. If a student holds a foreign passport (for example, from Peru) but through a student visa attends high school in the United States, he is still considered in the international category because he holds a foreign passport and does not hold a U.S. green card. However, if a student is a Peruvian citizen but attends high school in the United States and has a green card and permanent-resident status, he is not considered an international student. Finally, U.S. citizens who hold U.S. passports but attend high school abroad are not considered international students, either.

In short, international students, regardless of where they attend high school, are defined as citizens of foreign countries who do *not* hold a U.S. green card and are therefore not U.S. permanent residents. To quote from Dartmouth's information packet for international students, "Canadian citizens, U.S. permanent residents, and U.S. citizens living abroad are reviewed without the constraints of a limited financial aid budget."

Why bother to make such a fine distinction? The fact is that at all the highly selective colleges, Ivies included, the applications of international students are never read on a need-blind basis for the simple reason that financial-aid funds are severely limited for international students and non–green card holders cannot qualify for U.S. federal-aid funds, an important source of income for financial-aid packages. What does it mean for admission if you cannot be read on a need-blind basis?

Basically, those international students who check off "no" with regard to financial aid have a much greater chance of ad-

225

mission at all the highly selective colleges than do those who indicate that they will apply for aid. (There is no point in lying on the application, because if you are admitted and have indicated that you did not need financial aid, then if you can't afford the tuition, the college is powerless to help you and you will have to turn down the admission offer.) To oversimplify a little, international applicants at all the highly selective colleges are eventually divided up into the "don't need financial aid" and "do need financial aid" piles and then acted upon accordingly.

Most colleges have an officer in charge of international applicants and that person would normally be the first reader for all such files (since he is familiar with many foreign grading systems, tests, and other conventions that differ significantly from country to country). All international applications would go through the same process I outlined earlier, up to a certain point. That certain point is committee. Before international applications are distributed for committee consideration, all the ones that indicate a need for financial aid are removed for separate consideration in a different process, which I will discuss shortly. The no-need international students are sent on to committee and judged against the same standard that any other student would be judged against.

Thus, it is only those international students who apply for financial aid who will be treated differently and judged by different standards from those used for their U.S. counterparts. Money talks in international admissions.

How exactly does the process work for these international applicants who need aid? The process varies a little by college, since each college has its own budget for international financial aid (some have no budget and can take only full payers), but the general process is very similar. Once these applications have been read two or three times by the international officer and one or two additional officers, the international officer would sort out all the folders. If both readers voted "R," the student would be rejected. If both readers had negative leaning votes like "R" and "P-," or "P- and P-" ("P" stands for possible) or even "P and P-," or "P and P," the student would probably not be accepted. Those applications with stronger votes would be sorted by country and passed on to the financial-aid office for a partial read of about how costly it would be to accept these students. Then the international officer would usually meet with the head of the office and try to pick the strongest applicants, keeping an eye on the budget. If a very strong international student needed only a relatively small amount of financial aid, he would probably be accepted, but if he needed a large financial-aid award, the competition would be fierce.

To give a specific example, I helped the international officer read all the applicants from the People's Republic of China (PRC) for three years and was present at the final meeting with the director and the international officer. Typically, Dartmouth received between 80 and 150 applications from PRC students per year, but because of the Communist government, every single one not only required a complete aid package—they were so poor that they all qualified for fee waivers, as well.* Many of these students were brilliant; many were academic 8s and 9s. They were some of the most academically gifted students in the applicant pool. To give you an idea, many took the GRE (graduate record exam) that U.S. students take *after* they finish college, because the SAT I and II are not available in China. Even given the fact that English is not their native language, they routinely scored over 650 on the verbal (high for an intelligent, literate U.S. citizen) and sometimes a perfect 800 on both the analytical and quantitative sections of the test. The sad part is that with all these incredible students to choose from, Dartmouth accepted one or at the most two a year out of the entire group, since they needed a full aid package. As you can see, the odds are very great.

* The typical per capita income in the PRC is $120 a year.

The most competitive area is India/Pakistan. Over 220 students a year apply, but only a handful of high-need students will be accepted. Even among these brilliant students, those who do not need financial aid have a significant advantage over those who do. Of the ones who need financial aid, only a few are admitted a year out of the many who apply.

Besides India/Pakistan and the People's Republic of China, the countries with the largest number of international applicants to Dartmouth (and these numbers would be similar at the other highly selective colleges) are Canada, Ghana, Japan, and South Korea.

Overall, the acceptance rate for international students at Dartmouth was much lower than that of the rest of the applicant pool. From the classes of 1996 through 2000, the acceptance rate ranged from a high of 14.2 percent to a low of 10.5 percent. At some schools, it is even lower; Princeton typically accepts only 6 percent of the international applicants who apply. For the class of 2000 at Dartmouth, there were 1,272 international applicants from eighty foreign countries, from which 142 were admitted and 47 matriculated. These figures include both financial-aid and non-financial-aid applicants. I do not know the exact acceptance rate for each group, but obviously it is much higher for non-needy students than for high-need students. In total, two-thirds of the international applicants will apply for financial aid. For a typical year at Dartmouth, a roughly $400,000 international financial-aid budget supports around twenty-five students a year, while the other twenty or so students receive no aid.

On a final note, one very important test for international students is the TOEFL test, which measures proficiency in English. For some odd reason, it is not scored on an 800 scale—the highest score is 677. International students need to show a strong proficiency in English. If they score under 600, it will be nearly impossible to gain admission, particularly if they are in the aid category.

Now that we have looked at how financial aid affects admission, let us turn to some final aspects of the reading process.

23

Transfer Students

For the most part, the Ivies do not accept very many transfer students because of the tremendous number of applicants they get in the regular admissions process. Therefore, the odds of getting accepted as a transfer student are usually much stiffer than the odds of getting accepted as a freshman, depending on the school and the competition that year.*

The deadline for transfer students varies by college, but it is always much later in the year than the January first regular-decision deadline. For all of the Ivies, the deadline for transfer applicants is between March first and April first and applicants are notified by mid-May. (Note that international students who are applying as transfers and are also applying for financial aid need to get their transfer applications in at a much earlier date—at Dartmouth, by January first.)

In terms of admissions, the reading process for transfer applications is just a streamlined version of what happens during the regular-decision reading process. Usually only a few offi-

*At Harvard, the acceptance rate for transfer students is about 10 percent a year (roughly 100 are accepted out of 1,030); at Cornell, the rate is 18 percent for all seven schools (550 are accepted out of 3,000), but most are not for the Arts and Sciences, to which only 123 are accepted; at Columbia, the rate is about 6 percent (between 1,300 and 1,400 apply and between 60 and 100 are admitted); at Yale, 6 percent are accepted (about 600 apply a year); at Brown, 17 percent are accepted (100 out of 600); at the University of Pennsylvania, about 33 percent are accepted into the Arts and Sciences; and Princeton does not accept transfers on a regular basis. Dartmouth accepts about 45 students out of between 250 and 400. All these schools, with the exceptions of Brown and Columbia, are need-blind for transfer financial-aid applicants.

cers from each college would actually be involved in reading transfer applications, since the volume is comparatively smaller. All applications would be read two times and, if necessary, would go to the transfer committee. There still exist special categories, like athletes and minorities, so these tip factors would be weighed in the process. In fact, the process is almost identical to the regular one except that officers will look the most at your college transcript and recommendations, followed by your high school record. Note that your high school record and scores are still an important part of your file. To quote from the Dartmouth transfer application:

The Dartmouth transfer application makes it clear to all candidates that the primary emphasis is placed upon the student's college grades, the essay they submit as to why they want to transfer to Dartmouth, and the various recommendations from their professors and advisors. In addition, the admissions staff looks at the student's high school records, outside interests, and work experiences as well. And of course, the other, less tangible, qualities of the applicant, such as their personal qualities, are also taken into consideration by the committee. Personal traits such as creativity and intellectual curiosity are still very much sought by the admissions staff when it comes to transfers.

To generalize, most of the transfer admits *do not* come from other Ivy League schools. I was always pleasantly surprised by the wide variety of colleges from which Dartmouth accepted applicants. Here's a sampling of some of the schools from which Dartmouth accepted transfer students for the class of 2000: Boston University, Broward Community College, New York University, Ohio State University, Pennsylvania State University, Rockland Community College, Santa Monica College, Smith College, SUNY Binghamton, University of California at San Diego, University of Colorado, University of

New Mexico, University of Southern California, University of Texas at Austin, University of Vermont, University of Washington, Vassar College, Villanova University, Washington and Lee University, and Whitman College.

The highly selective colleges try not to just accept students from other highly selective colleges because they'd end up with a pretty boring transfer group. Instead, students come from around the country and from many lesser-known, lower-profile colleges. Since the process for transfer applicants is so similar to the regular application process, almost all the information I have discussed so far is also relevant to transfer students.

24

Do You Need an Independent Counselor?

The past few years have borne witness to a frenzied rush to gain acceptance to highly selective colleges, which in turn has spawned an entire industry of independent college counselors. In New York City, for example, these independent counselors often are paid extremely high consulting fees and are expected to work miracles for their clients. While I have spoken to many who do not really have the credentials or know-how to be truly effective, I have also met others who are very qualified to advise students and help them with the application process. To be fair, I have also met scores of extremely dedicated "public" counselors, the guidance counselors or college counselors who work for high schools and who in many cases are extremely knowledgeable and professional. When and under what circumstances, then, does it pay to invest in an independent counselor?

Before parents run out to find an independent counselor, they should make an effort to get to know the counselors at their child's high school, public or private. Many have years of experience and are tremendous resources. Sit down with the counselor early on in high school, ninth or tenth grade, and try to get a sense of how he envisions your child's college search, what kinds of colleges he thinks are realistic, and what advice he has for the college search in general. Does he have a time line for testing?

Does he have suggestions for course selections that will interest your child? It is a smart idea to get to know the counselor personally and to have a good working relationship, because the better the counselor knows your child, the more helpful his recommendation will be. As discussed earlier, the guidance counselor's letter of recommendation plays a key role because only the guidance counselor can provide insight as to where the student is ranked relative to the rest of his classmates and what teachers really think of him. This information is crucial to any application and is really not available to independent outside counselors, for how would they be aware of how the student was regarded by faculty and peers within the high school? There is simply no way for them to have access to that information.

Whether you decide to go to an independent counselor or not, you will need the high school counselor's help, for he will write the official high school letter of recommendation, so in no case should you alienate him from the process or tell him that you don't think he knows what he is talking about—even if that is what you happen to be thinking. I would also recommend the utmost discretion about the role of the independent counselor, because you will need to count on the high school counselor's official participation in your child's college admission process.

The most convincing reasons to hire an independent counselor would be (1) if the high school counselor seems underqualified for the job; (2) if the high school counselor has such a huge caseload that he cannot possibly spend enough time advising your child; (3) if your child has special needs, such as learning disabilities; (4) if your child has exceptional talents in an area like art or music that requires a specialized knowledge of different kinds of colleges, such as conservatories or design schools.

When should you contact an independent counselor? If I were an independent counselor trying to help students gain admissions to the most competitive colleges in the country, I would want to start meeting with the student and his family as early as eighth or ninth grade to make sure he was getting on the right track in terms of course selection in high school, certainly no later than eleventh grade. By the time many students are ready to apply for college, hiring an independent counselor will probably be too late in the game to have a major effect.

This brings me to the function of an independent counselor. Once you have made the decision to hire an independent counselor, what should you expect? In my view, the main function of an independent counselor should be to sit down with the student long enough to see what it is the student is really interested in and what ambitions he has for college, and to look at his transcript and achievements and try to match the student's talents and goals with colleges that will be able to address the student's needs. What independent counselors should *not* be expected to do is to get students accepted by the top colleges in the country. Remember: Only the student himself can get into college. There are no tricks, no shortcuts that will get a student admitted.

I have read all sorts of absurd claims by counselors, asserting they have gotten students accepted to certain colleges, but after having worked four years in admissions, I can tell you that for the most part, these stories are apocryphal. In fact, bad independent counselors can actually hurt a student's chance of admission by making the student look too "packaged," to the point that admissions officers suspect that many others beside the student have had too much input into the application. Remember, a counselor cannot create talent or intelligence— this must come from the student. After all, you can take vanilla ice cream and dress it up with all sorts of hot fudge, nuts, sprinkles, and whipped cream, but underneath it all, you still have plain old vanilla ice cream.

The best counselors are those who are able to match the student to the most appropriate colleges, and to guide them along in the process so testing is done at the right time, essays are written well in advance, requests for recommendations are well thought out, and all possible contingencies are provided for. A good counselor will know from experience what kind of college the student is capable of getting into and will include a few "reach" colleges, some real possibilities, and at least one "safety" school in case not all goes well. They will guide the student through the long and sometimes tiresome process, but they will not write the essays for him or try to invent talents that are just not there.

The best counselors take a very low-profile stance and never call the colleges directly or write letters on the student's behalf. Contrary to what you might think, the ideal independent counselor should be invisible as far as colleges are concerned. As discussed, the highly selective colleges under no circumstances want to give a privileged student an advantage over a nonprivileged student. If anything, these colleges bend over backward to attract talented students from modest backgrounds who do not have the money to hire an independent counselor in the first place.

Parents should be aware that if admissions officers know that the student has had an independent counselor, it can have a negative impact on the student's application. The natural response would be, "Doesn't the student think he is good enough to get in on his own without paying for extra help?"

The worst thing the counselor can do is to write a letter of recommendation to colleges on his client's behalf. Think about it: Colleges know that you are paying a consultant, so in effect they know that you are buying his words of praise—therefore, his letter has no value. The only letters taken seriously are those that come from the high school or from others who have known the student well.

The same applies to phone calls pestering admissions officers for feedback. The truth is, almost all highly selective colleges will give early feedback regarding decisions to guidance counselors they have grown to trust over the years, but only in rare cases would they ever give this information to an independent counselor. Many highly selective colleges will not even accept phone calls from independent counselors. I used to have phone appointments with both public and private school counselors a few weeks before letters were sent out, during which time I would run down the list of applicants from their high schools, giving them a "likely," "unlikely," or "possible" for each student. I knew I could trust them, especially because those decisions are not always final, although they are a good indication. Rarely, if ever, did I give information to an independent counselor.

25

The Final Rung of the Ladder: Last-Minute Adjustments

———•———

Consider that throughout the entire reading process, the regional officers never really had a chance to compare students from the high schools in their regions. Because of the logistics of the reading process, the regional officers would read applications from their regions over a three-month period, so it would be impossible to keep track of applicants from one particular high school group. In addition, remember that the applications of students from the same high school are usually read by a different combination of readers (that is, the regional officer, a second reader, and possibly a committee of four additional officers), so there are many variables in how applicants from the same high school are considered.

Are there checks built into the reading process to smooth out any inequities in the reading process? Of course. Each admissions office usually saves a few days at the end of the reading season for what is sometimes called "docket review." Other offices may have other terms for the same process. At Dartmouth, all the regional officers get a docket, or listing by high school and state, of every applicant in their region. This docket is updated daily and handed out every two weeks or so during the reading process. What usually happens is that officers are too busy getting their reading done to do a thorough review of decisions in their area (not to mention that it would be nearly impossible to locate a particular file until the end of the process), so they might not be aware of a problematic situation regarding a school group.

That is why most offices allow a few days for regional officers to take the time to go through their region school by school, using the basic information on the docket (the docket printout really just has test scores, CRS, AI, any special tags or flags, high school name, and admissions decisions). If, for example, an officer sees a list of seven applicants from the same public high school and notices that the college accepted one with a CRS that was significantly lower than the others, he might locate that file and reread it, or even pull all the files from that high school and check them out. In the vast majority of cases, the reason is obvious as soon as the officer rereads his comments and examines the ready sheet and master card. Still, every once in a while, you might find an odd case in which you turned down the number-one student from a high school but accepted a much weaker student. In these cases, the college might choose to wait-list the number-one student in order to avoid conflict, but rarely would it reverse the decision. In the case I just described, it's probable that the lower-ranking student was accepted either because of extenuating socioeconomic circumstances or because he had a major flag or tag.

It is commonplace to accept a lower-ranking athletic recruit at a high school and then turn down a much stronger student from the same high school who unfortunately was not a standout in the overall applicant pool. I think for the most part, guidance counselors understand that an athletic recruit will sometimes be accepted, even if he is not the high school's top student. The majority of complaints come from cases where the lower-ranking student's reasons for acceptance might be less obvious.

Suppose the angry family of the rejected student calls and accuses the college of accepting a student with a much lower ranking. The college cannot reveal any details about a decision regarding another student, but it is probable that the accepted student belonged to one of the special categories I have explained, such as recruited athletes, development cases, minority applicants, legacies, et cetera. Since it is impossible to try to smooth out all these differences, the regional officer does his best to catch real inequities or unfair cases during the docket review.

Even if the regional officer decides that there is a major problem in one particular high school and that one applicant who was rejected should have been admitted, the officer would still have to present that case to the director, who would have the ultimate decision-making power. In many instances, he will not be impressed and is not particularly worried about what the high school will think. I don't mean to portray admissions offices as devoid of compassion, but it is impossible to explain the nuances of all decisions to the public, especially to an angry parent who can't get over the fact that their number-one-ranked child was rejected, while another, lower-ranked student was accepted. If we could be honest, it would be tempting to give the real reasons, as dispiriting as they might be: "Yes, your child was number one, but his test scores were more than a hundred points lower than our averages in several areas. Plus, your child came across as dull and unimaginative. The student we did accept had much greater school support, much higher test scores, and impressed us as more interesting." Although it would be comforting from our standpoint (in fact, it was satisfying for me just to pen that sentence), that is a completely fictitious conversation that would never in a million years be heard from an admissions officer, even if it is exactly what he is thinking while talking to you over the phone.

26
Conclusion

————✦————

Though some of the smaller details may vary from college to college, the general knowledge presented in this book should give you a framework from which you can extract particulars for every other college in the highly selective category. In summary, it is evident that what I have described is a fallible process, although one that is not without merit.

As I reflect upon the entire process from start to finish (and I had the chance to do this at the end of four different admissions seasons), I am impressed with the overall quality of the decisions, despite the inequities of the AI formula. Every year when it came time for docket review, I expected to find a number of cases where final decisions were either unjust or insensitive, but I rarely found more than a handful out of the thousand or so cases in my region. Sure, there were always students for whom I was an advocate who were not ultimately accepted, but that's part of the democratic decision-making process.

At all the highly selective colleges I have listed, officers take their responsibility very seriously and read every folder, no matter how weak it may look at the outset. All applications get a thorough read, their day in court. Those that make it to committee are discussed by an even greater number of officers and therefore have a correspondingly higher chance to make an impression on someone on the admissions staff.

Is the system perfect? The obvious answer is no, but then again, very few systems work perfectly, especially when you consider that these colleges are trying to read and evaluate thousands of applicants in a short three-month span. The admissions officers at these colleges are bound to make occasional mistakes, misjudgments, and oversights that will work against applicants.

Should we *expect* the process to work perfectly? Here the answer is yes, by careful revision and reflection on the process itself. In my judgment, future revisions or refinements of Ivy League methodology should focus on the AI calculation. In some schools, the AI is used strictly for athletics; in others, the academic ranking for all applicants is based directly on the AI. The flaws of the AI are many:

1. The entire high school record is compressed into the CRS, which can be calculated in so many different ways that it does not do a fair job of comparing students from different schools around the country (for example, the difference between an academic 9 and an academic 4 can be the difference between a school that reports decile and another that reports a weighted GPA, even if both students were similarly ranked in their schools).

2. Two-thirds of the formula is derived from standardized testing.

3. It does not take into account the level of course load.

4. It is biased against lower-income and disadvantaged students because of the heavy emphasis on standardized testing.

5. It gives no extra points for attending supercompetitive high schools, where even being in the top 10 percent of the class is quite an achievement.

6. It doesn't take into account intellectual curiosity, which should be one of the primary factors for admission.

CONCLUSION

I don't think it is a bad idea to have a formula to rate applicants, but that formula would have to be much more equitable for all students. But how does one make a universal or ideal formula that is applicable to all individuals? One formula cannot take into account the wide variety of students from different backgrounds and different schools. There is no simple solution, but here are some elements that a fairer formula would have to take into consideration:

- Since class rank is the most accurate way to get a picture of where a student stands in relation to the rest of his class, only rank should be used in the computation of the formula. For schools that do not provide rank, the formula should simply not be used.
- Standardized test scores should only account for 50 percent or less of the formula so that high school performance counts for at least half of the student's academic achievement. I also think the verbal SAT should be given more weight than the math, since it is much more common to see high math scores than high verbal scores.
- The formula should take into account ratings assigned by guidance counselors and teachers. The boxes used by teachers and guidance counselors could be assigned numeric equivalents and could then be factored into the formula.
- The formula should take into account the student's writing ability as judged by admissions officers and teachers.
- The formula should take into account extreme socioeconomic disadvantage.
- The formula should take into account some kind of rating for intellectual curiosity.

As you can see, representing over ten thousand applicants with one formula is an impossible task. My final suggestion would be that even if the "ideal" formula was developed, that formula would be only *one* factor of many used in assigning an academic rating.

We have discovered in the last decade that computers are good for many complicated tasks involving formulas and managing large quantities of data, but computers are, as of this writing, not capable of making the finer judgments that humans are able to make. Therefore, I think the less number-based the process and the more people-oriented, the better the quality of the final decisions. What is most needed is not a formulaic panacea, but, rather, a process that involves deep thought, informed evaluation, input from faculty at the highly selective colleges (very few of the highly selective colleges ask for faculty input), and several different in-office readers to take into account various life experiences and points of view.

When I say "various life experiences," I mean not just those of the students but those of the officers, as well. What I envision is a system that relies more on checks and balances from officers and faculty who hail from all different walks of life, so that they can bring their own life experiences to bear on the evaluation of applicants. The more the evaluation takes the form of written comments from admissions officers and faculty, the more it will be able to take into account the more unquantifiable information, such as family background, passion for learning, potential to have a big impact at the college, and strength of intellect.

In the face of a new century, it remains to be seen whether the highly selective admissions offices will rise to the challenge of adopting their evaluation processes to the demands of a changing applicant pool. One fact is evident in the applicant pools I have seen, and that is that there are many motivated young people coming out of the nation's high schools who are burning with the will to excel. They all deserve the chance to be evaluated by colleges in a manner commensurate to their abilities and talents. Hence, the importance of developing an admissions process that recognizes the special student in any guise.

In the meantime, it is my fervent belief that the more you know about the admissions process, the better you will be able to do a thorough job of presenting yourself as a person with a vested interest in academics. By being intimately familiar with the process, you will avoid many of the common mistakes applicants make when applying to their first-choice college. My goal in writing this book has been to demystify the admission process, thereby making it accessible and more available to all applicants. I believe that any applicant, regardless of socioeconomic condition, place of residence, or high school attended, stands a better chance of gaining acceptance to the college of his or her choice if he or she is an *informed* applicant. *A Is for Admission* is a testament to this belief.

Appendix

Table A: Determining CRS from Class Rank

Rank	Class Size 1050–2000	1000–1050	950–999	900–949	850–899
1–2	80	80	80	80	80
3	79	79	79	79	79
4	79	78	78	77	77
5–6	78	77	77,76	76	76
7–8	77	76	75	75,74	75,74
9–10	76	75	74,73	74,73	73,72
11–14	75	74	73	73	73
15–19	74	73	71	71	71
20–24	73	72	70	70	70
25–29	72	71	69	69	69
30–39	71	70	68	68	68,67
40–44	70	69	67	67	67
45–54	69	68	67,66	66	66
55–69	68	67	66,65	65	65,64
70–84	67	66	65,64	64	64,63
85–99	66	65	64,63	63	63
100–124	65	64	62	62	62
125–149	64	63	61	61	61
150–199	63	62	60	59	59
200–249	62	61	58	57	57
250–299	61	60	56	56	55
300–349	60	59	55	54	54
350–399	59	58	53	53	53
400–449	58	57	52	51	52
450–499	57	56	50	50	50
500–549	56	55	49	49	48
550–599	55	54	48	47	46
600–649	54	53	46	45	45
650–699	53	52	45	44	42
700–749	52	50	44	42	40
750–799	51	47	43	40	38
800–849	50	44	40	38	34
850–899	48	42	37	34	27–22
900–949	40	34	34	27–21	
950–974	34	24	27		
975–999	21	21	21		

Rank	Class Size 800–849	750–799	700–749	650–699	600–649
1–2	80	80	80	80	80
3	79	79	78	78	78
4	77	77	77	77	77
5–6	76,75	76,75	76,75	75,74	75,74
7–8	74	74	74,73	74,73	74,73
9	73	73	73	73	73
10–14	72	72	72	71	71
15–19	71	70	70	70	70
20–24	70	69	69	69	68
25–29	69	68	68	68	67
30–39	68,67	67	67,66	67,66	66
40–44	66	66	66	65	65
45–54	66,65	66,65	65,64	65,64	64
55–69	65,64	65,64	64	64,63	63,62
70–84	63	63,62	63,62	62,61	62,61
85–99	62	62	62,61	61,60	61,60
100–124	61	61	60	60	59
125–149	60	60	59	59	58
150–199	58	58	58,57	57,56	56,55
200–249	56	56	55	54	54
250–299	55	54	53	52	52
300–349	53	50	52	50	50
350–399	51	49	50	49	48–46
400–449	50	47	48	47	45,44
450–499	48	45	46	45	43,42
500–549	46	43	44	43–41	40,39
550–599	45	41	42	40–39	38–33
600–649	43	38	40	38–33	31–21
650–699	41	35	35	31–21	
700–749	38	28	28–22		
750–799	34	22			
800–824	27				
825–849	22				

	550–599	500–549	450–499
1	80	80	80
2	79	79	79

Rank	Class Size 550–599	500–549	450–499
3	77	77	77
4	76	75	75
5	75	74	74
6	74	73	73
7–8	73	73,72	72
9	72	72	71
10–14	71	70	70
15–19	69	69	68
20–24	68	67	67
25–29	67	66	66
30–34	66	65	65
35–44	65	65,64	64,63
45–49	64	63	63
50–59	63	63,62	62
60–69	62	62,61	61
70–84	61	61,60	60,59
85–99	60	60,59	59,58
100–124	59	58	57
125–149	57	57	56
150–174	56	55	54
175–199	55	54	54
200–249	53	52	51
250–299	51	50–48	49–47
300–349	49	47–46	46–44
350–399	46	45–43	43–40
400–424	44	42	38,37
425–449	42	40	37–35
450–474	41	39–37	33–29
475–499	39	37–34	22
500–509	38	32	
510–519	37	29	
520–529	36	24	
530–539	35	24–21	
540–549	34	21	
550–559	32		
560–569	28		
570–584	24		
585–599	21		

APPENDIX

Rank	Class Size 400–449	350–399	300–348
1	80	80	80
2	79	78	78
3	77	76	75
4	75	74	74
5	73	73	73
6–7	72	72,71	72,71
8–9	71	71,70	70
10–14	69	69	68
15–19	68	67	67
20–24	66	66	65
25–29	65	64	64
30–39	64	64,63	63,62
40–44	63	62	61
45–49	62	61	61
50–59	61	61,60	60
60–69	60	60,59	59,58
70–79	59	58	58,57
80–89	58	57,56	57,56
90–99	57	57,56	56,55
100–124	56	55	54
125–129	55	53	52
150–199	53	51,50	50–47
200–249	50	48–46	46–43
250–274	48	45,44	42,41
275–299	45	44–42	41–39
300–309	44	41	37
310–329	43	40,39	36–31
330–339	42	38	27
340–349	41	36	23
350–359	40	34	
360–369	39	30	
370–379	38	30	
380–389	37	23	
390–399	35	23	
400–409	34		
410–419	31		
420–429	25		
430–449	22		

Rank	Class Size 250–299	200–249	150–199
1	79	78	78
2	77	76	76
3	75	74	73
4	73	72	71
5	72	71	70
6	71	70	69
7	70	69	68
8–9	69	69,68	67
10–14	68	66	65
15–19	66	65	63
20–24	64	63	62
25–29	63	62	60
30–34	62	61	59
35–39	61	60	58
40–44	60	59	57
45–54	59	58,57	56,55
55–59	58	56	54
60–69	57	56,55	53,52
70–74	56	54	51
75–84	55	54,53	51,50
85–94	54	52	50,49
95–99	53	51	49
100–124	52	50	48–45
125–149	50	49–46	44–41
150–174	48	46–43	39–34
175–199	46	42–39	31–23
200–209	44	38–36	
210–219	43	35–31	
220–229	41	29–27	
230–239	40	27–23	
240–249	38	23	
250–259	36		
260–274	32		
275–287	29		
288–299	23		

	100–149	95–99	90–94
1	76	76	75
2	74	74	73
3	72	71	70

Rank	Class Size 100–149	95–99	90–94
4	70	69	68
5	68	67	67
6	67	66	66
7–8	66	65,64	65,64
9	65	64	63
10–14	63	62	61
15–19	61	59	59
20–24	59	57	57
25–29	57	56	56
30–34	56	54	54
35–39	55	53	52
40–44	54	51	51
45–49	52	50	50
50–54	51	49	49
55–69	50	48–45	47–44
70–74	49	44	42
75–79	48	42	40
80–84	47	40	38
85–89	46	37	35
90–94	44	34	25
95–99	43	25	
100–104	42		
105–109	40		
110–114	38		
115–119	35		
120–134	32		
135–149	24		

	85–89	80–84	75–79	70–74	65–69
1	75	75	75	75	74
2	73	73	73	72	72
3	70	70	70	69	69
4	68	68	68	67	67
5	67	67	66	66	65
6	66	66	65	65	64
7	65	65	64	64	63
8	64	64	63	63	62
9	63	63	63	62	62
10–14	61	61	61	60	60
15–19	59	58	58	57	57

Rank	Class Size 85–89	80–84	75–79	70–74	65–69
20–24	57	56	56	55	55
25–29	55	55	54	53	53
30–34	54	53	52	51	51
35–39	52	51	51	50	49
40–44	51	50	49	49	47
45–49	49	49	47	47	45
50–54	48	47	46	45	43
55–59	46	45	44	42	40
60–64	45	43	42	39	35
65–69	43	41	39	35	26
70–74	41	39	35	26	
75–79	38	35	25		
80–84	35	25			
85–89	25				

	60–64	55–59	50–54	45–49	40–44
1	74	74	73	73	73
2	72	71	71	71	71
3	69	68	68	67	67
4	67	66	66	65	65
5	65	65	64	64	63
6	64	63	63	62	62
7	63	62	62	62	61
8	62	61	61	60	60
9	61	61	60	59	59
10–14	59	59	58	57	56
15–19	56	56	55	54	52
20–24	54	53	53	52	49
25–29	52	51	49	49	47
30–34	50	49	47	46	43
35–39	48	47	45	42	39
40–44	46	44	41	38	28
45–49	44	41	38	27	
50–54	41	38	27		
55–59	37	26			
60–64	26				

Rank	Class Size 35–39	30–34	25–29	20–24	15–19
1	72	72	71	70	69
2	70	69	69	68	67
3	66	65	65	64	62
4	64	63	62	61	59
5	62	61	60	59	57
6	61	60	59	58	55
7	60	59	58	56	53
8	59	57	56	55	52
9	57	56	55	53	50
10–14	55	54	52	49	49–41
15–19	52	50	47	43	39–28
20–24	48	45	41	30	
25–29	44	41	29		
30–34	39	29			
35–39	28				

	10–14	5–9	4	3	2	1
1	67	65	61	59	57	50
2	65	61	53	50	33	
3	60	56	47	31		
4	57	52	39			
5	54	45				
6	52	39				
7	50	35				
8	46	32				
9	43	32				
10	41					
11	35					
12–14	30					

Table B: Finding the CRS Using the Computer Program Formula Z=
$\dfrac{(2 \times \text{absolute rank}) -1}{2 \times \text{class size}}$

Converted Rank	Z	Converted Rank	Z	Converted Rank	Z
80	.0017	60	.1712	40	.8531
79	.0023	59	.1978	39	.8747
78	.0031	58	.2267	38	.8944
77	.0041	57	.2579	37	.9115
76	.0055	56	.2913	36	.9265
75	.0072	55	.3265	35	.9394
74	.0095	54	.3633	34	.9505
73	.0123	53	.4014	33	.9599
72	.0159	52	.4405	32	.9678
71	.0203	51	.4802	31	.9744
70	.0257	50	.5199	30	.9798
69	.0323	49	.5596	29	.9842
68	.0402	48	.5987	28	.9878
67	.0496	47	.6368	27	.9906
66	.0607	46	.6736	26	.9929
65	.0737	45	.7088	25	.9946
64	.0886	44	.7422	24	.9960
63	.1057	43	.7734	23	.9970
62	.1252	42	.8023	22	.9978
61	.1470	41	.8289	21	.0084
				20	1

Always round *up* to the highest decimal, so if Z = .5250, the CRS would be 49, not 50.

Example: Rank in class is 24/300

$$Z = \frac{2\times24-1}{2\times300} = \frac{47}{600} = .0783 \text{ which corresponds to a CRS of 64.}$$

Table C: General Conversion to Find CRS from High School GPA

CRS	4.0 Scale	Letter Grade Average	Percentage Average
80	4.30 and above	A+	98.00 and above
79	4.20–4.29		97.99–97.99
78	4.10–4.19		96.00–96.99
77	4.00–4.09	A	95.00–95.99
75	3.90–3.99		94.00–94.99
73	3.80–3.89		93.00–93.99
71	3.70–3.79	A–	92.00–92.99
70	3.60–3.69		91.00–91.99
69	3.50–3.59		90.99–91.99
68	3.40–3.49		89.00–89.99
67	3.30–3.39	B+	88.00–88.99
66	3.20–3.29		87.00–87.99
65	3.10–3.19		86.00–86.99
63	3.00–3.09	B	85.00–85.99
61	2.90–2.99		84.00–84.99
59	2.80–2.89		83.00–83.99
57	2.70–2.79	B–	82.00–82.99
55	2.60–2.69		81.00–81.99
53	2.50–2.59		80.00–80.99
51	2.40–2.49		79.00–79.99
49	2.30–2.39	C+	78.00–78.99
48	2.20–2.29		77.00–77.99
47	2.10–2.19		76.00–76.99
46	2.00–2.09	C	75.00–75.99
45	1.90–1.99		74.00–74.99
44	1.80–1.89		73.00–73.99
42	1.70–1.79	C–	72.00–72.99
40	1.60–1.69		71.00–71.99
38	1.50–1.59	D+	70.00–70.99
35	below 1.50	D	below 70

Glossary

Achievement tests: The old name for what are now known as SAT II subject tests. Most highly selective colleges require at least three SAT II tests for admission.

ACT: A standardized test offered nationwide, it can be used in place of the SAT I at most highly selective colleges. In some areas of the country, such as the Midwest, this test is taken more often than the SAT I.

Advanced Placement: College-level exams offered by the College Board in a number of different subjects. These tests are scored on a scale of 1 to 5, 5 being the highest score. Many highly selective colleges give college credit for high AP scores.

AI: Academic index. A formula used in Ivy League schools, particularly with regard to athletics, that averages three factors: the single-highest SAT I verbal and the single-highest SAT I math, the highest of three SAT II tests, and the converted rank score. The highest possible AI is 240.

All-American: A high school sports award reflecting an athlete who is one of the top players in the country.

All-county: A high school sports award reflecting an athlete who is one of the top players in the county.

All-state: A high school sports award reflecting an athlete who is one of the top players in the state.

AP Scholar: An award given by the College Board to students who score 3 or higher on at least three different AP exams.

Common application: A generic college application that can be used for many colleges around the country.

CRS: Converted rank score. An Ivy League convention intended to compare high school students' rank in class from all

256

over the country by putting them on a uniform scale of 1 to 80, with 80 being the highest.

Decile: A division used in breaking down class rank into tenths. Top decile refers to the top 10 percent of the class; second decile refers to top 10 to 20 percent of class, and so on. There are ten deciles.

Early action: An admission program offered by many schools that allows a student to apply by an earlier deadline and to hear from the college as early as December or January. The program is not binding, so if you are admitted, you can decline the offer. Harvard and Brown are the only Ivy League schools that have early-action programs.

Early decision: An admission program offered by many schools that allows a student to apply by an earlier deadline and to hear from the college as early as December or January. The program is binding, so if you are admitted, you are obliged to attend that college. All the Ivy League schools have early-decision programs except Harvard and Brown.

GPA: Grade point average—the average of an applicant's grades in high school. The two most common grading scales are 1 to 100 and the 4.0 scale.

International: Defined by colleges as a student who does not hold a U.S. passport, is not a permanent resident, and does not have a U.S. green card. International students are not treated as need-blind in terms of financial aid.

International Baccalaureate: College-level exams and full-diploma program offered by almost 300 U.S. high schools, with about 55 or so being added each year. The exams are scored on a scale of 1 to 7, 7 being the highest score. Many highly selective colleges give college credit for IB scores of 5, 6, or 7. For more information, call their North American office in New York at (212) 696-4464.

Legacy: The son or daughter of a graduate of a particular school. A student would be considered a legacy applicant at Yale if his father or mother graduated from Yale. This term refers only to sons and daughters of graduates from the school, not to those whose aunts, uncles, grandparents, et cetera, attended.

Magnet school: A selected high school (almost always a public school) that attracts top students from many different area school districts. Typically magnet schools offer high-level coursework for advanced students.

Mean: A mathematical term referring to the average score of a group of scores. It is calculated by adding up all the scores and dividing by the total number. The average of 3, 3, 4, 5, 9, 10, 20 would be 7.7: $3+3+4+5+9+10+20/7$.

Median: A mathematical term referring to the middle score of a group of scores. Half of the group scores over the median, while half scores under the median. In the following set—3, 3, 4, 5, 9, 10, 20—the median would be 5, because there are three numbers lower than 5 and three numbers greater than 5.

Minority: In the context of selective admissions, the four minority groups are Asian-Americans, African-Americans, Native Americans, and Hispanics. Only the last three are considered underrepresented minorities and are therefore subject to affirmative-action policies.

MVP: Most valuable player. A high school sports award designating the most valuable member of a particular team, usually voted upon by fellow teammates or the coach.

National Merit "commended": An award given out by the College Board for high PSAT scores by state. It is a runner-up to the higher designation of National Merit semifinalist.

National Merit semifinalist: An award given out by the College Board for high PSAT scores by state. Different states have slightly different formulas, but students awarded this honor tend to be among the top scorers in their respective state.

Need-blind: A term used in college admissions to describe the fact that the school does not take into account the applicant's ability to pay when making admissions decisions.

North country applicant: A designation used by Dartmouth College for applicants from Maine, Vermont, and New Hampshire whose parents did not graduate from college.

Postgraduate student: A student who opts to attend high school for a fifth year (thirteenth grade) before college.

Quartile: A division used in breaking down class rank into fourths. Top quartile refers to the top 25 percent of the class; second quartile refers to top 25 to 50 percent of class, and so on. There are four quartiles.

Quintile: A division used in breaking down class rank into fifths. Top quintile refers to the top 20 percent of the class; second quintile refers to top 20 to 40 percent of class, and so on.

Rank: A method used by high schools to express where the student stands in his or her high school class. A rank of 1/200 would mean that the student has the highest GPA in the class and has graduated ahead of the other 199 students.

Recentering: The process instituted in 1995 by the College Board when they changed the median scores on the SAT I back to 500 for both verbal and math sections. The median had dropped to well below 500 in both areas.

Recruited athlete: An elite-level athlete who is one of a college coach's top choices for his sport's team.

SAT I: Formerly known as the Scholastic Aptitude Test, now it stands for Scholastic Assessment Test. The test is designed by the College Board to evaluate students in the verbal and math areas. The two sections of the test are scored on a scale of 200 to 800, with 800 being the highest possible score.

SAT II: Formerly known as achievement tests, these tests are one-hour subject tests prepared by the College Board in over seventeen different academic subjects. Most highly selective colleges require two or three of these tests for admissions.

Squeeze play: A term specific to Ivy League athletics when an athlete gets an offer from one school well before the official notification date and has to force the other schools to make an early decision on his acceptance.

Transcript: The official high school record of grades and course work that is forwarded to colleges.

Unweighted: A high school treatment of grades on the transcript in which no extra points are added to give extra credit for difficult courses. Grades are reported exactly as they are earned.

Wait list: A list of students who were not accepted outright to colleges but were too strong to reject outright. These wait lists can include as few as ten students and as many as several hundred. Every school has a different policy with regard to putting students on the wait list.

Weighted: A high school treatment of grades on the transcript in which extra points are added to give extra credit for difficult courses.

Westinghouse finalist: One of the most prestigious national awards, given out once a year to students who have done exceptional scientific research. Since only a few students nationwide are awarded this designation, it is weighed very strongly by highly selective colleges.

Who's Who: Being listed in *Who's Who* is a somewhat meaningless designation at the highly selective college level, since so many students nationwide are listed in this yearly publication. The company's main object is to sell books to students whose accomplishments are listed therein.

Index

INDEX

ABOUT THE AUTHOR

The author, a native of New York City, graduated Phi Beta Kappa from Dartmouth College in 1989. After studying in Spain for a year at the Antonio de Nebrija Institute, she earned a master's degree in English and comparative literature from Columbia University. She has taught English and Spanish at the Putney School in Vermont. For four years, she was an assistant director of admissions at Dartmouth College. Currently, she is dean of faculty and chair of the English Department at North Broward Preparatory Schools in Coconut Creek, Florida. In her spare time, she pursues her scholarly interests and reads compulsively.